Burgess-Carpenter Library,
406 Butler
Columbia University
New York, N. Y. 10027

W9-BTJ-261

# Vietnam: The View from Moscow, Peking, Washington

*by Daniel S. Papp*

WITHDRAWN

McFarland & Company, Inc.,
Publishers

Jefferson, North Carolina

1981

*bur*
D S
558
. P36

**Library of Congress Cataloging in Publication Data**

Papp, Daniel S    1947-
Vietnam : the view from
Moscow, Peking, Washington.

Includes index.
1. Vietnamese Conflict, 1961-1975 — United States.
2. United States — Politics and government — 1945-
3. China — Foreign relations — 1949-1976.
4. Russia — Foreign relations — 1953-1975.
I. Title.
DS558.P36    959.704'32    80-20117

ISBN 0-89950-010-2

Copyright © 1981 by Daniel S. Papp

Manufactured in the United States of America

Published by McFarland & Company, Inc.,
Box 611, Jefferson, North Carolina, 28640

# Contents

Contents

# Preface

"Vietnam" ... even today, Americans often react to the word with mixed feelings of failure, frustration, and guilt. For 25 years, from the time when the first 35-member U.S. Military Assistance Advisory Group arrived in Vietnam in August 1950 to the time when the last Marines were lifted by helicopter from the soon-to-be-captured U.S. Embassy in Saigon in April 1975, the United States attempted to create a viable noncommunist state in the Southeast Asian nation. For 25 years, that effort achieved less than the desired results, finally ending ignominiously with the rout of the Army of the Republic of Vietnam and the collapse of the South Vietnamese state.

During the years immediately after the fall of South Vietnam, Americans in general preferred to ignore and to forget the American experience there. Recently, however, new interest has developed about what lessons the U.S. should learn from its Vietnamese experience. To uncover these lessons, it is first necessary to understand how American policy-makers perceived the situation in Vietnam as they made the critical decisions which led to involvement.

At the same time, it is somewhat myopic to perceive only American lessons, and incompletely useful to analyze only U.S. perceptions. The United States' involvement in Vietnam took place in a broader global context, and carried with it lessons for other nations as well — in particular the Soviet Union and the People's Republic of China. Given the major differences in worldview existing between these nations, it is reasonable to assume that the lessons they learned about the Vietnamese War may be considerably different from those learned by the United States. This observation has immediate relevance for the world today since in many cases, it is not too much to say that the lessons which the U.S.S.R. and the P.R.C. learned influence their current policies as much as the lessons the U.S. learned influence its current policies.

This book, then, compares American, Soviet, and Chinese perceptions of the Vietnamese War and contrasts the lessons each country learned, and continues to learn, from the U.S. involvement in it. It is hoped as well that it will contribute to the ongoing discussion of what in fact the United States should conclude — and what conclusions it should not draw — from the unhappy experience.

# I
# Vietnamese Conflict: An Overview

Throughout much of its history, Vietnam has been torn by conflict. Numerous accounts of Vietnam's past have stressed the Vietnamese peoples' efforts to maintain their independence from Chinese domination.[1] Its proximity to China gave Vietnam "the deep imprint of [its] neighbor to the North,"[2] and created an understandably ambivalent attitude within the Vietnamese for the Chinese. On the one hand, certain aspects of Chinese culture were admired; on the other hand, the potential expansion of Chinese political influence was feared. To a great extent, this ambivalence continued into the 19th century and beyond.

As Chinese power and influence waned during the 19th century, the traditional Chinese threat to Vietnamese independence was replaced by the more virile threat of European domination. In 1857, the persecution of French missionaries in Vietnam gave the French government a pretext for intervention. During the remainder of the century, the French gradually extended their influence in Indochina. It was not until 1917, though, that armed resistance to French dominion ended.

Under French rule, the colonial government was pervasive and strongly authoritarian. By 1930, there were about as many French colonial officials in Vietnam as British officials in India even though Vietnam's population was only one-twelfth of India's. The Vietnamese economy remained predominantly agricultural and Western social reforms were introduced slowly. Western education was brought to only a handful of Vietnamese; there were only 14 secondary schools in Vietnam by 1940.[3] During the century of French suzerainty, the seeds were gradually sown for revolution.

1

## The Development of the Vietminh

During the early 20th century, the French colonial administration offered little to the Vietnamese people. "Patriotic scholars" throughout Vietnam slowly built up organized opposition to the French. One of these "patriotic scholars" encouraged his son to serve as a messenger for the scholars. Ho Chi Minh followed his father's encouragement — and had taken his first step on the revolutionary path.[4]

Leaving Vietnam in 1911 at the age of 21, Ho Chi Minh traveled throughout much of the world supporting himself on a variety of odd jobs. During his stay in Paris, Ho read Lenin's *Theses on the National and Colonial Questions*, and this, according to one authority, marked the "beginning of Ho Chi Minh's conversion from a nationalistic patriot to an international Communist."[5]

Ho left France for Moscow during 1923. During his year and a half in the Soviet Union, he studied Marxism-Leninism, wrote for *Pravda*, and attended numerous revolutionary conferences and congresses. He also was active in Comintern affairs, being at one time a standing member of the Eastern Department of the Comintern.

By 1925, Ho was in Canton acting as the translator for Michael Borodin, the Comintern's advisor to Sun Yat-Sen and the Kuomintang. During 1925, Ho organized various Vietnamese political refugees into the Vietnamese Revolutionary Youth Movement, a precursor of the Indochinese Communist Party. Other Vietnamese who were in China at the time and would in the future become leaders of the Vietminh included Truong Chinh and Pham Van Dong.[6] By 1929, about 200 Vietnamese revolutionaries had trained in China and returned to Indochina to lead anti-French activities.[7]

Ho Chi Minh, however, was not one of them. Following the 1927 rupture of Kuomintang-Comintern relations, Ho returned to the Soviet Union. In 1930, the future president of North Vietnam founded the Indochinese Communist Party in Hong Kong. After a brief period in prison, Ho spent the remainder of the 1930s traveling throughout the Soviet Union, China and Indochina.

Throughout the 1930s, meanwhile, the Indochinese Communist Party attempted to provide leadership to various peasant rebellions in Vietnam. Despite the leadership of Pham Van Dong, Vo Nguyen Giap and Truong Chinh, the rebellions were not successful. Progress had been made, though. By the eve of World War II, despite limited successes and French repressions, the Indochinese Communist Party was the best organized and strongest anti-French underground group in Indochina. Since it was the strongest nationalist group, it attracted many Vietnamese who had no actual interest in communism or communist theory.

World War II further strengthened the nationalist movement in

Vietnam. After the Nazis invaded and defeated France, the Japanese concluded several agreements with the French administration in Indochina which left the local government in pro-Vichy hands, although it was under the overall direction of the Japanese. Consequently, the Japanese made no concession to Indochinese nationalists as they did to other Southeast Asian nationalists. The Indochinese nationalists stayed underground.

The Indochinese Communist Party increasingly became the focal point for the nationalist resistance against the Japanese occupation. In May 1941, Ho Chi Minh and the Indochinese Communist Party, operating under a national-front policy and emphasizing nationalism over Communism, formed the Vietnamese Doc Lap Dong Minh Hoi, or Vietminh.[8]

As the war continued, the Vietminh gradually extended their influence until, by the winter of 1944-1945, the Vietminh controlled wide regions of the three northernmost Vietnamese provinces. Meanwhile, the pro-Vichy French administration was becoming increasingly Gaullist as the Allied forces moved toward victory in Europe. The Japanese responded by removing the French administration and granting "independence" to Vietnam. Bao Dai, who had been the French-controlled emperor of the Annam region of Vietnam before the war, was appointed the new chief of state.[9]

The Vietminh, however, continued fighting. Two days after the Japanese surrender, a pro-Vietminh uprising occurred in Hanoi, and on August 29, 1945, the Vietminh formed the "Provisional Government of Vietnam." On September 2, Ho proclaimed Vietnamese independence.[10] In his Declaration of Independence, Ho declared: "We are convinced that the allied nations ... will not refuse to acknowledge the independence of Vietnam."[11] Almost immediately, the Vietnamese situation became uncertain. The United States, for the most part, still appeared to be guided by the deceased President Roosevelt's January 1, 1945, statement that the United States should not "get mixed up in any Indochina decisions."[12] With that the case, the British and the Chinese presided over the Japanese surrender in Vietnam. In the southern Cochin region of Vietnam, the British received the Japanese surrender and almost immediately gave control back to the French. In the northern Tonkin and Annam regions, the Chinese received the Japanese surrender but the Vietminh remained in control.[13]

The impasse continued for several months. Finally, on March 6, 1946, a formula was reached that was acceptable to both the Vietminh and the French. According to the agreement:

> The French government recognizes the Vietnamese republic as a Free State having its own Government, its own Parliament, its own Army and its own Finances, forming part of the Indochinese Federation and

of the French Union. In that which concerns the reuniting of the three "Annamite Regions" (Cochinchina, Annam, Tonkin) the French Government pledges itself to ratify the decisions taken by the populations consulted by referendum.[14]

By early 1946, then, it appeared as if the Vietnamese situation would be peacefully resolved. Vietnam had attained a degree of independence, and free elections were to be held to reunify the country. Actual events, however, did not follow this scenario.

## The Franco-Vietminh War

As we have seen, the United States did not intend to "get mixed up in any Indochina decisions" after World War II. Meanwhile the Soviet government and Mao's communist forces followed similar policies. Each had other problems with which to contend. Stalin's attentions were riveted on rebuilding a war-shattered country and solidifying the Soviet position in Eastern Europe. Southeast Asia was far from his mind, and far from Moscow. In the two years immediately after World War II, Stalin's interest in Southeast Asia was limited to efforts to support the French Communist Party's position on French colonial rule in Southeast Asia. Perhaps surprisingly, the French communists supported French colonialism in Indochina.

The Chinese communists, meanwhile, were preoccupied with the development of a base of operations to oppose Chiang Kai-shek. While Mao was sympathetic to Ho Chi Minh's cause, he himself was in a struggle for survival. Southeast Asia and Vietnam consequently were relegated to the corners of Mao's mind. Resolution of the Vietnamese situation was for the most part left to the Vietnamese and the French, at least for the time being. During the summer of 1946, Franco-Vietminh relations deteriorated significantly. Finally, on November 23, French naval units bombarded Haiphong and killed 6000 people.[15] The Franco-Vietminh War had begun.

For the next eight years, the French tried unsuccessfully to defeat Ho Chi Minh's forces. Borrowing heavily from Chinese guerrilla tactics and strategy,[16] the Vietminh controlled the countryside and the French controlled the cities. The French increasingly labeled anyone who opposed them "communists" until the term almost became a synonym for "nationalist."[17]

The actual relation between nationalism and communism in Vietnam during the postwar period is still a matter for debate. It does appear clear, however, that "the disciplined, well-organized, and well-led" Indochinese Communist Party "was strong enough to lead, but not to dominate Vietnamese nationalism."[18]

Finally, in January, 1950, the French Parliament ratified the Elysée Agreements, which recognized Bao Dai as the ruler of an independent Vietnam still within the French Union. On February 17, 1950, the United States recognized Bao Dai's regime.[19]

Both Peking and Moscow had recognized Ho Chi Minh's government previously. Peking's recognition was granted on January 18, 1950, and Moscow's was granted on January 31.[20] Vietnam had quite clearly become part of the Cold War.

Even with the Elysée Agreements, Vietnamese independence remained a facade. According to one authoritative spokesman:

> The various conventions signed by French and Indochinese representatives in 1949 and 1950 could not gloss over the hard fact that the Associated States were still colonies subject ultimately to control from Paris.[21]

The situation did much to discredit Bao Dai. Having served both the French and the Japanese, Bao Dai's position as leader of the new Vietnamese state appeared little more than a sham.

What was the United States' position on the conflict? One study indicated that:

> through 1949 American policy continued to regard the war as fundamentally a matter for French resolution.... The U.S. ... urged meaningful concessions to Vietnamese nationalism. However, the U.S. always stopped short of endorsing Ho Chi Minh, deterred by Ho's history of Communist affiliation.... At no point was the U.S. prepared to adopt an openly interventionist course. To have done so would have clashed with the British view that Indochina was an exclusively French concern.... Moreover, in 1946 and 1947 France and Britain were moving toward an anti-Soviet alliance in Europe, and the U.S. was reluctant to press a potentially divisive policy.... The U.S. considered the fate of Vietnamese nationalism relatively insignificant.[22]

The United States concluded that Ho seemed "quite capable of retaining and even strengthening his grip on Indochina with no outside assistance." The same appraisal of the Vietminh's leader stated that there was "no evidence of a direct link between Ho and Moscow." Such a link, however, was "assumed to exist."[23] The Soviet and Chinese recognition of Ho's government strengthened this assumption. On February 1, 1950, U.S. Secretary of State Dean Acheson, commenting on the Soviet recognition of the Democratic Republic of Vietnam, said that Moscow's action "removed any illusions as to the 'nationalist' nature of Ho Chi Minh's aims."[24]

Acheson's claim about Ho Chi Minh's aims was even then open to debate. There appears to have been limited Soviet interest in Vietnam through the spring of 1950. Hopes for communist rule in France collapsed in the spring of 1947, and even though the French Communist Party altered its position on independence for Vietnam, the Soviet Union regularly ignored the issue. Moscow identified Ho as a communist,[25] but for the most part Soviet attention remained elsewhere.

Until the end of 1949, Chinese communists similarly continued their benign neglect of Ho's efforts. Mao's attention was centered on his own revolution throughout this time. The 1947-1949 period saw the Communist Party of China and its forces wrest control of the mainland from the Kuomintang and establish its own state, the People's Republic of China.

Over the next four years, the Vietnamese situation became increasingly ominous to U.S. policymakers. The American thinking on Indochina during this period was dominated by three factors. First, Asia as a whole was recognized as an area of growing importance in world politics. Second, the world communist movement was viewed as a monolith. Third, the Vietminh's attempt to evict the French from Indochina was increasingly seen "as part of the Southeast Asian manifestation of the Communist world-wide aggressive intent."[26] American interest in Vietnam correspondingly increased.

Perhaps the major reasons for the increased American interest in the Franco-Vietminh War were the Chinese and Korean situations. Mao's victorious forces reached the Sino-Vietnamese border in December, 1949. To the Vietminh, it was an occasion for both rejoicing and apprehension. Material aid could now be obtained from the communist Chinese, but Chinese influence within Vietnam would almost inevitably increase.[27] To the United States, the situation was grim. According to Dwight Eisenhower, after Mao's victory the Indochinese struggle became:

> more intense and began gradually, with Chinese intervention, to assume its true complexion of a struggle between Communism and non-Communist forces rather than one between a colonial power and colonists who were intent on attaining independence.[28]

The exact amount of Chinese military aid to the Vietminh is uncertain. One of the most reliable estimates, however, placed Chinese military aid to the Vietminh as 400 tons per month in 1951, 1500 tons per month in 1952, and 3000 and 4000 tons per month in 1953 and 1954 respectively.[29] With added Chinese supplies and training, the Vietminh forces moved from primarily defensive to primarily offensive operations.

Coupled with the Chinese communists' victory in mainland China, at least in American eyes, was the North Korean invasion of South Korea. One of the several consequences of the Korean War as perceived by the United States was that China replaced the Soviet Union as the principal communist threat to Southeast Asia.[30]

General Mark Clark made this clear in a March 1953 statement warning that after the Korean conflict ended, China would turn to the south.[31] The following month, President Eisenhower reiterated this fear, saying that any Korean armistice which "merely released aggressive armies to attack elsewhere would be a fraud."[32] Several months later, Secretary of State John Foster Dulles linked Korea, China and Indochina and added a clear if implicit threat. Dulles declared:

> Communist China has been and now is training, equipping, and supplying the Communist forces in Indochina. There is the risk that, as in Korea, Red China might send its own army into Indochina. The Communist Chinese regime should realize that such a second aggression could not occur without grave consequences which might not be confined to Indochina.[33]

If the Chinese had in fact become more active in Vietnam following the creation of a Chinese communist state, what course had the Soviets followed? Following the outbreak of the Korean War, the Soviet media increased its coverage of the Franco-Vietminh fighting considerably. The Kremlin continually linked Korea and the struggle in Vietnam as two manifestations of American imperialism. Nonetheless, no Soviet aid apparently reached Vietnam. At one point, the Russians even went to the extreme of *denying* a report of an aid pact with Ho Chi Minh.[34]

This is not to say, however, that the Soviet Union was not concerned about the conflict in Vietnam. Moscow had "two good reasons for wanting to end the war at this time," according to Donald Zagoria.[35] First, U.S. Secretary of State John Foster Dulles had "unveiled" his massive retaliation doctrine which at least at the immediate time was a credible policy. Second, the French assembly was debating the European Defense Community proposal. If the "communist threat" in Vietnam was reduced, the Kremlin may well have believed that the French Assembly's perception of a "communist threat" in Europe may also have been reduced, thereby influencing the Assembly to cast a negative vote.[36]

Zagoria ignores yet a third factor, possibly the most significant one. Soviet attention was diverted from Southeast Asia not only by the new United States policy and the French Assembly's vote, but also by the on-going succession struggle in the Kremlin itself. Stalin's death had unleashed a struggle for power in the Kremlin which would not be resolved until 1957 when Khrushchev overcame the so-called Anti-Party Group.

American assessments of the situation overlooked the differences between the Chinese and Soviet positions. With McCarthyism running rampant in the United States, this was understandable. Even in 1953, though, the implications of events in Vietnam extended far beyond the country itself. The study mission of Walter Judd put forth a hypothesis that would eventually be called the "domino theory." Referring to Indochina as a whole, the Judd Commission argued that:

> The area of Indochina is immensely wealthy in rice, rubber, coal, and iron ore. Its position makes it a strategic key to the rest of Southeast Asia. If Indochina should fall, Thailand and Burma would be in extreme danger. Malaya, Singapore, and even Indonesia would become more vulnerable to the Communist power drive....[37]

John Foster Dulles agreed with this assessment:

> If they [the Soviets] could get this peninsula of Indochina, Siam, Burma, Malaya, they would have what is called the rice bowl of Asia.... And you can see that if the Soviet Union had control of the rice bowl of Asia that would be another weapon which would tend to expand their control into Japan and into India.[38]

Even with this predominant view, Eisenhower's so-called "New Look" defense concept precluded any large-scale direct American involvement in Indochina. American aid to the French in Vietnam was not, however, as severely limited. The increased American concern with the situation in Vietnam was reflected by soaring aid figures. In 1950, U.S. aid to French forces in Vietnam totaled $150 million per year. By 1954, annual aid was $1 billion, with a 33 percent increase contemplated for the following year.[39]

A number of factors other than the "New Look" defense posture contributed to the American hesitancy to intervene directly. Just before Dienbienphu, Army Chief of Staff General Matthew Ridgway sent a team of specialists to Vietnam to study the situation. The specialists' report concluded that any American ground involvement in Indochina would lead to a major military commitment with anticipated losses exceeding those incurred in Korea. Eisenhower's defense policy cut back conventional defense expenditures and could not permit such a commitment. At the same time, his domestic political position would not allow such a course of action since he had been elected with the promise that he would end the Korean War. If Eisenhower had authorized American involvement in Vietnam, the political capital he had accumulated from the end of the Korean conflict would have been considerably spent.

Meanwhile, the French position in Vietnam was rapidly deteriorating. By mid-1953, most of Tonkin and Annam were Vietminh controlled. Northern Cochinchina and the Mekong delta were also controlled by Ho's forces. At the close of 1953, a U.S. Central Intelligence Agency report stated that the Vietminh was attacking with 10,000-man main forces.[40] French domestic sentiment rapidly switched, now favoring withdrawal. Finally, on May 5, 1954, the French fortress at Dienbienphu surrendered to the Vietminh, and for all practical purposes, the Franco-Vietminh War was over.

Could the United States have done anything to change the outcome of the war? According to General Ridgway, the answer was yes. Ridgway did, however, add a major qualification:

> We would have fought in Indochina, could have won ... [at] tremendous cost in men and money. We could not afford to accept anything short of decisive military victory.[41]

An April 1954 U.S. Army position paper supported Ridgway's belief. According to the paper, American intervention in Indochina was militarily undesirable. A victory in Indochina could not be assured by the air force and navy alone, and the use of atomic weapons would not necessarily mean that ground troops would not be required. It was concluded that if ground troops were needed, seven to twelve divisions would be mandatory.[42]

The United States, then, did not intervene to prevent the French disaster at Dienbienphu. The French surrender came the day before the Indochinese phase of the Geneva Conference was to begin. Needless to say, the defeat weakened the French negotiating position.

After considerable discussion, the Geneva Agreements on Indochina were finalized. Chapter I, Article 1 of the "Agreement on the Cessation of Hostilities in Vietnam" declared:

> A provisional military demarcation line shall be fixed, on either side of which the forces of the two parties shall be regrouped after their withdrawal, the forces of the People's Army of Vietnam to the north of the line and the forces of the French Union to the south.

Chapter III, Article 16 commented on foreign military assistance to both parts of Vietnam, stating:

> the introduction into Vietnam of any troop reinforcement and additional military personnel is prohibited.[43]

Chapter VI, Article 33 listed the duties of the Joint Commission on Indochina. Ensuring "a simultaneous and general ceasefire," overseeing "the regroupment of the armed forces" of the two sides and enforcing "the observance of the demarcation lines" were some of the duties given to the Joint Commission.[44]

The "Final Declaration of the Geneva Conference" provided for the eventual unification of Vietnam. The declaration demanded that "general elections be held in July, 1956, under the supervision of an international commission." To prepare for the elections, "consultations [would] be held on this subject ... from July 20, 1955 onward."[45]

How did the concerned parties view the Geneva Accords? The Vietminh, who at the time "had the capability to eliminate the French from Tonkin with one major offensive,"[46] had apparently succumbed to Soviet and Chinese pressures to reach an agreement. The attitude of certain Vietminh representatives at Geneva was that they had been forced "to accept less than [they] rightfully should have attained...."[47]

The United States similarly was not pleased with the outcome. One Department of State official declared that "it would be an understatement to say we do not like the terms of the ceasefire agreement...."[48]

The Eisenhower administration was quite definitely in a difficult situation because of the agreements. If the administration supported the agreements, then it would have been open to McCarthyite charges that it had permitted part of Indochina "to turn Communist." If Eisenhower ordered intervention, then his claim to be the peacemaker of Korea would have been qualified. If Washington opposed the agreement, then French sentiment would have been inflamed against the United States. Secretary of State Dulles escaped the predicament for the time being by instructing the U.S. representative at Geneva, General Bedell Smith, to act as only an interested party. Dulles' instructions to Bedell Smith declared the United States "an interested nation which, however, is neither a belligerent nor a principal in the negotiation."[49]

The Soviet Union and China, on the other hand, were pleased by the outcome. Possible Soviet motivations for favoring a peace agreement on Indochina have already been discussed. China had many similar reasons for favoring peace. The specter of another Sino-American confrontation undoubtedly loomed large in the Chinese view. Although the United States had refrained from using nuclear weapons in the Korean War, Dulles' massive retaliation policy promised their use in subsequent conflicts. At the same time, lessening the possibility of war enabled the Chinese to concentrate on much-needed domestic programs, particularly in agriculture. Thus, both China and the Soviet Union supported the basic provisions of the Geneva Agreements.[50]

With the Geneva Agreements, the Franco-Vietminh war ended. The United States, dissatisfied by the outcome of the Geneva talks and convinced that Ho Chi Minh was indebted to and controlled by Peking and Moscow, set about creating a viable state in the south first under Bao Dai and then Ngo Dinh Diem. The Soviet Union and China, pleased at having avoided a confrontation with the United States, turned once again to more pressing domestic problems and other areas of foreign policy. Ho Chi Minh began building his socialist Democratic Republic of Vietnam in the north, and waited for the promised unification elections. Vietnam was at peace, but only temporarily.

## The Inter-War Period: Creation of Two Vietnams

Following Geneva, two centers of government were created in Vietnam, one under Ho Chi Minh in Hanoi, the other under Bao Dai in Saigon. These centers governed the two areas which would become North Vietnam and South Vietnam. Regroupment of the combat forces of the two sides proceeded as outlined in the Agreements.[51] An estimated 90,000 people left the South and regrouped in the North in 1954.[52] The northern government concentrated on the economic rehabilitation of the North and on marshaling support for the expected 1956 unification elections. Meanwhile about 900,000 people moved from the North to the South.[53] Ngo Dinh Diem, the American-supported prime minister of the nascent South Vietnamese state, based a major portion of his political power on these immigrants.[54] Engaged in a power struggle with the ever-present Bao Dai who was once again the chief of state, Diem found himself in a relatively good position to assume power during 1955. In October 1955, while Bao Dai was still in France, Diem arranged fraudulent elections in South Vietnam and declared himself to be the new president of South Vietnam. During the next few years, with considerable American backing, Diem consolidated his power.[55]

One of the primary means of U.S. assistance to Diem was the Military Assistance Advisory Group, or MAAG, established earlier to help strengthen and train Bao Dai's forces. Now, however, with the help of MAAG, Diem successfully overcame the challenges of the Cao Dai and Hoa Hao religious sects, as well as the Saigon-based Binh Zuyen vice syndicate.[56]

While Diem was solidifying his position, the time to begin preliminary negotiations for the unification elections had come and gone. On July 16, 1955, four days before the negotiations were scheduled to begin, Diem declared "We have not signed the Geneva Agreements. We are not bound in any way by these agreements."[57]

It was apparent that the United States supported his position. Five days earlier, the U.S. Department of State Bulletin implied that the United States opposed elections if certain unspecified conditions did not exist.[58] As time passed, the Saigon government refused to discuss new North Vietnamese overtures for elections, informal economic ties and informal diplomatic contacts.[59]

Within South Vietnam, the passage of the date for unification elections signaled the commencement of increased insurgent activity. Vietminh cadres who remained in the south after 1954 apparently consisted of two groups: the inactives, who had returned to civilian life and were no longer associated with the Vietminh, and whose attitudes toward the Vietminh ranged from loyalty to hostility; and the actives, who responded to the discipline and control of Hanoi and actively organized and propagandized for the Vietminh before the tentative 1956 unification election.[60] The active southern Vietminh cadres engaged in only limited sabotage and violence during 1954 and 1955.[61] Following 1955, however, attempts to undermine the Diem government increased. The Vietminh cadres who lived in the South became the core of the new insurgency, and from about 1959 on were reinforced by regroupees returning from the North. Much of their effort was devoted to increasing the displeasure of the Southern populace with Diem and to carrying out terrorist attacks against government positions and officials.[62]

Meanwhile, the Saigon government viewed all former Vietminh as threats to government security. In mid-1955, Diem launched an "Anti-Communist Denunciation Campaign," in many instances jailing those who were "neither Communist nor pro-Communist."[63] The government agents Diem employed to carry out the campaign were, on occasion, repressive, dishonest, and brutal, although it is unclear whether they were directed to persecute certain parts of the populace by the Saigon government itself.[64]

Diem's agrarian reforms also did little to endear him to the peasants. Peasants were forced to pay rent, whereas previously few had done so. Elected village councils were abolished and replaced by appointed officials, many of whom were Northern Catholics. Continual American prodding influenced Diem to improve conditions slightly, but peasant resentment remained.[65] By early 1957, South Vietnamese conditions had reached the point where a *Foreign Affairs* writer described the nation as "a quasi-police state characterized by arbitrary arrests and imprisonment, strict censorship of the press, and the absence of an effective political opposition."[66]

As Diem's repressions increased, Vietminh strength also increased.[67] The relationship between the increased repression by the Southern government and the increased strength of the Vietminh was extremely complex, and will not be approached here.[68] The following tables are presented, however, to illustrate the increasing scope of Vietminh activity, and to underline the decreasing ability of the Diem regime to protect its own people from that activity.[69]

### SOUTH VIETNAMESE GOVERNMENT REPORT TO U.S. EMBASSY ON CIVILIAN MURDERS AND KIDNAPPINGS

|  | Murders | Kidnappings |
|---|---|---|
| 1958 | 193 | 236 |
| 1959 | 233 | 343 |
| 5 months, 1960 | 780 | 282 |

### BERNARD B. FALL ESTIMATES OF MURDER OF LOW-LEVEL SOUTH VIETNAMESE OFFICIALS

| 1957 | 700 |
|---|---|
| 1958 | 1,200 |
| 1959 | 2,500 |
| 1960 | 4,000 |

While the campaigns of terror and repression were escalating in the south, North Vietnam was continuing its twin domestic tasks of economic rehabilitation and support for national unification. For the most part, at least through 1960, emphasis appeared to be placed on the former.

One of Ho's policies was an extensive agrarian reform. The reform program instituted led to a peasant revolt in the fall of 1956. Armed force was used to suppress the revolt.[70]

Industrialization also played a prominent role in the Lao Dong Party's (North Vietnamese Workers Party's) plans for North Vietnam. The Soviet Union and China extended considerable credit to North Vietnam in 1955, 1959, and 1960.[71] Despite these credits though, the D.R.V. had a "desire to avoid a new colonialism" and relied less and less on foreign aid as a percentage of its budget. According to Bernard Fall, 60.8 percent of North Vietnam's 1957 budget was based on foreign aid, with the figure falling to 21 percent by 1960.[72]

The emphasis on economic rehabilitation of the North did not mean, however, that northern leaders ignored the situation in the South. From 1954 on, North Vietnam had at least four sets of ties with the insurgents in the South. The first was the southern Vietminh cadres who had regrouped in the north. The second was the Vietnamese Fatherland Front, a political organization promoting national reunification. The third was some commonality of leaders and the fourth was the Lao Dong Party itself.[73]

Support of the southern insurgency posed a problem for the North Vietnamese leaders. After it became clear that Diem would not permit elections to be held, pressure mounted on Ho to aid the southern insurgents. The United States, as already shown, had become heavily committed to the Diem regime. Any North Vietnamese thought of insurgency in the South brought to mind the inevitable question, "What would the American response be?"[74]

Perhaps suprisingly, there was some indication that North Vietnam, possibly because of fear of American intervention, did not at first support any great escalation in insurgent activity in South Vietnam. Ho spoke to southern regroupees in 1956, telling them that "to work here [in the North] is the same as struggling in the South; it is to struggle for the South and for the whole of Vietnam."[75] Two years later, in mid-1958, the "Voice of the South Vietnam Liberation Front" radio station began broadcasting. The North Vietnamese periodical *Nhan Dan* condemned the broadcasts, saying that the radio operators were "using their broadcasts to distort Marxist-Leninist theories" and that they "falsified the policies of the Vietnam Lao Dong party and the Democratic Republic of Vietnam government."[76]

About all that can be said with any certainty is that by the close of 1960, the insurgency in South Vietnam, probably controlled by both northerners and southerners and caused at least in part by Diem's repressions and by an unclear combination of nationalism and communism, was rapidly growing. The South Vietnamese government was attempting to combat the insurgency, but with limited success. The second stage of the Vietnamese War was about to begin.

How did Washington, Moscow and Peking view the evolving situation in Vietnam? Washington's position has already been outlined. To the Eisenhower adminstration, Southeast Asia had become an integral part of the Cold War. The creation of the South East Asian Treaty Organization (SEATO) was one manifestation of this view. The division of Vietnam marked the boundary between freedom and communism. To protect freedom, the South Vietnamese government had to be supported diplomatically, politically, economically and militarily. Washington willingly supplied that support. Senators Hubert Humphrey and Mike Mansfield declared that Diem "deserves and must have the wholehearted support of the American Government and our foreign policy."[77] This statement of support was backed by economic and military aid. Between 1955 and 1960, the United States funneled nearly 1.5 billion dollars in aid to Diem.[78]

AMERICAN ASSISTANCE TO VIETNAM
(MILLIONS OF DOLLARS)

| U.S. Fiscal Year | Economic Aid | Public Law 480 | Total Economic Aid |
|---|---|---|---|
| 1955 | 323.6 | 2.2 | 325.8 |
| 1956 | 202.0 | 14.3 | 216.3 |
| 1957 | 258.3 | 22.8 | 281.1 |
| 1958 | 182.4 | 9.7 | 192.1 |
| 1959 | 200.6 | 6.5 | 207.1 |
| 1960 | 169.0 | 11.5 | 180.5 |
| Totals | 1335.9 | 67.0 | 1402.9 |

To be sure, Washington and Diem did not agree on everything. Washington chided Diem for not at least going "through the motions" of trying to organize free elections.[79] Similarly, Diem's much-heralded "agrarian reform program" was begun in 1958 only after considerable American prodding. Despite these minor disagreements, and despite a growing realization in the United States that Diem's version of democracy fell far short of contemporary American models, American support for and aid to Diem continued. Vietnam was firmly entrenched in the Cold War and the U.S. perception of the Vietnamese situation both reflected and caused this entrenchment.

The Soviet Union, on the other hand, appeared content to allow events in Vietnam to develop independently of large-scale Soviet involvement. As the date for the unification election in Vietnam came and went, the Soviet Union barely issued a protest in the United Nations. The Soviet media condemned Saigon and Washington for their refusal to participate in an election, but even this protest was muted. The Soviet Union was still diverted by more important matters—the growing Eastern European crisis and the resolution of its own continuing domestic power struggle. For the most part, it even appeared that the Kremlin tacitly recognized South Vietnam as an independent and legitimate nation. There are several pieces of evidence which support this conclusion. An April 1956 issue of *Kommunist* referred to "three Indochina states: Laos, Cambodia, and South Vietnam" under the protection of "the aggressive SEATO bloc."[80] In December 1956 *Kommunist* remarked that "such countries as the Philippines, South Korea and South Vietnam" had not yet attained "full political independence."[81] The first 1962 issue of the same journal stated that "Pakistan, Thailand, South Vietnam, South Korea, Iran, and other" countries had "anti-democratic, reactionary regimes."[82] In addition, in 1957, Moscow even proposed that both North and South Vietnam enter the United Nations.[83] Little should be read into this tacit recognition of a divided Vietnam. It was merely Soviet recognition of an international fact. Vietnam had simply been divided, much like Korea and Germany.

Soviet relations with North Vietnam meanwhile developed slowly. Following the Geneva conference, Moscow established an embassy in Hanoi. Ho Chi Minh journeyed to Moscow in July 1955, a trip which was greeted with "considerably less fanfare than Nehru's visit a few weeks earlier."[84] Nine months later Soviet Foreign Minister Mikoyan returned Ho's visit. The Soviet's apparently extended some economic aid to the D.R.V. as well during this period. Relations were cordial, but not close. According to one estimate, the D.R.V. sent over a dozen formal communications to Moscow between mid-1954 and late 1955 but the Soviets did not answer them "because of an apparent lack of interest ... in Moscow."[85]

During 1957, Soviet-North Vietnamese relations improved considerably; Hanoi apparently initiated this improvement as it adopted a more pro-Soviet stance. Dissatisfaction with Chinese aid and advisors (perhaps founded on traditional Vietnamese-Chinese antipathy), need for technology more advanced than China could supply, a new stress on economic development in the North, and an attempt to steer an "even course" in the slowly emerging Sino-Soviet feud may all have

precipitated the D.R.V.'s initiative. At any rate, Soviet President
Voroshilov traveled to Hanoi in 1957 and Ho made two trips to Moscow
the same year. The Soviet Union increasingly supplanted China as the
leading supplier of aid to North Vietnam.[86] Nonetheless, Soviet
economic interest in Vietnamese affairs remained limited through 1960.
According to Bernard Fall, Soviet aid to Hanoi between 1955 and 1961
totaled $365 million. Another observer estimated Soviet aid to Hanoi as
$130 million for the same period.[87] Clearly, to the Soviets, Vietnam was
not of major importance.

To the Chinese, North Vietnam was scarcely more important.
Diem's refusal to hold elections was a clear violation of the Geneva
agreements, Peking argued,[88] but China would and could do nothing except make several proposals for an additional Geneva Conference on Indochina. The Chinese continually and unequivocably condemned the
existence of South Vietnam as a "fraud" perpetrated by the "American
bandits." From 1950 through 1956, Chinese-North Vietnamese relations
remained exceedingly close. Gradually though, the D.R.V.'s one-sided
alignment with the P.R.C. disappeared. Between 1957 and 1960, at
least according to one observer, North Vietnam "appeared to have
taken a balanced position between China and the USSR."[89]

## The National Liberation Front of South Vietnam

During 1960, anti-Diem sentiment in South Vietnam rose considerably. Eventually this sentiment coalesced into the so-called
National Liberation Front of South Vietnam (NLFSV), which was created
in December 1960. The new movement, also known as the Vietcong,
consisted of several different anti-Diem factions including the Southern
Vietminh: the core of the NLFSV was apparently this group.

Although many of the Vietcong were indigenous southerners, an
increasing number of them were southerners who had regrouped in the
D.R.V. after 1954. Starting in 1959, more and more of the regroupees
returned to the South. Almost every year between 1959 and 1965, the infiltration rate went up, as the following chart shows.

THE INFILTRATION FROM NORTH VIETNAM OF SOUTH VIETNAM[90]

|         | Confirmed | Probable | Total  |
|---------|-----------|----------|--------|
| 1959/60 | 4,556     | 26       | 4,582  |
| 1961    | 4,118     | 2,177    | 6,295  |
| 1962    | 4,726     | 7,495    | 12,857 |
| 1963    | 5,362     | 3,180    | 7,906  |
| 1964    | 9,316     | 3,108    | 12,424 |
| 1965    | 23,770    | 1,910    | 25,680 |

The question of who controlled the insurgency was never answered satisfactorily during the 1960-1963 period. There were some indications that the infiltrators were being put into a position of authority over the southern indigents. Jealousies inevitably ensued, but none were serious enough to hurt the Vietcong. Infiltrators who were later interviewed were divided on the question of who controlled the insurgency. Some said the NLFSV ran the insurgency with limited northern assistance, while others said North Vietnam was in complete control.[91]

The United States, however, was convinced that the insurgency was directed by North Vietnam. This view was clearly stated in a December 1961 U.S. Department of State White Paper entitled *A Threat to the Peace: North Vietnam's Effort to Conquer South Vietnam*. The Department condemned Vietcong terrorism, declared that the communists were diverting the attention of the West from Vietnam with pressures on Berlin, Laos and the Congo and concluded that Hanoi directed the Vietcong.[92] The State Department was not alone in this view. Gradually, John Kennedy adopted a similar perception. During early 1961, Kennedy, aware of the danger of turning the conflict into a "white man's war,"[93] sent several fact-finding missions to Vietnam to assess the situation. These missions, particularly the Taylor-Rostow mission in October 1961, for the most part defined the situation as a military problem that could be handled by intelligent application of military force.

The Vietcong campaign of assassination and terror, which accelerated during the fall of 1961, apparently did more to change Kennedy's view of the Vietnamese situations than the reports of his fact-finding missions. Insurgents, to Kennedy, became "agitators and subversives" to be dealt with by applying "counter-insurgency techniques" including relocation of villages, tight population controls, development of an efficient police force and the establishment of military forces throughout the country that could meet any "subversive activity."[94] In December 1961, following the accelerated wave of Vietcong violence, Kennedy told Diem that the United States was:

> deeply disturbed by the assault on your country. Our indignation has mounted as the deliberate savagery of the Communist program of assassination, kidnapping, and wanton violence became clear.[95]

Following this, the American presence in Vietnam gradually increased. At the end of 1961, there were 1,650 U.S. advisors in Vietnam. The following year, 12,000 Americans were advising Diem's forces. By mid-1963, the number was 15,000. American deaths per year had also increased in the three-year period, climbing from three, to 50 to 111.[96]

In February 1962 the U.S. Military Aid Command for South Vietnam was set up under General Harkins. Militarily, a "Strategic

Hamlet Program" was instituted in South Vietnam. The program, extending from late 1961 to late 1963, provided for the relocation of the populace from the countryside into defended hamlet and town areas.[97]

It was evident that the United States was not about to abandon Diem. The U.S. decision to continue and increase its support for Diem must be viewed in light of several events. These included Khrushchev's January 1961 speech maintaining that wars of national liberation were just ones, which did not threaten international peace or carry with them the danger of precipitating a nuclear war and therefore should be supported and even encouraged by the Soviet Union[98]; the Cuban situation, particularly the abortive Bay of Pigs invasion that shattered American prestige and opened doubts about American resolve; the Kennedy-Khrushchev meeting in Vienna, during which Khrushchev apparently attempted to intimidate Kennedy; the recurrent Berlin crisis; Kennedy's belief in counterinsurgency, particularly the Green Berets; the U.S. perception of a lurking and malevolent People's Republic of China; and of course previous American experience in Korea and Indochina.

Despite increased U.S. aid, the Diem regime was unable to permanently stem Vietcong advances. The increased support succeeded in maintaining a temporary military balance during 1962 but by 1963 the Vietcong forces were on the offensive once again. American frustration in Vietnam was compounded by reports in September 1963 that Ho Chi Minh had advanced a proposal to Diem that suggested if Diem were to ask American advisors to leave, then the Vietcong would cease their attacks.[99] Diem was rumored to be considering the proposal favorably. Diem's brother Nhu had already called for the withdrawal of half of the 13,000 advisors in the South,[100] and was rumored to be setting up "secret channels of communications with Hanoi."[101] At the same time, opposition within South Vietnam, primarily from the Buddhists, was further undermining Diem's authority. By late October, leaders of the South Vietnamese Armed Forces decided to act to rectify the deteriorating situation in South Vietnam. On November 1, amid numerous rumors and reports that the U.S. supported such a move, Diem was killed in a coup engineered by General Duong Van Minh.

Three weeks after the Saigon coup, Kennedy was assassinated. His successor, Lyndon Baines Johnson, almost immediately reaffirmed Kennedy's policies toward Vietnam, emphasizing that the United States and South Vietnam "should seek to turn the tide not only of battle but of belief."[102] Johnson also confirmed that the Kennedy plan for the withdrawal of U.S. forces from Vietnam by the close of 1965 would be followed if possible.[103]

Within two months, the Johnson administration abandoned the withdrawal program. U.S. Ambassador to South Vietnam Henry Cabot

Lodge told Saigon military leaders that Washington foresaw no neutral solution for Vietnam and that the Kennedy disengagement plan had been discarded.[104] To Johnson, "the neutralization of South Vietnam would only be another name for a Communist takeover."[105] Perhaps using the new U.S. position as a cue, General Nguyen Khanh led a January 30 coup against the ruling military junta of Duong Van Minh since, to Khanh, the Minh regime was paving the way for neutralism.[106] Thus, by the beginning of 1964, the American perception of the Vietnamese problem had not changed. It was still defined in a Cold War context. The American commitment to Vietnam, however, had deepened considerably. To Washington, the stakes had become much larger.

To Moscow, on the other hand, the stakes in Vietnam had been reduced. Between 1960 and 1964, Soviet-North Vietnamese relations had deteriorated. Despite the emphasis the Third Lao Dong Party Congress placed on economic construction in the North and support for Soviet ideological tenets,[107] Hanoi's interest in the South continued. Through 1962, the only apparent disagreement between Hanoi and Moscow was over the wisdom of infiltration.

Not surprisingly, with the D.R.V.'s increased support for the revolution in the South, Sino-Vietnamese relations improved. The hallmarks of the new cordiality in these relations were Chinese President Liu Shao-chi's May 1963 visit to Hanoi and the July 1963 issue of *Hoc Tap*, the Lao Dong theoretical monthly, which completely adopted the Chinese view of just wars and wars of national liberation.[108] Also, despite Soviet pressure, the North Vietnamese sided with China and refused to sign the nuclear test ban treaty.[109] In February 1964 *Hoc Tap* continued the anti-Soviet trend and dismissed statements that implied an increased NLFSV effort in South Vietnam would lead to a greater American involvement in the war, including attacks on the North. The article stated that if the United States attacked North Vietnam, it would have to deal with the People's Republic of China. No mention was made of the Soviet Union. Obviously, Soviet-D.R.V. relations were less than satisfactory. By the summer of 1964, relations had deteriorated to the point where Khrushchev was willing to abandon Soviet concern in Southeastern Asia. On July 27, the Kremlin threatened to resign its co-chairmanship of the Geneva Control Commission on Indochina.[110]

Soviet relations with the NLFSV made Khrushchev's threat even more credible. Ever since the NLSFV was formed in 1960, it presented a problem to the Soviet Union. The basic Soviet dilemma, in view of its expressed support for national liberation movements and its obvious desire to avoid a conflict with the United States, was whether the NLFSV should be aided and if so, how much?

In September 1960 the Third Lao Dong Party Congress issued a public appeal for the people of South Vietnam "to bring into being a broad National United Front directed against the U.S. and Diem and based on the worker-peasant alliance."[111] This North Vietnamese appeal was in marked contrast to Hanoi's earlier insistence upon "a struggle [in the South] on the political level alone."[112]

Whether because of "Hanoi's order"[113] or because of "Southern initiative in response to Southern demands,"[114] the NLFSV was finally established on December 20. Although it would be of interest to examine the background to the establishment of the Front, it would not be pertinent here.[115] It is clear that Hanoi at least approved of the NLFSV's creation. What is pertinent is that the Soviet Union did not acknowledge its establishment until January 31, 1961.[116]

Why did the Soviet Union wait for over a month to acknowledge the creation of the NLFSV? The most apparent reason was that the Soviet Union was not particularly pleased with the event. The previously-stated dilemma now became a reality that had to be faced.

Khrushchev indicated the actual Soviet feeling toward national liberation movements in general and the insurgency in South Vietnam in particular in his famous speech of January 6, 1961. Khrushchev cited Vietnam as an example of the type of war the Soviet Union supported. A careful reading, however, indicated that it was Vietnam's war against the French and not the ongoing Vietcong insurgency to which Khrushchev referred.[117]

To the Soviets, a war of national liberation was defined as a war in which an attempt was being made either to remove a colonial power or to remove the regime of a juridically independent state which was both oppressive and tied to a colonial power.[118] When the South Vietnamese National Liberation Front was established, these criteria were not met. Thus, the Kremlin undoubtedly viewed the Front as an entity which could only produce policy problems for the Soviet Union.

Even more strikingly, it was not until January 19, 1962, that Soviet papers referred to the NLFSV as a "national liberation movement" or the Vietnam War as a war of national liberation.[119] One indication of changing Soviet-NLFSV relations was the first official visit of an NLFSV representative, Huynh Van Tam, to the Soviet Union.[120] The visit occurred in December 1961 and was perhaps connected to the American decision in November to increase substantially the number of U.S. advisors in South Vietnam.

Despite the Soviet recognition of the Front and the increased American involvement in South Vietnam, Soviet aid to the NLFSV was very limited throughout 1962. Thus, while the increased U.S. involvement in South Vietnam may have precipitated the Soviet recognition, it did not lead to a significant improvement in the Soviet-NLFSV relations. Throughout the early years of the existence of the Front, then, it appeared as if the Soviet Union were less concerned with the group in Vietnam than with the Pathet Lao in Laos.[121] Even the Soviet concern for the Pathet Lao, however, was diminishing. In December 1963 Khrushchev turned over to the D.R.V. the Ilyushin 14 aircraft which had been engaged in the Hanoi-Laos airlift. Soviet interest in all of the Southeast Asia, by the end of the 1963, was dying.

Soviet policy toward and relations with the National Liberation Front of South Vietnam did not change noticeably throughout the remainder of Khrushchev's tenure. Moscow maintained its policy of verbal support for the Front and material neglect of it. The Soviet Union continued to indicate its preference for a conference on all of Indochina, a preference which undoubtedly displeased the NLFSV.[122] By early 1964, then, Khrushchev undoubtedly wished that Indochina would simply "dry up and blow away."[123]

To the Chinese, however, the Vietnamese situation was more complicated. While it did present myriad possibilities to underline the legitimacy of the Chinese position in the on-going ideological dispute with the Soviets, the painful fact remained that any American reaction to the stepped-up insurgency in South Vietnam would bring American military strength near China's borders once again, *à la* Korea. The Chinese leadership, then, faced a perplexing problem: how could support for Hanoi be shown, but at the same time the threat of nearby American military power be reduced?

Peking responded with typical Chinese brilliance. Throughout 1960 and 1961, the Chinese argued for political struggle, small shows of military force in South Vietnam and diplomatic negotiations.[124] Chou En-lai and other Chinese leaders appealed for a return to the Geneva Accords and a peaceful reunification of Vietnam,[125] and after the conclusion of the 1962 Laotian Agreements, called for a similar agreement to be acted on in South Vietnam. On July 21, 1962, Foreign Minister Chen Yi supported "neutralization for Vietnam" on the basis of the Laotian model of a tripartite government. To the Chinese Foreign Minister, the settlement in Laos showed that "acute and complicated international disputes can be settled through negotiations" and that "a new starting point in the relaxation of tensions" had been reached.[126]

Through the end of 1962, then, China played both ends against the middle. Verbal encouragement of southern insurgency solidified China's ideological claims as a supporter of national liberation efforts and appeals for negotiations emphasized Peking's more pragmatic concern about limiting the possibility of U.S. military intervention. During

1963, however, as the Soviets gradually reduced their interest in Southeast Asia, Sino-Vietnamese relations improved. Liu Shao-chi visited Hanoi in May, and in June the North Vietnamese adopted China's ideological stance on questions of war and peace. By early 1964, North Vietnam had turned to China as its primary protector in case of American attack. China was clearly scoring points in Hanoi and at the same time the threat of further American involvement had not appreciably increased.

In early 1964, the Vietnamese conflict presented almost an ideal situation for the Chinese. The Russians had already indicated their lack of interest in Southeast Asia, the North Vietnamese had made clear their commitment to support the NLFSV, the domestic situation in South Vietnam was unstable at best. The requirements for a successful war of national liberation existed, according to the Chinese. Additionally, by supplying North Vietnam with military and economic assistance, Peking could *indirectly* support the revolution in South Vietnam, thereby minimizing the possibility of a Sino-American confrontation. The D.R.V. would serve as the "reliable rear base" for the NLFSV in much the same way as China had served the Vietminh against the French. Success for the NLFSV appeared imminent.[128] Best of all, the National Liberation Front's success could be translated into immediate political and ideological capital by the Chinese on almost every issue in the Sino-Soviet dispute. The American "paper-tiger" would be defeated, Soviet "capitulationism" would be proven, Chinese policies on détente and national liberation would be confirmed, Soviet fear of confrontation with the United States would be proved groundless, and the subordination of peaceful socialist assumption of power to violent assumption of power would be affirmed. To the Chinese, the stakes were great, and the probability of success high.

# II

# Prelude to Escalation

During 1964 the South Vietnamese military situation took an abrupt turn for the worse. In the first half of the year, the Vietcong made a successful concerted effort to eliminate the South Vietnamese strategic reserves by luring them from their bases and ambushing them. In neighboring Laos, still a vital infiltration route into the South from the North despite the 1962 agreement, the Pathet Lao seized large sections of the strategic Plain of Jarres. Perhaps the most discouraging aspect of the situation was the decreasing amount of South Vietnam's territory under the control of the Saigon government. The following table, prepared from official South Vietnamese estimates "themselves suspect of being overly optimistic,"[1] reflected the worsening situation.

### THE NUMBER OF RURAL VILLAGES CONTROLLED

|  | September, 1963 | April, 1964 |
| --- | --- | --- |
| Saigon | 1,682 | 1,485 |
| Vietcong | 709 | 866 |
| Contested | 139 | 187 |

By December 1964, the chairman of the Central Committee of the National Liberation Front of South Vietnam, Nguyen Huu Tho, claimed that three-fourths of South Vietnam's land and half of its people were under Vietcong control.[2] Clearly, the Saigon government was in a serious position.

## The American Response

The United States was aware of its ally's predicament. One U.S. government publication described the situation as follows:

This attitude of cautious optimism changed gradually by the early summer of 1964 to one of deepening gloom. No radical shift marked this

23

transition; it was one of a heightened awareness of instability in the
government in Saigon..., of a deteriorating situation in the countryside,
and of the discovery that things had been worse to begin with than the
U.S. expected.[3]

National Security Action Memorandum 288 of March 1964 supported this assessment. Commenting on the deteriorating situation, the
memorandum noted that 40 percent of South Vietnam's territory was
controlled by the Vietcong; the South's population was increasingly indifferent to who controlled them; South Vietnam's army (ARVN) had an
increasing desertion rate; both draft dodging to escape service in the ARVN
and recruitment conducted by the Vietcong were alarmingly high;
the hamlet militias and self-defense corps had poor morale; 17 hamlet
militia in the I Corps area had turned in their weapons; in the III Corps
area, certain hamlet militia had been disarmed because of suspected dis-
loyalty; in the northern II Corps area, strategic hamlets under government control had dropped from 413 to 275 in one year; and the Vietcong controlled "virtually all facets of peasant life" in the southern IV
Corps area.[4] Secretary of Defense McNamara unintentionally gave a
much more terse summation of the entire South Vietnamese situation
nine months later, in December. Reporters overheard McNamara say
that if a particular press conference were held, it would leave the impression "the situation is going to hell." The press conference was not
held.[5]

Throughout 1964, then, the United States was faced with an un-
pleasant choice. It could expand its involvement, possibly becoming
committed to a major military effort, or it could keep its involvement at
a relatively low-level and risk the loss of South Vietnam.

One of the first pressures to expand the war was applied by South
Vietnam's President Khanh. On May 4 Khanh told the U.S. ambassador
to Vietnam, Henry Cabot Lodge, that the way to solve the southern
problem was to invade the North. On May 12 and 13, Khanh reiterated
his desire to McNamara and General Maxwell Taylor. On July 19, the
South Vietnamese leader publicly advocated *Bac Tien* ("forward to the
North").[6] Khanh further pressured his American allies by maintaining
that there were no major differences between Washington's and Saigon's
policy wishes, but only minor differences about the timing and what to
announce publicly. This statement followed Air Force Commander
Nguyen Cao Ky's advocacy of air attacks on North Vietnam.[7] In the
same vein, Khanh reportedly interpreted Senator Barry Goldwater's
presidential nomination by the Republican Party as a support for his *Bac
Tien* desire.[8] General Khanh declared that, "We [the South Vietnamese]
are already victims of a North Vietnamese aggression. Any response
from us would be a counter-attack."[9]

Although it was probably not known to Khanh, the U.S. Joint Chiefs of Staff privately had advocated air attacks on North Vietnam since mid-February. While the Joint Chiefs' support of air attacks stopped well short of Khanh's purported desire for a land invasion of the North, it was clear that domestic pressures were being applied to the Johnson administration to escalate. Although the Joint Chiefs' position did not become publicly known until late June,[10] several staff memoranda had privately reached the conclusion that bombing North Vietnam was necessary: JCSM 136-64 of February 18, JCSM 174-64 of March 2, and JCSM 222-64 of March 14 had all advocated such a policy.[11]

Certain concrete actions had already been implemented against North Vietnam. Most noteworthy was the covert action program begun against the North on February 1, 1964. The goals of the program were harassment, diversion, political pressure, the capture of prisoners, physical destruction, intelligence and the diversion of North Vietnamese resources.[12]

Following McNamara's March 1964 visit to Vietnam, the United States decided to construct more strategic hamlets, train more South Vietnamese army units and send more U.S. equipment to South Vietnam. Three months later, General Maxwell Taylor, the foremost American theorist on counterinsurgency warfare, replaced Henry Cabot Lodge as U.S. ambassador to South Vietnam. The implication of the Taylor appointment was obvious. Washington wanted its leading expert on guerrilla warfare on the scene to direct operations.[13]

The United States also attempted to internationalize the conflict in Vietnam during the same summer of 1964. A July ANZUS meeting was designed in part to lend an international flavor to the war in Vietnam. The United States also sought to have other non-ANZUS nations introduce troops into Vietnam.

The American position on negotiations similarly implied that the United States intended to increase its involvement in Vietnam. The Soviet Union called for a reconvening of the Geneva Conference on Laos in the summer of 1964 and threatened to resign its co-chairmanship of the Conference if its desires were not accepted. North Vietnam supported the Soviet position.[14] The United States and South Vietnam, however, opposed such a conference.[15]

President Johnson indicated that the United States would not permit the Southeast Asian situation to deteriorate further. Speaking in Minneapolis at the end of June, Johnson asserted that the United States "when necessary would not hesitate to risk war" to preserve the peace.[16] At the instigation of Johnson himself, J. Blair Seaborn, the Canadian delegate to the International Control Commission on Vietnam, traveled to Hanoi during the same month and warned the D.R.V.'s leaders that

"U.S. patience was running thin." Even more forebodingly, Seaborn told the North Vietnamese that "great devastation" would occur "in the D.R.V. itself" if the war in the South was escalated.[17] Through the first half of 1964, at least, American policy toward Vietnam appeared resolute. As an American ally, South Vietnam deserved additional support, Washington reasoned. All that was needed was an incident to popularize that support.

The needed incident shortly occurred. On August 2, the U.S. destroyer *Maddox*, patrolling 30 miles off the North Vietnamese coast, reported that it was attacked by three North Vietnamese patrol boats. Three days later, the *Maddox* and another destroyer, the *C. Turner Joy*, were attacked 65 miles off the coast. That night, planes from the U.S. Seventh Fleet attacked patrol boat bases and support facilities in the D.R.V. In response to the crisis, the U.S. Congress passed the Gulf of Tonkin Resolution, which permitted the President "to take all necessary measures to repel any armed attack against the forces of the United States and to prevent further aggression." To many observers, in retrospect, the entire incident seemed to have been staged as a pretext to enable Johnson to carry out his threat against the North.[18]

After a period of relative quiet that preceded the U.S. presidential election, renewed pressures for escalation buffeted Johnson. In November, the Joint Chiefs of Staff once again advocated broadening the conflict. It was also reported that Ambassador Taylor supported bombing of the Ho Chi Minh Trail in Laos and staging areas in North Vietnam. The following day, Taylor traveled to the United States to present his views to the administration.[19]

Some Congressional sentiment also favored a wider war. On November 26, Chairman of the Senate Armed Service Committee Richard B. Russell said, "We either have to get out or take some action to help the Vietnamese.... I can't figure out any way to get out."[20]

Indications of desires for a wider war were numerous in December. A December 13 *New York Times* article reported a debate within the U.S. government over whether the war should be carried to the North.[21] Early in December, the United States and South Vietnam concluded an aid agreement that increased the number and quality of the military, paramilitary and police forces, improved the South Vietnamese air defense system and gave more economic assistance to the South Vietnamese government.[22]

Military operations also picked up in tempo in December. The first contingent of Air Force F105 Thunderchiefs arrived in Vietnam and Thailand on December 16[23] and almost immediately joined Operation Barrel Roll, a program of armed reconnaissance of the infiltration routes in Laos that had begun two days earlier.[24]

These indications all pointed to an increased U.S. war effort. There were, however, opposite signs as well. For some time, the U.S. government had disavowed *Bac Tien*, denied it wanted an expanded war, disavowed Taylor's statements and failed to respond to several Vietcong provocations. Chief spokesman for the so-called antiwar faction was Lyndon Johnson himself.

Johnson criticized those "who want to go north," meaning General Khanh, in a late September speech in Texarkana, Texas.[25] Two weeks afterwards, Maxwell Taylor criticized Khanh, declaring that Khanh's desire for *Bac Tien* was contrary to U.S. policy.[26]

Taylor himself was reprimanded by Johnson in November, after he had argued for an expanded war. On November 23, just prior to Taylor's visit to the United States, the State Department released a statement that said that his views were not the policy of the U.S. government.[27] Apparently the U.S. government felt that the State Department statement was not convincing enough since the government reasserted that the Taylor-Johnson talks would not result in a wider war only four days after the original assurance.[28]

Johnson's campaign statements also indicated that the United States would practice restraint in Vietnam. Although some of the statements were clearly motivated by considerations of the presidential campaign, declarations such as "we do not want our American boys to do the fighting for Asian boys" and "the United States will not get tied down in a land war in Asia," became quite common as the campaign went on.[29] Lyndon Johnson quite definitely appeared as the peace candidate, and his convincing victory over Barry Goldwater in the November elections indicated the America people supported his views.

By far the strongest indicator pointing to a restrained U.S. policy toward Vietnam, however, was the American inaction following two Vietcong raids on American installations in South Vietnam. When U.S. inaction was viewed in light of Johnson's post-Tonkin Gulf statement that "provocation would force a response," the resoluteness of U.S. policy appeared greatly qualified.

The two Vietcong raids occurred on November 1, 1964, and December 24, 1964. In the first attack, the Vietcong launched a mortar barrage on Bien Hoa Airport, killing several Americans and damaging several aircraft. The U.S. military recommended reprisals against the North, but Johnson refused, possibly because elections were two days away.[30] In the Christmas Eve attack, a Vietcong bomb killed two Americans and wounded 58 in a U.S. billet in Saigon. Once again, Johnson did not permit reprisal attacks against North Vietnam.[31]

Secretary of State Dean Rusk furthered the impression that an inertia had taken hold of American policy toward Vietnam. Appearing on a January 3, 1965, television program, Rusk said that the United States would neither expand the war nor withdraw.[32]

An Associated Press survey of the U.S. Senate in early January, 1965, showed that Congress neither wholeheartedly supported the war effort nor desired an expanded war. Of the 63 senators surveyed, 31 advocated a negotiated settlement in Vietnam after the anticommunist bargaining position was improved, ten favored immediate negotiations, eight wanted an American commitment against North Vietnam, three supported immediate withdrawal, and 11 advocated only a strengthening of the South Vietnamese government.[33]

Obviously, then, by February 1965, U.S. policy toward Vietnam presented a confusing picture. Advocates of different policies, each with their own perception of the Vietnamese problem, struggled for influence within the American government. The final decision maker, Lyndon Johnson, was not only enmeshed in this web of conflicting advocacy, but also trapped by his own campaign rhetoric and the awareness that the South Vietnamese situation was deteriorating rapidly. If Johnson acted to "save Vietnam from Communism," he would lay himself open to the charge of having deceived the American people. If he did nothing, the possibility increased that South Vietnam would collapse. As 1964 drew to a close, Johnson himself was perplexed and U.S. policy reflected both his perplexity and the internal government debate. Contingency plans for attacks on the D.R.V. had been drawn up, but would they be used? The answer, even from the perspective of the Presidency, was still open.

Overshadowing the vagaries of American policy was another immense problem. During late 1964 and early 1965, the South Vietnamese domestic situation became increasingly unstable. The United States was well-aware of the importance of the stability of the South Vietnamese government. Maxwell Taylor observed that the Southern government's instability was the most important reason why "unsatisfactory progress [was] being made in the pacification of the Vietcong."[34] The Saigon government's difficulties began to multiply just after the Tonkin Bay incidents. On August 7, Khanh declared a state of emergency in South Vietnam supposedly because of the Tonkin incidents and because of Buddhist rioting. Khanh also proclaimed himself president. Internal opposition in Saigon forced Khanh to resign the presidency within a month, but he remained in the government as premier. Following this change of position, a rumor circulated that the United States would "reconsider its role" in the fight against the National Liberation Front if Khanh did not remain in the South Vietnamese government as a full participant. Washington immediately denied the rumor.[35] By mid-September, the situation in Saigon had become so unstable that *The New York Times* wondered how much longer there would be a "South Vietnamese structure" for the United States to support.[36]

Yet another government was soon to come to power. On November 3, a civilian government led by Premier Tran Van Huong replaced Khanh's government. Khanh became the army commander-in-chief.[37] By the end of November, Buddhists had once again rioted in opposition to the new government and martial law had been declared.[38] In early December, the Buddhists threatened to assume an anti-American posture if the U.S. persisted in its support of the Huong regime.[39]

South Vietnamese generals tried to take advantage of the unrest in Saigon and on December 19, 1964, they attempted to remove the civilian government but failed. They did succeed in creating an Armed Forces Council under General Khanh, thereby weakening Premier Huong. The Buddhists, however, were not pleased with this limited change and proclaimed themselves to be in a "life or death struggle" with the civilian government.[40]

Meanwhile, U.S. Ambassador Taylor urged Premier Huong not to cooperate with the military.[41] The American government warned the Vietnamese military leaders that American support was contingent on the maintenance of a government free from improper interference by the military.[42] In response to this warning, General Khanh stated that the South Vietnamese would not fight "to carry out the policy of any foreign country."[43] Khanh furthur declared that the South Vietnamese government needed independence from "foreign manipulation," cautioned the U.S. not to impose "unwanted leaders" on Vietnam and warned Ambassador Taylor to stay out of South Vietnam's internal affairs.[44] The Buddhists supported Khanh's statements, as well as his later declaration that U.S. policy "impose[d] a new colonialism on South Vietnam."[45]

Perhaps in response to Khanh's statements, and definitely in response to the increased South Vietnamese military influence in Saigon, speculation that the United States would withhold a recently approved aid increase to South Vietnam of $70 million soon followed.[46] For almost a month, the South Vietnamese situation simmered. Then on January 20, 1965, Premier Huong granted portfolios to four generals including Major General Nguyen Van Thieu, the commander of the IV Corps area, and Air Vice-Marshal Nguyen Cao Ky. Both men were regarded as pro-American.[47] Buddhist reaction was instantaneous. Rioting broke out in Saigon, directed against both the Huong government and the United States. The USIA library in Saigon was burned and calls were made for U.S. Ambasssador Tayor's removal.[48] On January 27, in another coup, Nguyen Khanh once again resumed power on behalf of the military. The United States did not immediately recognized the new government.[49]

The new Khanh government was rumored to be favoring neutralism as January drew to a close. *The New York Times* reported that neither Khanh nor the Buddhists feared neutralism.[50] President Johnson's special assistant for national security affairs, McGeorge Bundy, arrived in South Vietnam on February 4 and found the *Times* report to be accurate.[51] Rumors emanating from Paris that "unofficial" representatives of Saigon and Hanoi were holding peace discussions in both Paris and Saigon were even more disturbing to Washington.[52] Meanwhile in Saigon, various correspondents speculated on "the emergence within six months of a government" that "will present an ultimatum-invitation to the United States to get out of Vietnam."[53]

*The New York Times* also commented on the possiblity, editorializing that the United States might soon be faced by two questions. First, what would Washington do if a South Vietnamese government came to power that demanded the withdrawal of the United States from Vietnam? Second, even assuming that that did not occur, should the United States expand the war or voluntarily withdraw?[54]

Coming on top of all the other problems in South Vietnam, and more urgent than any of the other problems, was the fact that the Vietcong had launched a massive offensive in January 1965 that threatened to sweep the Vietcong and the National Liberation Front to victory.[55] According to a North Vietnamese document captured two years later, North Vietnam itself expected a military victory in the south in early 1965. The captured document declared that "we [the North Vietnamese and Vietcong] were about to defeat the enemy" and added "but [we] had not yet definitely defeated his special war."[56]

By February 1965, then, the United States position in Vietnam was extremely precarious. The 23,500 American "advisors" had not turned the tide of battle for the South and even military defeat was foreseeable. The South Vietnamese government was becoming increasingly anti-American. The United States government itself was divided on its view of the situation. Some within the government persisted in viewing the Vietnamese conflict in a bipolar Cold War context, while others viewed it in a multipolar nationalistic context. Johnson had not yet made a decision on policy, but it was clear that he was keeping his policy options open. Washington's statements and actions reflected this presidential indecision. Johnson and his government gave the impression that they were unsure whether to expand the war, maintain the existing level of commitment or reduce the commitment and even withdraw. From the perspective of Washington, confusion reigned supreme.

## *The Soviet and Chinese Views: America Constrained*

As might be expected, the ambivalent American attitude toward Vietnam created some confusion and uncertainty in the Soviet Union and China. Perhaps surprisingly, though, by the beginning of February 1965 both Moscow and Peking had given numerous indications that they did not expect a large-scale American intervention. These perceptions developed slowly throughout 1964.

At the beginning of 1964, with North Vietnam closely following the Chinese ideological line, Soviet interest in and concern for events in Vietnam remained minimal. To be sure, American presence in Vietnam was continually condemned and General Khanh's January coup was interpreted as an American-initiated effort to cast aside "old agents who had compromised themselves or proved incapable of continuing the pro-American game."[57] Even with this Soviet interpretation of the events in South Vietnam, the Kremlin apparently made no effort to render additional material assistance to North Vietnam. During February 1964 First Secretary of the Lao Dong Party Le Duan traveled to Moscow via Peking. Negotiations in Moscow were not successful, apparently foundering on the issue of the war in the South. According to the communiqué issued at the close of Le Duan's stay in Moscow, the "exchange of opinions that [took] place was fruitful for mutual understanding and comradely cooperation."[58] In other words, no agreement was reached. According to one observor, Soviet aid to the D.R.V. was even further curtailed following Le Duan's visit to Moscow.[59] *Hoc Tap*, the North Vietnamese party journal, supported at least the view that no agreement was reached in Moscow. In its February issue, the journal warned the United States that if it attacked North Vietnam, it would not only have to fight the D.R.V. but also China.[60] The U.S.S.R. was not mentioned.

American intentions in Vietnam were undoubtedly more aggressive in appearance to both Moscow and Peking after United States Secretary of Defense Robert McNamara's March 26 speech in which he recalled Khrushchev's 1961 speech defining wars of national liberation. In his speech, McNamara claimed that Khrushchev referred to Vietnam as "a sacred war. We recognize such wars."[61] As previously noted, Khrushchev had been referring to the Vietminh's concluded war of liberation against the French and not to the ongoing insurgency, as the Vietnamese conflict was then regarded. Consequently McNamara's statement may have appeared as a deliberate American attempt to overemphasize external support for the NLFSV, which in turn could be used to legitimize increased U.S. involvement in South Vietnam. The Soviets, well aware of their own decreasing interest and concern for

Southeast Asia, loudly condemned McNamara's speech. The Chinese viewed it as another manifestation of American aggressiveness.

The Soviet isolation was further illustrated by the Soviet reaction to a mid-May French proposal for a new conference on Indochina. While the North Vietnamese and Chinese at first opposed the conference, *Pravda* avidly supported the idea. Soviet policy was thus two-faceted: it supported proposals for a peaceful settlement of the Vietnamese situation and it supported the NLFSV whenever possible as long as no immediate threat of a conflict with the United States presented itself. In line with this second facet, mass meetings were held throughout the Soviet Union in March and April protesting the "aggressive American actions" in Vietnam but no significant material aid was sent to the D.R.V.

Maxwell Taylor's appointment as ambassador to South Vietnam was understandably condemned by Moscow. A July 5 *Pravda* article commented on the appointment:

> For what does this newly minted prophet call? For continuation of the bloody war in South Vietnam, for expansion of this war, for unrestrained oppression of all who belong to the camp of opponents of the existing puppet regime....
>
> ... It is the idea of the American military that Taylor, promoted to the rank of ambassador-prophet, will spare no effort for the implementation of this policy.[62]

The Soviet Union was cognizant of Taylor's lack of diplomatic experience and was also familiar with Taylor's leading role in the development of American flexible response and counterinsurgency theory.[63] At the same time, Johnson's declaration that the United States "where necessary would not hesitate to risk war" to preserve the peace and McNamara's statement that "we are prepared for all possible developments in Southeast Asia" lent a militant posture to American policy, in Moscow's view. Numerous Soviet broadcasts in late June made it clear that to the Soviets, the United States was entirely prepared to risk a major war in Southeast Asia.[64] The "hints of the possibility of a large scale conflict" pointed "the direction in which U.S. policy is heading.[65] The American-South Vietnamese disagreement over *Bac Tien* was a minor one, the Soviets believed.

By the end of July 1964, then, the Soviet position in Southeast Asia was not enviable. Moscow viewed the United States as intent on carrying out its commitment to the South Vietnamese government. At the same time, according to the Soviet definition of a war of national liberation, the National Liberation Front was worthy of Soviet aid but to grant aid would risk a confrontation with a United States that was apparently willing to accept almost any risk to honor its commitments and achieve success. Compounding the Soviet problems was the challenge presented by Communist China to the Soviet interpretation of Communism and charges by North Vietnam that the Soviet Union was failing to protect the socialist bloc. It was little wonder that on July 27 the Soviet Union threatened to resign its position from the International Control Commission on Indochina if its proposal for a conference was not accepted.[66] According to *Pravda*:

> The Soviet Union, for its part, is ready as always to promote efforts which are directed at accelerating the calling of the aforementioned conference. A negative attitude on the part of other states toward this proposal will place the Soviet government in a position where it will be forced to reconsider the question of the possibility of the fulfillment of the functions of co-chairman by the Soviet Union, since the role of co-chairman is being made useless and fictitious by the significant and systematic violations of the Geneva Agreements by some states.[67]

The following day's issue of *Izvestiia*, as if to emphasize the threat of resignation, moved the threat from the last paragraph, where it had appeared in the declaration as printed in *Pravda*, to the second paragraph.[68] At the same time Khrushchev indicated to British Foreign Secretary R.A. Butler, who was in Moscow at the time, that the Soviet Union had decided to defer a decision on its withdrawal from the co-chairmanship.[69] The threat, though, still remained.

Two questions were almost immediately asked. First, was the Soviet threat a real one or was it designed for propaganda purposes? Second, if the Soviet Union was seriously considering the resignation of the co-chairmanship, what were its motivations?

The general impression at the time the Soviet threat was made was that the Soviet Union was, in fact, serious. After the British exchange in Moscow with the U.S.S.R., Western officials "expect[ed] the Soviet Union to carry out its threat to withdraw as co-chairman."[70] China and Albania also apparently considered the Soviet resignation threat to be genuine. A mid-August Albanian radio broadcast declared that "in recent times the Soviet Union has tended to dissociate itself from events in Southeast Asia."[71] Peking had a similar impression. In a note dated August 2, China appealed to Soviet leaders not to withdraw from the co-chairmanship and supported their call for a new conference.[72]

If it is accepted that the Soviet threat was genuine, what motivated the Soviet action? While the strained state of Soviet-North Vietnamese relations was undoubtedly one of the factors which influenced the Soviet action it is doubtful if the Soviet-North Vietnamese ill will would have led the Soviets to indicate that they would resign the co-chairmanship. The Soviets had nothing to gain if they resigned their position solely because of their disagreements with North Vietnam. What other factors, then, could have been determinants?

Probably the most significant other factor was the danger of a Chinese-American confrontation in Southeast Asia. Before the Soviet Union threatened that it would quit the co-chairmanship, the Chinese government had indicated that it would come to the assistance of North Vietnam if the D.R.V. were attacked. On June 24, Chinese Foreign Minister Chen Yi implied for the first time that Chinese assistance would be forthcoming:

> The Chinese people absolutely will not sit idly by while the Geneva Agreements are completely torn up and the flames of war spread to their side.[73]

The Chinese response to a North Vietnamese note condemning U.S. provocations made the Chinese position more explicit:

> the Chinese people naturally cannot be expected to look on with folded arms in the face of any aggression against the D.R.V.[74]

Later in the month, Chen Yi linked Vietnam and Korea:

> Should United States imperialism dare to embark on an adventure of extending the war [in Vietnam], it would end up in the same way it did in its war of aggression in Korea.[75]

On July 19, Chen Yi reiterated that Communist China would come to the assistance of North Vietnam if it were attacked by the U.S.[76]

With these Chinese promises of assistance to North Vietnam, the Soviet threat of withdrawal from the co-chairmanship of the Geneva Conference on Indochina may be more easily explained. If the Soviet leaders were convinced that the Chinese position was genuine and at the same time believed that the United States would take a firm stand in South Vietnam which would possibly include expanding the war to North Vietnam, then the Soviet threat to resign its co-chairmanship may be viewed as a Soviet effort to disengage itself from an area of imminent Chinese-American confrontation.

The Soviet reasoning probably went along the following lines: if the United States accepted the Soviet proposal for a new conference specifically on Laos, the possibility of a Chinese-American confrontation would decrease. If the United States did not accept the proposal, then a continuation of the June-July situation — an increasing U.S. resolve in Southeast Asia and a convincing Chinese promise to come to the assistance of North Vietnam — could have compromised Khrushchev's efforts to improve Soviet-American relations and possibly could have led to a Soviet-American confrontation for the benefit of China and North Vietnam.

Thus, if the Soviet proposal was not accepted, the Soviet Union was willing to disengage from continental Southeast Asia. Such a Soviet disengagement would have prevented a deterioration of Soviet-American relations because of occurrences in that area and would have also lessened the possibility of the Soviet Union's involvement in the event of a Chinese-American confrontation.

The Soviets probably also perceived a third benefit which would accrue to a policy of disengagement, given an American rejection of their proposal for a conference on Laos. The Soviet Union, through its disengagement, would have been dissociated completely from the more strident Chinese ideological position of support to national liberation movements. Thus, the groundwork would have been laid for a decisive condemnation of the Chinese ideological position at the proposed conference of world communist parties.[77]

Khrushchev's July 8 speech to a graduating class at a military academy in Moscow may also be construed in this light. In his speech, Khrushchev emphasized various successes of the Soviet Union's foreign policy, mentioning things such as the Test Ban Treaty and the decrease in the manufacture of nuclear materials. The alleged goals of Moscow's diplomacy, *i.e.*, lasting peace, the removal of the threat of war and peaceful coexistence between countries with different social systems, were also stressed.[78] Later in his speech, the Soviet premier referred to national liberation wars and their dangers in general:

> We do not need war; war brings only calamity for nations.... However, when I say that we are against wars, I mean aggressive expansionist war. But there are other wars — national liberation wars where the suppressed nations are rising in the struggle against their oppressors, colonialists and imperialists. Such wars we consider just and sacred. We support the people who take up arms and fight for their independence and freedom. And we support them not only with words but with concrete actions.

Although Khrushchev appeared to support national liberation wars, he immediately followed the above statement with a warning to the Soviet people that they:

> must realistically see and appraise the international situation, the situation in which we live. The hotbeds of international tension which now exist — and these hotbeds, unfortunately, are in many parts of the world — are dangerous. *They are dangerous because in these regions local wars, in certain instances, could lead to a large conflict, and could even provoke a world conflagration* [emphasis added].

Khrushchev's warning about the danger of a local war escalating to a world war was followed by a reference to Vietnam:

> In South Vietnam, the United States has waged an aggressive bloody war for many years. The U.S. is in the role of world gendarme, striving to overcome the national liberation movement of the people of South Vietnam. This is a dangerous policy, and we have pointed this out to the government of the United States more than once. The people of South Vietnam have a full right to struggle with the force of arms for their freedom and their rights. They have a sacred fight for their freedom, and we support the people of South Vietnam in their struggle.

In one speech, then, Khrushchev had succeeded in emphasizing the Soviet desire for peace, underlining the Soviet support for national liberation wars, cautioning the world about the dangers of a local war escalating to a world war and confirming Soviet support for the South Vietnamese people. Later newspaper articles echoed Khrushchev's remarks, reiterating Soviet support for the South Vietnamese people[79] and restating the Soviet fear of the escalation of a local war into a world war.[80]

How may these statements be interpreted? Since Soviet aid to the National Liberation Front of South Vietnam was insignificant during 1964,[81] the Soviet proclamation of support for the people of South Vietnam was undoubtedly for propaganda purposes, the silencing of Chinese criticism, and/or the silencing of domestic criticism that may have been emanating from various Soviet hardliners. The same was probably true for the Soviet espousal of national liberation wars. The stated Soviet desire for peace was part of Khrushchev's standard rhetoric.

The Soviet warning about the dangers of a local war escalating into a world war cannot be quite as easily dismissed. Although it is true that Khrushchev's 1961 typology of wars had warned of the precise danger of escalation of which Khrushchev spoke at the graduation exercises, the Soviet leader did not habitually warn of the danger. Even more curious was the reference to Vietnam which immediately followed the warning. While he did refer to Soviet conversations with the United States and Soviet support for the people of South Vietnam, his reference was both vague and subdued. The combination of all these factors seemingly indicated that Khrushchev was asking the United States not to fall into a "Chinese trap" in Southeast Asia.

Khrushchev's July 8 speech, the Soviet threat to resign as co-chairman of the Geneva Conference on Indochina, the Soviet reaction to the American rejection of proposals to negotiate, the Soviet reactions to U.S. military buildups in South Vietnam and South Vietnamese calls for attacks on North Vietnam, and the Soviet reaction to Maxwell Taylor's ambassadorial appointment can all be explained if the Soviet Union considered U.S. policy to be operating relatively free of constraints in regard to a continued military buildup in South Vietnam and to possible land or air attacks against North Vietnam.

If these were the Soviet calculations during the first seven months of 1964, what was the comparable Chinese position? For the most part, it appears as if the Chinese People's Republic accepted American intentions in Vietnam at face value but was not intimidated by them. The Chinese, confident in the ideological correctness of their advocacy of national liberation, argued that the Vietnamese could "cope with their

[own] situation."⁸² Thus, while the Chinese vehemently condemned American involvement in the Khanh coup, the appointment of Maxwell Taylor as ambassador and American threats of escalation, they also attempted to have the best of both worlds. By stressing the correctness of the North Vietnamese policy *vis-à-vis* the South Vietnamese, they ideologically supported national liberation. Conversely, by stressing the necessity of self-reliance in national liberation, the Chinese could improve their freedom of action in a potential crisis situation with the United States. The earlier Chinese promises of aid (see above) could in reality be interpreted in numerous ways, several of which did not obligate the Chinese to direct support for the D.R.V. For example, China could conceivably act as a "reliable rear area" for D.R.V. activity. This is almost exactly what happened. China verbally warned that the two Asian communist countries were like "lips and teeth" and would act in concert.⁸³ At the same time Peking moved troops, aircraft and supplies into Chinese provinces bordering North Vietnam. Airfields were built in southern China which on the basis of their location (12 miles from Vietnam) could have been intended as much for North Vietnamese defense as for Chinese defense.⁸⁴ This interpretation of a relatively flexible Chinese strategy which maximized China's freedom of action was further supported by the Chinese position on negotiations. China supported the D.R.V.'s appeal for reconvening the Geneva Conference on Laos and generally supported various proposals for negotiations throughout the summer.

In retrospect, the motivation behind Chinese statements and actions before the Tonkin crisis is clear. The Chinese perceived the opportunity for considerable ideological gain at the expense of the Russians in Vietnam. To benefit from this potential, they had to make their commitment to North Vietnam credible. Steps to achieve this were undertaken. At the same time, potential confrontation with the United States, which was viewed as committed to the Saigon regime, was a distinct possibility. To minimize this possibility, a certain flexibility had to be built into Chinese policy. Consequently Peking stopped short of unequivocable support of Hanoi.

The Tonkin Gulf incidents of August 2 and 4 confirmed the wisdom of both the Soviet and the Chinese policy, at least to Soviet and Chinese leaders. Soviet disengagement had apparently been the best policy for Moscow, since the Kremlin had neither the means nor the inclination to respond to the American counterattack on North Vietnam. Conversely, Chinese flexibility permitted Peking to condemn the United States, to support North Vietnam and the NLFSV and to do nothing.

In actuality, the Soviet reponse to the American attack on North Vietnam was difficult to categorize. On August 6 an official TASS news agency statement reported that "authoritative Soviet circles emphatically condemn" the U.S. bombing of North Vietnam. Continuing, the statement said that future provocations could lead to a "broad armed conflict with many ensuing dangerous consequences" and that the U.S. would bear the responsibility for any "dangerous consequences."[85]

At first glance, this indicated strong Soviet support for the North Vietnamese government. However, the August 6 issue of *Pravda* in which the TASS statement was printed weakened the impact of the statement by printing an equally large joint Soviet-American statement issued on the anniversary of the Test Ban Treaty entitled "To Advance Further on the Path Toward Mutual Understanding and Peace." Both the TASS statement and the joint Soviet-American statement received front page coverage.[86] Viewed in isolation, this occurrence was relatively insignificant. An August 6 *Izvestiia* article, though, continued to present a rather ambivalent Soviet attitude. After drawing a distinction between Senator Barry Goldwater, Khanh and the Pentagon on the one hand and the American people on the other, *Izvestiia* declared:

> The forces of peace have all the possibilities of putting out the flames of conflict in Southeast Asia and of insuring all the countries, all the people of this area a stable peace under conditions of freedom and independence. No effort must be wasted in the pursuit of this objective.[87]

On August 7, 8 and 9, *Pravda* carried considerable coverage of world commentary on the bombing, but had little editorial comment.[88] At the same time, Radio Free Europe noted that European communist radio stations were reporting the North Vietnamese attacks and the American retaliation "almost without comment."[89] *Pravda's* coverage of China's statement on the American bombing also indicated that Moscow feared further escalations in Southeast Asia.[90] *Pravda's* coverage completely omitted China's warning that "aggression against the D.R.V. is aggression against China" and its declaration that "no socialist country can sit idly by."[91]

Khrushchev's remarks during the several days immediately following the American bombing were the most telling indication that the Soviet Union saw a necessity both to confirm its backing of a fraternal socialist country and to maintain cordial relations with a United States perceived to be operating free from constraints in Vietnam. Speeches by Khrushchev or interviews with the Premier were carried by *Pravda* on three consecutive days following the TASS statement. Not until the third day did Khrushchev mention Vietnam.

On August 7, *Pravda* printed a long conversation between Khrushchev and several collective farm leaders.[92] On August 8, *Pravda* carried an interview with Khrushchev on the Soviet economy.[93] Finally, on August 9, *Pravda* printed a lengthy speech which Khrushchev had

Townhin made some change mind about disengagement

delivered in Ordzhonikidze the previous day in which he stressed the Soviet intent to defend the socialist bloc.[94] According to the Soviet premier:

> The Soviet Union does not want war and will do everything to prevent it. But if the imperialists want war with the socialist countries, the people of the Soviet Union will fulfill their sacred duty; they will defend their homeland and other socialist nations.

Khrushchev also delivered a condemnation of the American bombing, and then warned certain individuals of the futility of their efforts to overcome national liberation movements. The warning was notable for its vagueness as well as its restraint:

> We would want to forewarn all who are mad and half-mad, sane and insane, not those who want to live in peace and who want to respect the independence of nations. Let them not intervene in the internal affairs of other countries. Let them finally understand that in our time no one can act like a pirate. Nations will not live as they did in the past, will not be slaves to capitalism or colonialism. They fight and will continue to fight for their freedom, and no aggressive forces, no gendarme action of the U.S.A. or other imperialist power can defeat them. We would want to forewarn all so that they understand and assimilate these truths. If the imperialists want a war, then this war will spell the full and utter defeat of capitalism, although it will also bring many victims of tragedies to the nations of peace.

The content and timing of Khrushchev's speech gives rise to several questions. First, why did it take three days for the Premier to respond to the attack? Second, how did Khrushchev's remarks mesh with previous Soviet reaction? Third, to whom were Khrushchev's remarks addressed? Finally, why did the Soviet leader refrain from making a stronger promise of support?

One explanation for the delay in Khrushchev's reaction to the bombing was that he was touring the Russian countryside at the time of the bombing. However, this in itself is not a sufficient explanation. A more satisfactory explanation of Khrushchev's delayed statement was that there was a debate within the Soviet leadership over how strong a position to take. It was obvious that the Soviet Union could not follow its preferred policy of Southeast Asian disengagement. To take that course would have left the Soviet Union open to Chinese criticism that American imperialism had succeeded in intimidating the Soviet Union. A new policy had to be decided upon. If the Soviet leaders held different views about the future course of U.S. policy toward Vietnam, then the three-day delay before Khrushchev's statement may have indicated that a debate within the Soviet leadership was taking place and, at least in the short-run, the Soviet Union was adopting a "wait and see" attitude with respect to America policy. A "wait and see" attitude also gave Soviet leaders a chance to see whether the U.S. attack was an isolated event or part of a more extensive plan. From Khrushchev's vantage point, the hard-line ideologues and militarists would likely be satisfied with the warnings that national liberation movements were unstoppable, that the Soviet Union would defend the socialist bloc in the event of an attack and that capitalism would be utterly destroyed in a world war. On the other hand, the softline state bureaucrats, managers and technicians would likely be appeased by Khrushchev's realization that the capitalist leadership was not monolithic and by his reaffirmation that a world war would bring great suffering to the socialist countries as well as to the capitalist countries.

Internationally, a similar rationale was sufficient to explain Khrushchev's speech. The same arguments which he used to placate hard-line domestic pressures could be used to answer Chinese claims that the Soviet Union was a revisionist power. At the same time, the arguments which he used to placate softline domestic pressures could be used to indicate to the American leaders that the Soviet Union was not necessarily ready to have Soviet-American relations deteriorate because of the bombing of North Vietnam.

To the Soviets, the Tonkin Gulf incidents had shown an American willingness to disregard China as a constraint on U.S. actions if these actions remained limited to involvement in South Vietnam and minor efforts against North Vietnam. Since the Soviet Union had already made it evident that its interests in continental Southeast Asia were practically nonexistent, the Kremlin realized that its own effect as a constraint on U.S. policy in the area was negligible. The Soviet leadership believed that the United States had considerable latitude in choosing its options during the summer of 1964.

The Chinese, meanwhile, had had the wisdom of their flexible policy confirmed. China and North Vietnam both condemned the Soviet effort to bring the Tonkin Gulf incidents to the United Nations.[95] While the Soviet leadership decided what course of action to take following the incidents, the Chinese quickly came out against "the aggression against China."[96] To underline the sincerity of their position, the Chinese quickly moved over a dozen MIG 15s and 17s into North Vietnam[97] and began to conduct large-scale army manuevers in southern China.[98] Chen Yi again promised Chinese support for North Vietnam.

The Chinese reaction to the Tonkin Gulf incident was predicated on an attempt to maintain Chinese credibility in Southeast Asia. While all the above efforts did, to a degree, save Chinese face in Southeast Asia, *The New York Times* reported the attempt was only partially successful. The feeling which reportedly became prevalent in Southeast Asia was that if there was a "paper tiger," it was China.[99]

Why did the Chinese choose the rather limited methods of

response they did? Probably the most obvious answer was the extreme Chinese military inferiority in relation to the United States. Despite Peking's bombastic rhetoric about American imperialism, the P.R.C. clearly sought to avoid a direct confrontation with the United States while at the same time to benefit from its avowed opposition to imperialism. In other words, the Chinese would do all they could to support North Vietnam without risking a military confrontation with the United States. Peking believed the United States was resolute in its intent to maintain a separate South Vietnamese government and consequently would encourage the North Vietnamese and the NLFSV to pursue a course of "resolute opposition to imperialism" based on "self-sufficiency" while at the same time reducing risk to itself.

Following the Tonkin Gulf incidents, both socialist countries reviewed their perceptions of American policy toward Vietnam. Their review led to surprising conclusions: the United States would not become involved in a full-scale intervention in Vietnam, and would even accept the loss of South Vietnam. To both countries, the leading reason for this perceived U.S. hesitancy to become sizably involved was the ongoing Presidential election. At first, to the Kremlin, the Presidential election served as a pressure to escalate the war effort. Although there were occasional allusions to U.S. domestic criticism of the war in Vietnam during the summer of 1964, most Soviet commentaries instead criticized "the activization of the 'ultras' in the U.S.A., who increase the danger of all types of foreign policy adventures." To the Soviet Union, this activization was in itself "assuming an international significance."[100] Chief among the "ultras" was Senator Barry Goldwater. To *Pravda*, instead of being sent "to a madhouse or a court," he received the nomination as the Republican Presidential candidate.[101] Another publication believed that Goldwater "reflected the adventuristic position of the most chauvinistic and aggressive circles of American reaction."[102] To the Kremlin leaders, Goldwater's increased influence carried a threat of increased world tension.

During the early stages of the Presidential campaign, President Johnson was not excluded from this Soviet criticism. Maxwell Taylor's appointment as ambassador to South Vietnam was one act viewed as an attempt by Johnson "to confirm his 'hardness' for the 'ultras.' "[103] The Soviet Union made similar observations about the Tonkin Gulf crisis. "Unofficial Soviet sources" told American reporters that the U.S. reprisal strikes against North Vietnam were, from the Soviet viewpoint, dictated by the twin necessities of the U.S. Presidential campaign and placating General Khanh.[104] *Pravda* implied the same thing as it observed that:

> Following the aggressive act of August 5, leaders of the Republican Party congratulated leaders of the Democratic Party, saying that national unity was attained on the question.[105]

Gradually, though, as Goldwater continued to make statements such as the United States should "prosecute the war in Vietnam with the object of ending it,"[106] and Johnson countered them with statements such as neither American nor South Vietnamese interests would be served "by a big offensive against North Vietnam,"[107] the Soviet Union accepted the dichotomy between the two candidates. In the words of one Soviet periodical published after the election:

> For the first time, pre-election foreign policy declarations of Republicans and Democrats differed significantly from each other on a number of points, and in this way the American electorate received the possibility to make known its attitudes on a major international problem — the problem of war and peace.[108]

The same article continued, saying that the leaders of the Democratic Party took "a serious and determined stance in the area of international relations in opposition to the ragings of Goldwater." It was even posited that "in the final analysis," Johnson's position on war and peace had "determined the outcome of the Presidential election." Johnson's opposition to nuclear war, the use of tactical nuclear weapons, and nuclear proliferation were all cited as examples of his "realistic" position.[109] On another occasion, it was recalled that Johnson had opposed a contemplated blockage of Communist China during the Quemoy and Matsu crisis of the 1950s.[110] To the Soviet Union, Johnson's position "on the question of war and peace were his trump cards in the pre-election struggle."[111] This position not only helped him defeat Goldwater, but also acted as a constraint on U.S. policy toward Vietnam. A major escalation in the war would have hampered Johnson's campaign position, and therefore, in Soviet eyes, American diplomats were

> doing everything possible so that there is not a new political explosion before the November presidential elections in the United States.[112]

The perceived effect of the election on actual U.S. policy in Vietnam was underlined to the Soviets after the Vietcong raid on the Bien Hoa airbase. The attack, which occurred immediately before the U.S. Presidential election, destroyed five B-57 bombers, damaged eight B-57s, and killed four Americans.[113] Even though the United States immediately warned China and North Vietnam that Washington did not intend to disengage from Vietnam after the election, the United States did not retaliate.[114] In contrast to China and North Vietnam, which termed the attack on Bien Hoa a "brilliant victory,"[115] the Soviet media, for the most part, carried factual reports of the incident, as well as an occasional picture of the destroyed B-57s.[116] Once again, though, when it became clear that after the election the United States would not retaliate, the Soviet media adopted a more strident tone, referring to the Bien Hoa attack as "the victory of the Patriots."[117]

President Johnson's impressive election victory implied that American foreign policy would retain its continuity. In the Soviet Union, new leaders had come to power as well. Following Khrushchev's removal in October, the new Soviet leaders—Leonid Brezhnev and Alexei Kosygin—exerted efforts to confirm that continuity in Soviet foreign policy would also remain. One area where continuity did not exist, however, was in Soviet policy toward Southeast Asia. Almost immediately, Soviet-North Vietnamese and Soviet-NLFSV relations improved. On November 17, 1964, Premier Kosygin sent a message of solidarity directly to the Central Committee of the NLFSV, something which Khrushchev had never done. On December 20, *Pravda* carried the statement of the chairman of the NLFSV's Central Committee, Nguyen Huu Tho, that three-fourths of South Vietnam's land and half of its people were under Vietcong control. *Pravda* commented that much of this accomplishment was due to "moral and material support" from the Soviet Union.[118] On January 1, 1965, the NLFSV established a permanent delegation in Moscow. Clearly Soviet policy toward Vietnam had changed.

The Chinese were also aware of this. Although published a year after the collective leadership removed Khrushchev, the following Chinese perception of the new team was probably adopted during late 1964. According to the Chinese, the new leaders of the Soviet Union

> came to realize that it was no longer advisable to copy Khrushchev's policy of "disengagement" in its totality. So they switched to the policy of involvement, that is, of getting their hand in.[119]

Even with the new Soviet involvement in Southeast Asia and Johnson's impressive election victory, the Kremlin did not believe that there would be "preordain[ed] change in the foreign policy of official Washington."[120] Instead, it was posited that "the forces which moved [Goldwater] to the front of the stage are still there and have maintained their influence."[121] The only difference to the Soviets, was that after Goldwater's defeat, the U.S. "ultras' " plans for expanding the war were "afraid of the light of day" and were "hidden under lock and key."[122]

The Soviet leaders were aware that contingency plans for the bombing of North Vietnam were being discussed in Washington.[123] As these Washington discussions continued, the Soviet media began to talk of a "great decision" which would be forthcoming from Washington about the future course of American policy toward Vietnam.[124] It also appeared as if the Soviet Union had no firm idea as to what the decision would be. *Izvestiia* quoted one Washington paper, saying that Johnson's point of view was "not known to even his closest advisors."[125] A Soviet broadcast called on Johnson to "confirm words [uttered during the election campaign] with real deeds."[126]

The new Soviet leadership, possibly attempting to influence the decision-making process in Washington, chose to make its first promise of aid to North Vietnam during late November when Taylor journeyed to the U.S. to discuss future policy. The Kremlin's promise coincided with a threat against "adventuristic plans":

> Those who nurture adventuristic plans in the Indochinese peninsula must be aware that the Soviet Union will not remain indifferent to the fate of a fraternal socialist country [North Vietnam] and is prepared to extend to it the necessary assistance.[127]

Moscow apparently wanted to make sure that Washington was cognizant of the Soviet position. Throughout December, Soviet leaders and media continued to warn against "adventuristic plans" and promised "necessary assistance." A December 1 *Izvestiia* article equated the debate over Vietnam with the 1952 debate over Korea, and then reprinted the warning.[128] Three days later, a Brezhnev speech was printed which carried the same comments,[129] to be followed the next day by a Soviet-Czechoslovakian communiqué which once again promised "the necessary assistance" to North Vietnam if it was attacked.[130] Foreign Minister Andrei Gromyko's speech to the United Nations reiterated the warning a few days later,[131] and Kosygin's December 9 speech to the Supreme Soviet promised assistance to both North Vietnam and Cuba if they were attacked.[132] *Pravda* followed up the already abundant restatements of the warning just a few days later with two more reiterations.[133]

The Soviet Union also maintained its call for a return to negotiations on Indochina throughout December.[134] At first, when viewed in light of the increased successes of the National Liberation Front of South Vietnam during November and December, this Soviet position may appear to be an anomaly. However, when it is remembered that the Soviet-American rapprochement maintained its importance under the collective leadership despite its desire to improve Soviet-North Vietnamese relations, the anomaly becomes more readily explainable. The Soviets may have again been striving for the best of both worlds, a success which they had achieved once before at the Geneva Conference on Indochina in 1954. If a conference were arranged, the United States could have more easily found a way out of an uncomfortable situation. At the same time, the NLFSV would have been in control of considerable areas of South Vietnam. Therefore, assuming a conference were arranged, the Soviet Union could have achieved a continued Soviet-American rapprochement and a continued improvement in Soviet-North Vietnamese relations.

The Soviet attempt to insert itself as a constraint on U.S. policy toward Vietnam continued from late December through early

February. Deputy Chairman of the Council of Ministers A.N. Shelepin, delivering an address to the National Assembly of the United Arab Republic on December 27, 1964, confirmed that the Soviet Union would not "stand by with its arms folded while Vietnam is subjected to aggression."[135] A week later, Soviet Foreign Minister Gromyko sent a note to North Vietnam's Foreign Minister Xuan Thuy promising "the necessary assistance" in case "the aggressors dare to encroach upon [the D.R.V.'s] independence and sovereignty."[136] *Krasnaia Zvezda* echoed Gromyko's statement,[137] and *Pravda* warned that the United States should not have "illusions" about the Soviet willingness to aid the Hanoi regime. The same article warned that continued American and South Vietnamese provocations of North Vietnam threatened an "outbreak of a big military conflict."[138] Two later *Pravda* articles carried similar promises of Soviet aid to North Vietnam if the D.R.V. was attacked.[139]

The worsening position of the United States in South Vietnam itself was discussed at great length by the Soviet media.[140] After pointing to the various military and political failures in South Vietnam, and noting that the U.S. also had to "be aware of the position of the socialist countries," a February 1 *Pravda* article concluded that "it can be said quite definitely" that Washington "had proved unable to solve the task of suppressing the liberation movement in South Vietnam."[141] A Soviet journal implied that the United States had sufficient reason to limit or decrease its involvement in Vietnam. Referring to Johnson's pre-election promises on war and peace, the journal declared that "he had a great opportunity to carry out these promises."[142] A different article in the same journal noted that:

> Three years of the undeclared war of the American imperialists against the people of South Vietnam have not brought them closer to their objective.[143]

Thus, by the beginning of February 1965, the Soviet Union perceived the U.S. position to be extremely serious. At the same time, the Russians were aware of the apparent lack of resolve that characterized U.S. policy and themselves had embarked on an extensive program to improve Soviet-NLFSV ties and Soviet-D.R.V. relations. By February, 1965, the Russian position in Vietnam had improved tremendously in relation to its August 1964 position, and its February perception of American intentions in Vietnam was diametrically opposed to its earlier view. These changed positions were magnified by the announcement that Kosygin would visit North Vietnam in the near future. This visit marked the first time a member of the Soviet hierarchy had gone to Vietnam since 1957 when then-President Voroshilov had visited Hanoi.

Why did Kosygin go to Vietnam? There are a number of indications that one of the primary factors may have been a Soviet desire to become more closely identified with a successful national liberation movement. As the NLFSV became more successful in late 1964, Soviet relations with both the Front and North Vietnam improved. As the Soviet Union adopted the perception that the United States was increasingly constrained in Vietnam, declarations of Soviet support for North Vietnam not only had the effect of further constraining the United States, but also of identifying the Soviet Union more closely with the struggle in the South. A closer identification of the Soviet Union with the NLFSV and the D.R.V. carried the added benefit of quieting the Chinese claim that the Soviet Union was not revolutionary. It was similarly clear that Kosygin's February 7 declaration that the Soviet Union supported a new conference on Indochina "to achieve a peaceful settlement" did not contradict Hanoi's position. As Western and Eastern sources all agreed, Hanoi, not Saigon, would have benefitted from such a conference since the NLFSV controlled much of the South.

Other interpretations of the motivation behind Kosygin's trip are also possible but not as persuasive. Kosygin's visit may also be viewed as a way to open a "second front" in Asia in the Sino-Soviet dispute and as an attempt to persuade Ho Chi Minh to attend the upcoming Moscow meeting intended to arrange a new world conference of communist parties. Regardless of the actual motivation, two things were clear. A distinct improvement had occurred in Soviet-North Vietnamese relations and the Russians clearly did not expect an American attack on North Vietnam.

The Soviet perception of American intentions was quite similar to the Chinese view at the time. Both before the Gulf of Tonkin crisis and after, the Chinese had stressed their intention to come to the aid of North Vietnam if the D.R.V. were attacked. Peking's parallel emphasis on revolutionary self-sufficiency enabled Peking, to a degree, to rationalize its limited aid to North Vietnam and at the same time maintain its revolutionary credentials. Throughout the fall of 1964, the Chinese continued to pursue this line of policy.[144]

The Chinese perception of constraints on U.S. policy, meanwhile, was somewhat similar to the Soviet attitude. The American presidental election was recognized as a factor in limiting U.S. courses of action in Vietnam but was dismissed in the long run as having "no genuine impact" on future American policy. Johnson's protestations of having no desire to expand the war were viewed as "campaign rhetoric" which would be abandoned after the election.[145] Goldwater was continually condemned as a dangerous candidate as the Chinese issued warnings to the United States not to extend the war.[146]

If the Chinese dismissed the American election as a possible constraint on American policy, the same was not true of the South Vietnamese domestic situation. As the NLFSV extended its influence and control over wider territories of South Vietnam, the Chinese increasingly praised the inevitability of its success. The continual coups in Saigon were similarly interpreted as proof that the United States could not maintain its position in Vietnam.[147] To Mao and the other Chinese leaders, the United States was in fact a "paper tiger" in Vietnam during late 1964, in no small degree because of the precarious internal situation of the South Vietnamese government.

China, just as the Soviet Union, was aware that a policy debate was going on in Washington during November. However, in contrast to Moscow's uncertainty, Peking apparently expected Washington's decision to be against sizeable escalation. (It will be remembered that in November the Soviets predicted that "only time will tell" what future American policy would be. See above.) Nonetheless, China cautioned that "aggression against North Vietnam is aggresssion against China" on several occasions in early December.[148] The timing of Peking's announcement may be attributed to two factors. First, the Chinese hoped to further sway American policy-makers toward a decision opposing new escalation in Vietnam. Second, Mao probably hoped to offset any gains the Soviet Union had made in Hanoi following Moscow's promise of "necessary assistance" to the D.R.V.

The renewed Soviet interest in Vietnam in particular and Southeast Asia in general was motivated, in the Chinese view, by the desire of the Kremlin's new leaders to "get their hand in" with an imminently successful national liberation movement.[149] If Brezhnev and Kosygin could successfully do that, Mao reasoned, then the successes of the NLFSV and by implication the ideological correctness of Hanoi's conduct of the national liberation wars would be shared by Moscow as well as Peking. It is little wonder, then, that the Chinese resented Moscow's new interest in Southeast Asia. The November explosion of a Chinese nuclear weapon had greatly boosted the Chinese image in Asia, and the success of the NLFSV would further improve China's prestige.

As January drew to a close, with the exception of the apparent improvement in Soviet-North Vietnamese relations, the Chinese position in Southeast Asia was secure. Khrushchev's fall, the Chinese nuclear explosion, a new Jakarta-Peking agreement and Peking's success in avoiding a world conference of communist parties originally scheduled for December at which Khrushchev had intended to seek expulsion of the Communist Party of China from the movement all contributed to the Chinese confidence. Additionally, and importantly, the specter of conflict with the United States that had appeared so possible in August had diminished considerably. In January, 1965, at the same time the

Soviet Union was anticipating eventual American withdrawal from Vietnam, Mao was predicting that the United States would accept defeat in Vietnam within two years or less.[150] Chinese support of unconditional negotiations on Vietnam was probably linked directly to this view of a for all practical purposes defeated United States.[151] If the United States rejected negotiations, China would appear as the "peace-loving" nation. If the U.S. accepted negotiations, then its bargaining position would be almost untenable. To Peking, the Vietnamese situation was under control.

# III
# Escalation: 1965-1966

Early in the morning of February 7, 1965, Vietcong guerrillas attacked American advisers' barracks in Pleiku and a helicopter base at Camp Holloway four miles away. Nine U.S. soldiers died, and 128 others were wounded. Within 14 hours, 49 U.S. navy jets retaliated against North Vietnamese barracks and staging areas at Dong Hoi, 40 miles north of the demilitarized zone. The next day, 24 more planes launched a second attack against a military communications center in North Vietnam, again just north of the border. These raids, known as FLAMING DART, marked the beginning of an entirely new era of the war in Vietnam. Although the raids were originally designed as a limited reprisal operation, it soon became clear that they in fact were the first stage in a new wave of escalations.

## Americanization: The View from the Oval Office

Why were the FLAMING DART raids any more noteworthy than the previous August attacks following the Tonkin Gulf incidents? Two reasons were most apparent. First, the public rationale for the raids linked them directly not only to the attacks on Pleiku, but also to "the continuing infiltration of personnel and equipment from North Vietnam." Additionally, it was stressed that "the key to the situation remains the cessation of infiltration from North Vietnam."[1] For the first time, the United States government was arguing that the South Vietnamese rebellion was primarily the product of North Vietnamese infiltration.[2] One fundamental change in the U.S. public position on the conflict was thus readily apparent.

The second major change was the linkage between the reprisal attacks on North Vietnam and three separate Vietcong attacks in the South, only one of which was against an American installation.[3] By linking the FLAMING DART operations with Vietcong attacks on both American and South Vietnamese personnel, earlier arguments that the

49

Vietnamese conflict was being fought primarily by indigenous South Vietnamese units with U.S. forces participating only in advisory and support capacities were considerably altered. In the future, military options previously closed to U.S. policy-makers would be open. Although the raids were officially described as "appropriate reprisal actions," these differences clearly existed. Even more pointedly, shortly after the first press statement concerning FLAMING DART was released, President Johnson issued another statement in which he declared that a turning point in the war had been reached and directed

> the orderly withdrawal of American dependents from South Vietnam.... We have no choice now but to clear the decks and make absolutely clear our continued determination to back South Vietnam....[4]

On February 10, the Vietcong ignored the warnings and attacked a U.S. enlisted men's billet at Qui Nhon. Once again, American and South Vietnamese planes responded to the attack, raiding targets just north of the demilitarized zone. Unlike the first FLAMING DART attacks, this mission, labeled FLAMING DART II, was not characterized as a reprisal. Instead, it was linked to "further direct provocations by the Hanoi regime" and "continued acts of aggression" by the North against the South.[5] American resolve, much to the surprise and consternation of both the Soviets and the Chinese (not to mention the North Vietnamese) had hardened.[6]

What led to this new American firmness and the decision to upgrade American involvement in the conflict? The decision to launch FLAMING DART I was reached in a 75-minute National Security Council meeting the night of February 6. In addition to the usual NSC members, Senate Majority Leader Mike Mansfield and Speaker of the House John McCormack were present.[7] Although no detailed description of the events of that meeting has been released, it is probable that the decision to launch the strikes was made because of a growing feeling that something had to be done to indicate to the North Vietnamese that the United States did not, in fact, intend to abandon its ally. Three months after the raids, Ambassador Taylor reported to Washington that throughout February the D.R.V. and Vietcong's outlook was "probably still favorable" for victory in the South, implying that Washington had been at least partly motivated to agree to the strikes because of North Vietnam's expected success.[8]

Similarly, McGeorge Bundy's mission to Saigon had returned to Washington and issued a memorandum reflecting the mission's views of the Vietnamese situation. Originally filed as "top secret" and not released till the unauthorized publication of the so-called *Pentagon Papers*, the Bundy memorandum pulled no punches about the seriousness of the situation in South Vietnam:

> The Situation in Vietnam is deteriorating, and without new U.S. action defeat appears inevitable — probably not in a matter of weeks or perhaps even months, but within the next year or so. There is still time to turn it around, but not much.
>
> The stakes in Vietnam are extremely high. The American investment is very large, and American responsibility is a fact of life.... The international prestige of the United States, and a substantial part of our influence are directly at risk in Vietnam ... any negotiated U.S. withdrawal today would mean surrender on the installment plan.
>
> The policy of graduated and continuing reprisal ... is the most promising course available....
>
> There is one grave weakness in our posture in Vietnam which is within our own power to fix — and that is a widespread belief that we do not have the will and force and patience and determination to take the necessary action and stay the course.
>
> This is the overriding reason for our present recommendation of a policy of sustained reprisal. Once such a policy is put in force, we shall be able to speak in Vietnam on many topics and in many ways, with growing force and effectiveness.[9]

Thus, in one memorandum, the seriousness of the situation was outlined, the supposed causes for the seriousness were listed, the importance of improving the situation was argued and the method to achieve the needed improvement was put forth. Bundy rejected the possibility of withdrawal summarily and unhesitatingly advocated escalation.

Bundy defined his concept of sustained reprisals as "a policy in which air and naval action against the North is justified by and related to the whole Vietcong campaign of violence and terror in the South." The cost of a program of sustained reprisals "seem[ed] cheap" when "measured against the costs of defeat in Vietnam." Once the program was initiated, "it should not be necessary to connect each specific act against North Vietnam to a particular outrage in the South." While the entire Bundy recommendation was developed before the original FLAMING DART raids, it had not yet been delivered to Johnson and was not a factor in the decision to proceed with the strikes. However, as the Bundy memorandum pointed out, FLAMING DART created "an ideal opportunity for the prompt development and execution of sustained reprisals."[10]

Ambassador Taylor argued along similar lines. In a series of top secret cables to Johnson, Taylor argued for "graduated reprisals" against the North. These reprisals would be designed to weaken the will of Hanoi's leaders in particular and North Vietnam in general and damage installations in North Vietnam from which the D.R.V. could aid the Vietcong.[11] At the same time, the Joint Chiefs argued for a series of continuing raids against the North.[12] The quantity and intensity of the various arguments finally swayed Johnson and a new course was set.

By February 13, Johnson had agreed to inaugurate regular bombing attacks against North Vietnam.[13] These operations, which would
become known as Operation ROLLING THUNDER, were originally
scheduled to begin on February 20 but a combination of bad weather,
another political crisis in Saigon[14] and a hope that the Soviet government
would cooperate in consultations on Vietnam with the British as co-
chairmen of the Geneva Conference,[15] forced its delay until March 2.
Again, the war had been escalated. The public rationale for the ROLLING
THUNDER raids had been developed in the releases explaining FLAMING
DART and reiterated after the commencement of ROLLING THUN-
DER — aggression from the North was continuing.[16] On the upper
decision-making level, it was evident that the new view was different
if only in the degree of seriousness. To Johnson, pressure had to be increased on North Vietnam not only because of infiltration but also
because South Vietnam was in danger of falling to the Vietcong. For the
most part, Johnson, Rusk, McNamara, Bundy and Taylor simply accepted the view that South Vietnam was too important to lose. American
involvement would be gradually escalated until the threat to the existence
of South Vietnam was eliminated. By March 15, Johnson had decided
that the strikes should be planned on a weekly basis, could be carried out
by U.S. planes alone, did not have to be specifically related to Vietcong
actions and would be designed as signals of American determination.[17]
According to a memorandum written by Assistant Secretary of Defense
John McNaughton shortly after Johnson's decision, American objectives
were:

> 70% — to avoid a humiliating U.S. defeat (to our reputation as
> a guarantor)
> 20% — to keep SVN (South Vietnam) territory from Chinese
> hands
> 10% — to permit the people of SVN to enjoy a better freer way
> of life
> Also — to emerge from crisis without unacceptable taint from
> methods used
> Not — to "help a friend," although it would be hard to stay in if
> asked out[18]

Additionally, NcNaughton asked if the situation in South Viet-
nam could be "bottomed out" without extreme measures against North
Vietnam or deployment of large numbers of United States troops. To the
Assistant Secretary, the answer was "perhaps — but probably no."[19]

McNaughton's question was perhaps initiated by the March 8
landing of two marine battalions at Da Nang, supposedly for purposes of
base defense. The landing of the marines signaled a major change in the
quality of U.S. involvement in Vietnam. Whereas previously U.S.

ground forces were officially advisors, they were not engaged in active defense. Now, they were.

Why had the decision to change from an advisory capacity to an active capacity been made? According to *United States-Vietnam Relations*, it was the result of at least two different perceptions developing in Washington. On the one hand, "official Washington ... [with the] possible exception of General Westmoreland, his staff, ... and General Johnson in Washington," took the deployment of the marines "at face value," that is, to "insure the security of U.S. lives and property." Westmoreland and Johnson, on the other hand, "saw in the deployment of the marines the beginning of greater things to come." Thus, to most decision-makers, including Lyndon Johnson, the two-battalions decision was a relatively insignificant one and therefore was not opposed.

At any rate, American combat troops, admittedly few in number, were in Vietnam. Two distinct and different decision-making processes had been followed in introducing combat troops and in bombing North Vietnam. In the case of the bombing attacks, the decision was made as a product of "a year's debate," while the introduction of troops had occurred "without much fanfare — and without much planning."[20] In both instances, though, the motivation behind the escalations was that South Vietnam was in danger of falling and unless American support was forthcoming, would fall. During the next several months more American combat troops were introduced to Vietnam and bombing raids against the D.R.V. expanded in both scope and intensity.

Even while the military escalations proceeded, criticism directed against Johnson's policies in Vietnam strengthened. To many, the U.S. was demanding an end to North Vietnam's support of the Vietcong, but was offering nothing in return. In response to this cricitism, Johnson delivered a speech at Johns Hopkins on April 7 in which he affirmed that the United States would "never be second" in the search for peace in Vietnam. During this speech, Johnson proposed the concept of the Mekong River project, which if acted upon would "dwarf even our TVA." Hanoi, however, denounced the proposal as a method to conceal U.S. aggression, instead putting forth its own famous "Four Points" proposal. As other Western peace feelers were turned aside,[21] Johnson viewed continuing military pressure as the only way to offset pressure against South Vietnam. "Our objective in Vietnam remains the same," Johnson told the American people, "an independent South Vietnam."[22]

This very American objective, despite U.S. protests to the contrary, precluded any serious efforts to negotiate. With the NLFSV near final victory in the South, any successful negotiated settlement would have had to take into account the prevailing balance of forces in the

South. Johnson could not and would not accept this. Thus on February 25 the United States rejected Kosygin's February 7 appeal for a negotiated settlement, claiming no negotiations would be acceptable until the D.R.V. "indicate[d] a willingness to end its aggression."[23] Several months later, a similar view was expressed by Bundy in an interview with Philippe Devillers. Bundy's attitude was even more striking in its indication that no negotiations would take place in the foreseeable future. Bundy told Devillers that there was:

> no chance of a political settlement for at least two or three years, during which time ... we shall have rebuilt the social structure of the countryside, the peasants will be so disgusted with the VC that they will denounce them.[24]

From the American point of view, then, the bottom line on negotiations was the same as the rationale which led to the increased military involvement: above all else, South Vietnam must survive as an integrated and independent national unit. Until this was guaranteed, no effective negotiations could occur. United States military strength was to be used to bring this about.

By late April, the additional American involvement had not yet guaranteed the survival of South Vietnam. During the one-day Honolulu Conference of April 20, it was made exceedingly apparent that U.S. leaders both in Washington and Saigon did not expect "the DRV/VC to capitulate, or come to a position acceptable to us, in less than six months." According to John McNaughton, "the participants" did not see "a dramatic improvement in the South in the immediate future."[25] Following a week-long bombing halt in May and a trip to Saigon by Secretary of Defense McNamara, American officials almost unanimously agreed that additional measures were necessary. Militarily, the situation in South Vietnam was continuing to deteriorate. Vietcong strength in the South was still growing in preparation for an expected monsoon offensive[26] and U.S. advisors, after assessing South Vietnamese military casualties, predicted that American forces would be introduced *en masse* to prevent defeat. In early June, the South Vietnamese were defeated in a major battle.[27] By mid-July, 1965, the situation within South Vietnam had become so grave that, following an inspection trip to Southeast Asia, Secretary McNamara concluded:

> The situation in South Vietnam is worse than a year ago.... A hard Vietcong push is now on to dismember the nation and to maul the army. The Vietcong main and local forces ... have the initiative, and, with large attacks (some in regimental strength), are hurting ARVN forces badly.... Cities and towns are being isolated.... The economy is deteriorating....[28]

Obviously, the situation was bad. President Johnson himself

commented on the condition of South Vietnam in early June, saying, "Suffice it to say, I think it [the military situation] is serious."[29]

On July 28, President Johnson held a press conference in which he discussed the American response to the worsening situation. Johnson announced that the U.S. government had decided to "commit its strength" to defend South Vietnam. Lamenting that "we did not choose to be the guardians ... but there is no one else," Johnson confirmed "one of the most solemn pledges of the American nation," to defend South Vietnam. Johnson left no room for questioning why an additional 100,000 U.S. troops were being sent to Vietnam: "We intend to convince the Communists that we cannot be defeated by force of arms or superior power."[30] By the end of 1965 there were 184,314 U.S. combat soldiers in Vietnam. The war had been Americanized.

From the viewpoint of Washington, then, the U.S. involvement in Vietnam was escalated during 1965 to prevent the imminent collapse of South Vietnam as an independent nation. While the policy of increased involvement had its critics both within and outside the administration, by far the dominant view was that American prestige, already deeply committed to the Saigon government, had to be protected and therefore South Vietnam had to retain its independence. Already, American strategists had moved from the so-called "strategy of base security" as a rationale for U.S. involvement to an "enclave strategy," and sentiment was mounting for acceptance of a "search and destroy strategy."[31] A short war was not expected, increased commitment was. Significantly, according to one McNaughton memo,[32] both the probability of success and the probability of failure of the U.S. intervention increased as time passed:

PROBABILITY OF SUCCESS/INCONCLUSIVE/COLLAPSE

| | |
|---|---|
| 1966 | .2/.7/.1 |
| 1967 | .4/.45/.15 |
| 1968 | .5/.3/.2 |

During 1966, Johnson's view changed little. Again, a combination of continued North Vietnamese support for the Vietcong, rebuffed peace feelers, and slow military progress led to the maintenance of the perceived necessity to continue the U.S. buildup. One of the most significant factors contributing to this view was the rebuff of the so-called "Peace Offensive" in late December 1965 and January 1966.

During the month-long "offensive," American bombing raids against North Vietnam were halted. Meanwhile, United States Ambassador to the United Nations Arthur Goldberg visited Pope Paul VI,

French President Charles De Gaulle, and British Prime Minister Harold Wilson. Ambassador-at-Large W. Averell Harriman journeyed to Poland, India and Yugoslavia in an attempt to arrange negotiations. Ambassador to the Soviet Union Foy Kohler met with Soviet President Nikolai Podgorny. Secretary of State Dean Rusk talked with Hungarian officials and Presidential Assistant McGeorge Bundy traveled to Canada to meet with Prime Minister Lester Pearson. From Washington's viewpoint, no results were obtained and bombing was resumed.

Shortly after resumption of the air raids on the D.R.V., Johnson met with South Vietnamese President Thieu and Premier Ky in Honolulu. The Honolulu Conference, called as much for its impact on the American domestic political scene as for planning additional steps for the U.S. effort in Vietnam,"[33] left no doubt (if there was any remaining) about the direction of U.S. policy. The declaration and communiqué issued at the conclusion of the conference called for a "two front war" in South Vietnam, one directed against communism and the other against South Vietnamese poverty.[34] Johnson's administration became not only more deeply committed to the military confrontation in the aftermath of the Honolulu Conference but more closely tied to the Thieu-Ky regime as well.

Johnson and other American policy makers had long recognized the necessity of creating a stable government in South Vietnam[35] but had been for the most part unable to achieve this objective. After the Thieu-Ky government came to power during the summer of 1965, the U.S. government pressured particularly Ky into numerous references to the need for social and economic reforms.[36] The Honolulu Conference may in part be viewed as a continuation of that effort. It was soon evident, however, that the process of popularizing Ky and stabilizing the government had failed. In March, anti-Ky Buddhist rioting broke out. By April 14, Ky had been "persuaded" to hold elections during the fall of 1966. Although these elections were eventually held, considerable doubt remained about their legitimacy. In the United States, the September elections were hailed as a success for Vietnamese democracy by the U.S. government; in South Vietnam, they were viewed as a "politically irrelevant gesture."[37]

The United States government had become in essence not only the guarantor of South Vietnamese independence but also of the Thieu-Ky government. The recognized need for stability and the absence of leaders other than Thieu and Ky who shared the objectives of the U.S. government practically guaranteed continued American support for Thieu and Ky. Throughout 1966, this support was manifested not only in diplomatic-political advocacy but also in the continued influx of

*Honolulu, early 1966: South Vietnamese Premier Nguyen Cao Ky hears out President Lyndon B. Johnson during a break in formal talks. Courtesy The White House.*

American men and materiel to South Vietnam. By the end of 1966, over 383,000 U.S. soldiers were fighting in Vietnam. To Washington, this deployment of troops had been marginally effective. In the words of Secretary of Defense McNamara in a memorandum addressed to Johnson following McNamara's December 1966 return from South Vietnam, "any military victory in South Vietnam the Vietcong may have had in mind 18 months ago has been thwarted by our emergency deployments and actions."

McNamara sounded more somber notes as well. The Secretary saw "no reasonable way to bring the war to an end soon," described pacification as "a bad disappointment," and could find no evidence that the morale of Hanoi had been "cracked." McNamara's conclusion was both foreboding and prophetic:

> In essence, we find ourselves ... no better, and if anything worse off [than before]. This important war must be fought and won by the Vietnamese themselves. We have known this from the beginning. But the discouraging truth is that, as was the case in 1961 and 1963 and 1965, we have not found the formula, the catalyst, for training and inspiring them into effective action.[38]

McNamara argued that the U.S. had to "continue to press the enemy militarily" and develop a posture in Vietnam that would make "trying to wait us out less attractive." He advocated a five-point program to achieve this: stabilize United States force levels at eventually 470,000 men, construct an infiltration barrier along the 17th parallel, stabilize the ROLLING THUNDER program against the D.R.V. at 12,000 sorties per month, pursue an active pacification program in the South, and press for negotiations.

Thus, by the end of 1966, after two years of escalation, U.S. leaders still did not see the proverbial "light at the end of the tunnel." The specter of a military defeat had been removed, from the viewpoint of Washington, but the hope of guaranteeing the continuation of an independent South Vietnamese state had not been achieved. It was still argued that Southern instability and political violence was the result of North Vietnamese infiltration. From Johnson's perspective, the United States would pull out of Vietnam as soon as "the infiltration, the aggression, and the violence ceases."[39] With Hanoi arguing that Vietnam was rightfully one nation, there was little probability of this happening. The political frailty of the South Vietnamese government demanded continued American presence if Saigon's independence was to continue and since this was both Washington's and Saigon's objective, there was no other choice. With the D.R.V.-NLFSV side and the U.S.-Saigon side at loggerheads on the issue of infiltration, Johnson believed he had no choice but to pursue military victory. A political settlement was ruled out.

If anything, because of the increased U.S. commitment to the Saigon government, Washington viewed the situation as possibly worse in 1966 than it had been in 1965. The stakes had increased considerably, and the implications of winning or losing had expanded as well. In December 1965, Washington could contemplate withdrawal. By December 1966, such a thought was impossible. The battle had been joined and it had to be won.

## *The Johnson Doctrine: The View from Moscow*

The Kremlin, as might be expected, was placed in an uncomfortable and even embarrassing position by the American air attacks on the North. Put simply, the Soviet Union could do nothing militarily to prevent American attacks on a "fraternal socialist nation" because of its military inferiority to the United States. The escalations were embarrassing in a political sense since the first escalations, the FLAMING DART raids, occurred while Soviet Premier Kosygin was still in Hanoi as an official guest of the North Vietnamese government. The day before the air attacks, the Soviet premier had again promised to give "necessary assistance" to the Hanoi regime if North Vietnam were attacked by the United States. The Soviet reaction to the February 7 and 8 air raids did much to elucidate the Soviet predicament and to clarify the Soviet perception of the situation.

The first official Soviet government statement on the bombings was released on February 9. Condemning the raids, the statement was rather restrained in tone, and was in marked contrast to the D.R.V.'s statement to fight "until victory."[40] On the whole, Soviet commentary was rather limited. While *Pravda* carried reports of anti-American demonstrations throughout the world,[41] it was evident the Soviet leaders were uncomfortable over developments in Vietnam. Although a relatively small but violent demonstration was organized in front of the American Embassy in Moscow,[42] Soviet commentary remained restrained. Soviet papers even appeared to be making a conscious effort to treat Kosygin's visit to the D.R.V. and the American bombing of that country as two completely independent events. In no single *Pravda, Izvestiia,* or *Krasnaia Zvezda* article was it observed that the American bombing had occurred simultaneously with Kosygin's visit to Hanoi. Soviet leaders were obviously aware of the concurrent events. They were also obviously trying to minimize the strategic, tactical and political implications of the simultaneous timing of the two events.

Did the Soviet Union consider the timing of the attacks against North Vietnam to be a "provocation," especially in light of Kosygin's presence in Hanoi? While the Soviet Union occasionally took this position,[43] it was quite likely that the claim of "provocation" was intended for propaganda effects. The Soviet Union knew that the U.S. destroyer patrols in the Gulf of Tonkin, which were scheduled to begin the day after Kosygin arrived in Hanoi, had been suspended so that they would not give the appearance of "provoking the Soviet Union."[44] The Kremlin had also been informed that the attacks on the D.R.V. were for retaliatory purposes only. These two facts, coupled with the month-long respite on the North which followed the FLAMING DART raids, probably influenced the Soviet Union to picture the raids as "a futile last-ditch effort by Washington to strengthen its bargaining position rather than as a prelude to a new escalation."[45]

It soon became evident that the Soviet Union intended to fulfill its promise to extend additional assistance to North Vietnam. In the week immediately preceding the February 7 bombing raid, *Pravda* offered "necessary assistance" to North Vietnam on February 1, 3 and 7.[46] After the February 7 raid, the Soviet Union confirmed its promise, even though other terminology was used. On February 8, Kosygin spoke at a reception at the Soviet embassy in Hanoi and warned that the Soviet Union "could not remain indifferent" to the fate of another socialist country.[47] A Soviet government statement carried in the same issue of *Pravda* warned that the Soviet Union intended to fulfill its "international duty to a fraternal socialist country," while an editorial in the same paper promised that Moscow would "safeguard the security and strengthen the defense potential" of North Vietnam.[48] *Krasnaia Zvezda* warned that the Soviet armed forces were "raising their vigilance even more in the face of the war provocations of imperialism." The article also underlined the Soviet Union's ability "to protect the fraternal Vietnamese people."[49] In the same vein, a lengthy *Pravda* editorial declared that the D.R.V. had "reliable and strong friends" and that the Soviet Union would "strengthen the defense capacity" of North Vietnam. The editorial stressed that no one should "have any doubt that the Soviet Union will do this."[50] Finally, the communiqué issued after the close of Kosygin's trip again promised "necessary assistance" to North Vietnam, condemned American "imperialism," confirmed Soviet support for "just struggles" and appealed for negotiated settlement of international disputes and for peaceful coexistence between countries with different social systems.[51]

Two questions must now be asked. First, why did the Soviet Union reemphasize its intent to aid North Vietnam? Second, in Soviet eyes, why did the United States attack the D.R.V.? Several answers were possible to the first question. First, it must be remembered that the U.S. attacks on February 7 and 8 were specifically labeled retaliatory attacks. The same was true of the February 11 attack, which was in retaliation for a February 10 Vietcong raid on a Quinhon barracks in which 23 Americans were killed.[52] The air attacks on North Vietnam may thus have appeared to be a passing phenomenon similar to the air attacks following the Tonkin incidents in 1964.

Second, the Soviet Union still perceived certain constraints to be operating on American policy toward Vietnam, although the raids did cause the Soviet Union to question their influence on U.S. policy. *Izvestiia* even published in full a *New York Times* editorial which wondered whether the three days of raids had been a mistake.[53]

Third, the Soviet leaders may have reasoned that additional aid and continued promises of necessary assistance would have made it clear to American leaders that the Soviet Union was indeed committed to support North Vietnam. The importance of the Soviet promise itself as a constraint on American policy would have been increased.

Fourth, the Soviet Union and North Vietnam were still convinced that a Vietcong victory in the South was imminent. The Soviet Union undoubtedly wished to be as closely identified as possible with such a victory as long as danger to the Soviet homeland was not increased.

Lastly, in its eyes, the U.S.S.R. may simply have been unable to afford the decrease in prestige of any other course. With the conference of 19 communist parties scheduled to begin in early March, the People's Republic of China would have been delighted to take advantage of any indication of Soviet collusion with the United States.

Why, then, did the Soviet Union believe the United States had launched the three raids? While the retaliation rationale was undoubtedly accepted by the Soviets as the public reason for Washington's action, the Kremlin made it clear that it believed another reason provided the actual motivation. That reason was that the United States' position in South Vietnam as well as the ability of the South Vietnamese government to govern was near collapse.[54] To the Soviets, then, the raids were designed to improve the immediate U.S.-South Vietnamese position. This interpretation was further supported by Kosygin's report to the Russian people on his trip to North Vietnam, China and North Korea. In his report, which was delivered on television, Kosygin commented on the South Vietnamese situation:

> Now, when the Saigon regime is on the brink of collapse, the United States is embarking on the path of spreading the aggression and the organization of military provocation against the D.R.V. and other independent countries in Indochina. It wishes to create a situation which would allow it to place in South Vietnam new detachments of American soldiers in order to undertake yet another attempt to break the desire of the people for independence and freedom.[55]

The Soviet perception of U.S. policy toward Vietnam during February thus closely paralleled the actual considerations being debated in Washington. The Soviet leadership was in fact cognizant of the policy debate. One Soviet newspaper spoke of pressures on President Johnson to "increase the acts of aggression against the D.R.V.,"[56] while another source believed that the American "ship of state is increasingly inclining toward the side of the ultras."[57] Later, the same publication declared:

> The real threat on the part of the rabid ones in the United States not only continues to exist but is increasing.... They are poisoning the general political climate in the U.S. and, as is seen, they are moving the U.S. more and more toward a reactionary course within the country and toward a course of military adventure in the international arena.[58]

Following the FLAMING DART operations, the Soviet Union cautioned the United States that further raids on North Vietnam could cause a deterioration in Soviet-American relations.[59] Some fear was expressed that the war in Vietnam "might flare into a big war,"[60] but more significant than that was the emphasis the Soviet Union began to place on "socialist unity." According to one Soviet broadcast:

> What does defending peace from imperialist attack mean? It means, first of all, *strengthening the socialist system ... by all available means* and to contribute comprehensively to the development of the national liberation movement.... It means ... *closing the ranks of all peace-loving forces*, opposing imperialism in a decisive manner, and struggling for the pursuit of the policy of peaceful coexistence between countries with different social systems, for the settlement of controversial international problems by negotiations [emphasis added].[61]

In keeping with the perceived importance of socialist unity, Soviet newspapers continually appealed for socialist unity. *Pravda* printed both the Soviet and Chinese letters which were exchanged on the anniversary of the Soviet-Chinese Friendship Treaty,[62] and *Izvestiia* declared that Kosygin's stops in China and North Korea following the trip to Hanoi were intended "to strengthen the cohesion of socialist countries in every way."[63] Despite various Sino-Soviet disagreements, it was emphasized that:

> The most important factor encountered by the U.S. military in Indochina is *the firm position of the Soviet Union, the People's Republic of China, and the other socialist countries* and their unity and determination to render every possible support to the fraternal Democratic Republic of Vietnam [emphasis added].[64]

Numerous other Soviet sources also referred to and emphasized the unity within the socialist camp, maintaining that this unity would defeat the imperialists.[65] Judging by the stress being placed on socialist unity, it was evident that the Soviet Union was attempting to dissuade the United States from attaching too much significance to disagreements within the socialist bloc.

Nonetheless, the Soviet Union probably was not totally surprised by the commencement of ROLLING THUNDER in March. Official U.S. statements clearly showed U.S. resolve had suddenly increased, and a public opinion poll taken in February showed that 83 percent of those surveyed supported Johnson's decision to order the FLAMING DART raids.[66] At the same time, "socialist unity" simply did not exist. Only 18 of 26 communist parties invited to the March 1-5 conference of communist parties agreed to send representatives. China and North Vietnam did not.

How did the Russians react to ROLLING THUNDER? As was to be expected, the commencement of the raids was immediately condemned.[67] It was observed that the retaliation rationale for the air attacks had been abandoned[68] and that the raids had been resumed to avert military defeat in the South.[69] The Soviet government, meanwhile, issued a statement which warned that the declarations of February 9 and 11 were "fully in force."[70] The statement also cautioned that if U.S. leaders thought the bombing would frighten anyone, they were "mistaken" and would have to "assume the full responsibility for [their] course of action."[71]

The introduction of Marine contingents into South Vietnam was just as unsettling to the Soviet Union as was the bombing of the North. The landing of the Marines was quickly condemned[72] but following Soviet statements were more illustrative of the actual Soviet apprehension. *Pravda* mentioned the possibility of a naval blockade of North Vietnam, the introduction of more soldiers to Vietnam and the establishment of a "multinational command" as had existed in Korea.[73] A few days later, *Krasnaia Zvezda* referred to the same first two possibilities and added that American leaders were contemplating landing sabotage teams in North Vietnam and using tactical nuclear weapons against North Vietnam.[74]

Soviet spokesmen also voiced their fear of an American invasion of the North. Shortly before Maxwell Taylor went to Washington in March, Radio Moscow reported that:

> Taylor told a correspondent of the Canadian Broadcasting Corporation in Saigon that South Vietnam was being invaded from the north, the frontier was being crossed from the north to the south daily and probably hourly. Why should they not cross the frontier from the south to the north in self-defense? *This is a blunt call to invade the D.R.V. territory by U.S. ground forces in addition to the air raids.* Is not Taylor carrying these plans to Washington? [emphasis added].[75]

It can be seen, then, that the Soviet Union viewed the bombings and the troop landings as indications of strengthening American resolve. One indication of the second thoughts caused in the Kremlin by this new resolve was the decreased emphasis the Kremlin placed on its aid to the D.R.V. While it was true that Soviet references to support were con-

siderably less frequent in the week immediately preceding the commencement of Operation ROLLING THUNDER than they had been in the week
preceding the beginning of Operation FLAMING DART,[76] no references to
"necessary assistance" were made in the week following the beginning of
ROLLING THUNDER. During this week, the Soviet government itself
released a statement on the bombing which only implied material support and the Consultative Conference of Nineteen Communist Parties
released both a statement on the bombing and a final communiqué
which were similar to the Soviet government statement in their references to Vietnam.[77] No one promised "necessary assistance, to the D.R.V."
Thus, even though the Soviet Union may have expected the raids and the
troop buildup, it was not sure about what course of action to take since
the raids and the buildup implied a strong American resolve to support
the South Vietnamese government.[78]

There was one brief exception to this pattern. On March 23,
*Pravda* printed an appeal from the NLFSV "to send volunteers to South
Vietnam" if the United States continued its buildup.[79] The day after the
Liberation Front's request was made public, the Soviet Union offered to
send volunteers if they were needed and requested. The Soviet offer was
made by Leonid Brezhnev during a speech honoring the just-returned
Soviet cosmonauts of Voskhod II. After heaping praise on the
cosmonauts' feat, Brezhnev abruptly changed the subject and tenor of
his speech. Brezhnev condemned U.S. action in Vietnam, and, with no
prior introduction, declared that many Soviet citizens had volunteered
to go to Vietnam and fight for freedom.[80]

Western diplomats immediately voiced their doubt that the
promise of volunteers was seriously meant.[81] The Soviet handling of the
promise lent some credence to the Western doubt. Not until April 1 did
*Pravda* again mention the Soviet willingness to send volunteers. During
the intervening week, the main *Pravda* editorial on Brezhnev's speech
did not refer to volunteers.[82]

Why, then, did the Soviet Union make such statements if it did
not actually wish to send volunteers? Two reasons appeared evident.
First, the Soviet offer tended to increase the Soviet standing within
North Vietnam. The North Vietnamese government paper *Nhan Dan*
said that the offer was "a great encouragement."[83] Second, it must be
remembered that Maxwell Taylor went to the United States in late
March to discuss American policy toward Vietnam. Previous Taylor
trips had led to escalations, and the Soviet Union felt that the March trip
would be no exception. Soviet leaders may have feared that Taylor
would return to South Vietnam with permission to further escalate the war,
including possibly an invasion of North Vietnam. The Soviet promise to
send volunteers may have been an attempt to forestall such a possibility.

The Soviet hesitation to send volunteers to North Vietnam did not imply, however, that the Soviet Union was unwilling to supply the D.R.V. with other types of aid. In early April, it was reported that the Soviet Union had sent North Vietnam 550 million dollars in military aid.[84] Later in the month, the First Secretary of the Lao Dong Party, Le Duan, thanked the Soviet Union for its "contribution to the strengthening of the defense potential" of North Vietnam in the communiqué issued at the close of his trip to the Soviet Union.[85]

How did the increased American commitment to Vietnam, in Soviet eyes, fit in with other U.S. policies? Until the end of April 1965 the Soviet Union viewed the American escalations in Vietnam as little more than a relatively major segment of an old policy — containment.[86] The Kremlin was aware, however, that the outlines of a more resolute position were beginning to influence American policy toward Vietnam. Finally on April 28 an event occurred in a part of the world completely dissociated from Vietnam, at least in a geographical sense, which to the Soviets placed U.S. policy in Vietnam in a new context[87]: United States Marines landed in the Dominican Republic. Immediately, the two interventions were linked. Increasingly Vietnam came to be regarded as a relatively major segment of a new policy — the "Johnson Doctrine."

What exactly was the "Johnson Doctrine" as perceived by the Soviets? One source stated that "this new doctrine — the 'Johnson Doctrine' " — encompassed all "the territories of the capitalist world into the zone of interest of the U.S.A.,"[88] while another declared:

> The new doctrine — Johnson's "globalism" — is shown as an effort to impose American law everywhere. The U.S. wants the right to intervene anywhere that, in the opinion of the American ruling circles, their interests are infringed upon.
>
> The grand strategy of the reactionary American circles is to frighten the world's nations by its might....[89]

Why did the United States have an "illusion of a global government?" According to one article, the "illusion" was based on three factors: the world-wide U.S. military structure, vast overseas investments, and the world's largest gross national product.[90] How, in Soviet eyes, did the United States intend to use these factors to implement the Johnson Doctrine? Four major methods were to be employed. First, anticommunist propaganda was to be used. Second, military opposition to national liberation fronts was to be expanded. Third, escalation was to be employed to test the validity of the theory of limited war adopted by the U.S. government. Finally, alliances were to be reemphasized.

To the Soviet Union, it appeared as if the United States was attempting to use anticommunist propaganda to equate the national interest of the United States with the national interest of various Asian and African countries.[91] Repeated U.S. claims that Patrice Lumumba of the

Congo, various Buddhists in Vietnam and "numerous presidents from a score of Latin American countries" were communists were interpreted to be part of the U.S. tactic.[92] The Soviet leaders believed the United States was using this method — the creation of a fear of communism — to establish more foreign military bases from which to launch operations against national liberation movements.[93] Premier Kosygin, speaking to the first graduating class at Patrice Lumumba University in Moscow, referred to this perceived ideological offensive:

> Neocolonialism does not only mean new forms of economic exploitation. It also means a considerable intensification of the ideological offensive of imperialism in Asia, Africa, and Latin America. The purpose of this onslaught is to throw the liberated people into confusion....[94]

In Soviet eyes, the U.S. propaganda effort was intended to be combined with open military activities to prevent successful national liberation movements throughout the world.[95] According to *World Marxist Review*:

> The ominous thing that emerges from President Johnson's actions and his "doctrine" is this: *The U.S. government has openly declared war on all the national liberation and democratic movements of our time* [emphasis in the original].[96]

Vietnam was considered to be "the first battlefront in the American war against the national liberation movement."[97] The U.S. military effort in that country, to the Soviets, was designed "to intimidate other freedom-loving people."[98] It was similarly asserted that the U.S. was using Vietnam as a laboratory for its military theory of limited wars.[99]

Escalation was viewed as one of the ways to implement the theory. To the Soviets, escalation combined both propaganda efforts and military efforts in an extensive assault against national liberation movements.[100] The Soviet Union felt that by employing this tactic the United States hoped to prevent a coalescing of the antiwar movement throughout the world and to influence the world to accept gradually increased bombing of North Vietnam.[101]

In addition to propaganda, military efforts and escalation, it was believed that the United States intended to reemphasize military alliances as part of the Johnson Doctrine. One of the paramount Soviet fears was the creation of a "NEATO," or Northeast Asian Treaty Organization. Operating under the aegis of "collective colonialism,"[102] the hypothetical NEATO was supposed to include Taiwan, the Philippines, Japan, the United States and some European countries. The Japanese-South Korean Treaty of January 1965 was termed the first step in the creation of "NEATO," while the American Seventh Fleet's use of Japanese ports and the South Korean introduction of troops into South Vietnam was interpreted as further proof that "NEATO" would soon become a reality.[103]

Thus, after the U.S. intervention in the Dominican Republic, the Soviet Union gradually adopted the idea that the United States was embarking on an active policy of opposition to national liberation movements throughout the world, intending at the same time to avoid the "strongholds" of socialism so that the new U.S. policy could be more successful.

Johnson's July 28 announcement which "Americanized" the war was viewed within the context of the "Johnson Doctrine." Soviet treatment of the Johnson press conference indicated both Soviet deference to North Vietnam on the issue as well as Soviet uncertainty over what policy to adopt following Johnson's announcement. The Soviet newspapers reported Johnson's speech on July 29[104] but there was no reference to Vietnam or Johnson's conference the following day. Instead, *Pravda* carried a front page editorial on the American intervention in the Dominican Republic.[105] *Pravda* did not print anything on Johnson's speech until August 4 and this was merely a summation of North Vietnam's statement on Johnson's speech.[106] The D.R.V.'s statement, which had been released two days before the Soviet summation, was printed in full in the August 5 *Pravda*.[107] Not until August 7 did the Soviet government release a statement through its news agency TASS. The TASS release, as usual, condemned the United States and supported North Vietnam.

The Soviet statement simply warned that the Soviet Union would continue to improve the defense potential of North Vietnam. U.S. desires for peace were dismissed as "hypocritical." In the words of TASS:

> TASS is authorized to state that in the leading circles of the Soviet Union the new steps of the United States government are regarded as aggressive actions tending to escalate the war in Vietnam. The statesmen who make the policy of the United States should not fool themselves into believing that the American aggression will go unpunished. It will invariably bring increasing rebuff and will ultimately suffer a disgraceful defeat....[108]

While the TASS statement revealed nothing new, it was still significant that it took the Soviet Union ten days to respond officially to the Johnson news conference — indicating both a Soviet desire to adopt a position congruent with North Vietnam's and Soviet policy confusion. It was clear that the United States intended to adopt a major portion of the war as its own. This factor combined with other Soviet goals and with strident Chinese calls for strong opposition to the United States gave the Soviet Union ample reason to hesitate.

The Soviet Union believed the U.S. decision to Americanize the war was based on several things in addition to the "Johnson Doctrine" and the deteriorating conditions in South Vietnam. While some Soviet authors felt that Johnson's July 28 speech indicated that the United States would remain in Vietnam for a long time,[109] others felt that the purpose of Johnson's speech and the concomitant buildup was primarily to "neutralize [the Administration's] Republican critics."[110] Washington's policy was also considered to be a success for "the acrimonious bard of the American ultras," Barry Goldwater.[111] Yet another Soviet article stated that the American buildup was to display American might, to demoralize the NLFSV and to bolster the morale of the South Vietnamese.[112] Clearly, the Soviet Union believed that the United States was beginning to prepare for an attempt to attain a military victory in South Vietnam.

As American men and supplies continued to flow to Vietnam throughout the remainder of 1965, this Soviet perception solidified. United States policy in Vietnam corroborated the Soviet view. On October 17, the United States attacked a missile base for only the second time,[113] and on November 7 and 8, six more SAM sites were raided.[114] One of the primary reasons that the sites were attacked was because the missiles were becoming more effective. Nonetheless, it was clear that the United States was willing to take the risk of injuring Soviet personnel who were manning the bases.[115]

The fact that Soviet personnel had been covertly sent to man the SAM sites raised an interesting point. If the Soviet Union sincerely wanted to deter the United States, why were Soviet personnel sent to North Vietnam secretly? Would not their presence in the D.R.V. be a more effective constraint on American action against the North if their presence were publicly known?

The Kremlin's reasoning may have gone along the following lines: Since the United States appeared to be strongly committed to achieving its goals in Vietnam and since the Kremlin realized that Hanoi and the Vietcong were just as intent on achieving their objectives, it was probable that sizable U.S. ground forces in the South and prolonged U.S. air strikes against the North would be forthcoming. Despite Soviet interest in and concern for North Vietnam, Moscow did not desire a confrontation with the United States precipitated by North Vietnam. On the other hand, the Soviet Union found it necessary to fulfill its commitment to North Vietnam and provide effective air defenses. These air defenses, the SAM missiles, required trained personnel to be effective. The only personnel who were trained in their use were Soviet technicians, who therefore had to be sent to the D.R.V. To minimize the possibility of confrontation with the United States, the presence of Soviet

Top: *August 1965, in North Vietnam:* SAM *missiles supplied by the Soviet Union were moderately effective against U.S. aircraft.* Bottom: *October 1966, Phuc Yen Airfield, 20 miles northwest of Hanoi: two Soviet-supplied* MIG-17 *jet fighters. Official U.S. Air Force photographs.*

personnel at the North Vietnamese missile sites was not publicized. In effect, the Soviet Union signaled the United States that it did not desire a Soviet-American confrontation. At the same time, the lack of official American comment on the Soviet technicians was a U.S. signal to Moscow that the U.S. similarly did not desire a confrontation.

Rumors of escalation accompanied stepped-up U.S. raids against North Vietnam during December. Following McNamara's late November inspection tour of Vietnam,[116] it was reported that many people in Washington wanted Haiphong harbor to be mined.[117] In mid-December the United States bombed the Uong Bi powerplant in North Vietnam and a few days later authorized U.S. troops to pursue retreating Vietcong units even if they retreated into Cambodia.[118] The general feeling that prevailed in Washington was that, during 1966, U.S. reserves would be mobilized, U.S. military strength in Vietnam would be increased from 175,000 men to 350,000 men and the war would be extended in North Vietnam to include attacks on Hanoi and Haiphong. At the same time, the Soviet Union perceived these measures and rumors to indicate an American attempt to achieve a military victory. As early as September, the Soviets had speculated that the United States was considering a partial mobilization.[119] McNamara's November trip to Vietnam was viewed as simply another precursor to another escalation.[120] Permission to pursue Vietcong cadres into Cambodia was condemned,[121] as was the increased U.S. military budget for the next fiscal year.[122] The Uong Bi attack was perceived to be merely the forerunner for more extensive raids on other North Vietnamese industrial targets.[123] The depth of the Soviet uneasiness was made clear by a December radio broadcast:

> Rumors are now rife in Washington that U.S. government circles are seriously discussing the necessity of a declaration of war by Congress against North Vietnam.[124]

Thus, by the end of 1965, the Soviet Union believed that the United States was striving for a military victory in Vietnam while using claims of a desire for negotiations as a smokescreen behind which further escalations could be undertaken. Since the Soviets also realized that North Vietnam and the NLFSV were striving for a win in the South, and since it was clear that the introduction of U.S. combat forces into South Vietnam made North Vietnam and the Vietcong's hoped-for victory in 1965 unlikely, the Soviet leadership undoubtedly anticipated a long and arduous struggle in Vietnam. As opposed to the situation in the summer of 1964, when the Soviet Union expected a Sino-American confrontation in Southeast Asia, the Soviet Union did not attempt to withdraw from the area. Such a move would have been ideologically and politically difficult to justify. Instead, the Soviet Union reconfirmed its interest in Southeast Asia and its commitment to North Vietnam. There were several indications of this Soviet interest and commitment. In early November, the Soviet Union sent a high-level delegation to a meeting in Bangkok, Thailand, which was discussing the establishment of an "Asian Development Bank." Although the Soviets did not immediately join the enterprise, they did indicate that they would report back to the bank on whether they would help finance and operate the bank.[125] Of much greater significance, however, was the Soviet reaction to the American "Peace Offensive."

According to Soviet propagandists, the "Peace Offensive" was nothing more than a "smokescreen" for "more escalations."[126] "The Diplomatic Offensive," *Pravda* declared, was "very similar to a diversionary maneuver" since the American Government wanted "to make an impression" on congressmen before it requested the allocation of large new expenditures "for the war in Vietnam."[127] *Izvestiia* observed that a nation "can talk endlessly about peace and still carry out a war."[128] When the expected escalations did occur, and when the February Honolulu Conference proclaimed a two front war against "North Vietnamese infiltration" and "hunger, injustice and disease," the Soviet Union viewed its earlier perceptions as being vindicated.[129] The resumption of bombing and the Honolulu Conference "proved the falseness of the peace initiative," a TASS statement on the conference declared.[130] More American escalations continued to be expected and more continued to come. Put simply, the "American escalations" in Vietnam were needed "to offset defeats."[131] The "Johnson Doctrine," though still the core of American policy, had been unexpectedly slowed by military difficulties.

During the January bombing halt, the Soviet Union moved to strengthen its ties with North Vietnam. Soviet Communist Party Secretary A.N. Shelepin traveled to Hanoi, probably both to illustrate Soviet support for the D.R.V. and to prevail upon North Vietnam to attend the upcoming 23rd Congress of the CPSU, scheduled for March.[132] There were several indications that Shelepin and the North Vietnamese leadership could not reach an understanding on the conduct of the war in the South. The clearest indication was the joint Soviet-North Vietnamese communiqué issued at the end of Shelepin's visit. While the communiqué did promise more Soviet aid for the D.R.V., it was also vague on a number of points, clearly implying Soviet-North Vietnamese disagreement.[133] Most of the implied disagreement centered around the conduct of the war in South Vietnam. The Soviet delegation, the communiqué revealed, was "impressed" by the courage and valor of the North Vietnamese leadership.

If the Russian delegation found a North Vietnamese leadership which sought to follow a more intransigent line than that advocated by

the Kremlin, why then did Moscow increase its aid commitment to the
D.R.V. following the Shelepin visit? Several interrelated explanations
are possible. Moscow often adopted a deferential posture in regard to
North Vietnamese positions on the war[134] and with the Sino-Soviet
dispute increasing in intensity, Moscow may have felt that an ideal opportunity existed to put the lie to Peking's position that the Kremlin did
not support national liberation movements. At the same time, the once-
feared imminent success of the "Johnson Doctrine" in Vietnam had
receded and the possibility of Soviet aid to an unsuccessful national
liberation movement, leaving the Soviets open to the Chinese charge
they had provided insufficient aid, was reduced. Increased Soviet aid to
North Vietnam became therefore a viable policy alternative.

  With the "Johnson Doctrine" having been stalemated, the
Kremlin looked upon President Johnson's July 12, 1966, speech in White
Sulphur Springs as the framework for a new policy. In his speech, Johnson affirmed the "determination of the United States to fulfill its commitments in Asia as a Pacific Power." Later, Dean Rusk reiterated Johnson's position, declaring that the United States would "collectively or
unilaterally intervene" where its interests were threatened "whether or
not the U.S. has treaty commitments." The Kremlin interpreted these
declarations as an American attempt to justify a "right to intervene in
any part of Asia" and provide "some political pretext for the war
declared by the United States on the national liberation movements."[135]
As a replacement for and "improvement" on the "Johnson Doctrine," the
new "Asian Doctrine" sought to supplement a "discredited SEATO" with a
"more flexible and more elaborate system of military and political
alliances."[136] Maintaining that the United States placed "an even greater
stake on military solutions" with the new policy, *Pravda* described the
"Asian Doctrine" as an attempt to "create a new block that would be
linked to the U.S.A. by military and economic bonds." "The military
beachheads of the United States in Thailand, South Korea and South
Vietnam" would be connected with the Philippines, Australia and New
Zealand, thereby creating "an American bridge to Asia, as it were,
across which the imperialists could further their desire for military and
economic expansion."[137] The U.S. was viewed as creating "a major complex of military bases as a long-term beachhead for a major war in this
area of the world."[138] Specific bases mentioned included Sattahip in
Thailand and Camranh and Danang in Vietnam.

  Why had the United States adopted the "Asian Doctrine"? The
Soviet Union, apparently, discerned two reasons. First, because of the
importance of the area and the problems besetting the "Johnson Doctrine," a successful policy had to be conceived. The "Asian Doctrine,"
which was according to the Soviets "designed to determine American

policy in [Asia] for the next half century," was adopted because Washington considered the Pacific Ocean, the countries of South and Southeast Asia, Australia, New Zealand and the Indian Ocean as "a strategic whole of which Indochina is the core."[139] Thus, when one policy proved less than successful a new one had to be implemented.

Second, the Soviet Union believed that the United States was taking advantage of China's opposition to Soviet policies and attitudes. American activities in Vietnam "exploited events in China" and "set up a military mechanism for the suppression of liberation movements."[140] While much of this explanation was undoubtedly a product of the ongoing Sino-Soviet polemic, there may have been some validity to the Soviet proposition. George Kennan's observation that "it would be foolish" for the United States to ignore the Sino-Soviet disagreement was cited as proof that American policymakers were using the disagreement to their own advantage. The possibility was even discussed that "all of the escalations in Vietnam were undertaken only after a thorough sounding of Peking's reaction."[141] Other sources charged that Maoists "aided American escalation in Southeast Asia.[142]

By the end of 1966, then, the Soviet Union believed the United States had replaced the so-called "Johnson Doctrine" with a more insidious concept, the "Asian Doctrine," but was pursuing basically the same objective in Vietnam as before—a military victory to maintain its neocolonial position in South Vietnam.[143] American-Soviet relations had correspondingly deteriorated as Soviet policy-makers moved to implement Brezhnev's September 1965 warning that "normalization of [U.S.-Soviet] relations [was] incompatible with the armed aggression" in Vietnam and that U.S.-Soviet relations had "a clear tendency to freeze" because of American actions in Vietnam.[144] Even more pointedly, Soviet Premier Kosygin emphasized that the Vietnamese War overshadowed all Soviet-American relations and that a meeting between President Johnson and Soviet leaders was impossible while the bombing of North Vietnam continued.[145] Additionally, the Soviet Union delayed or canceled several technical exchanges,[146] the Geneva disarmament talks were downgraded[147] and negotiations on the nuclear nonproliferation treaty were slowed.[148] While Soviet-American contacts had not terminated, they had in fact "frozen," just as Brezhnev had warned. Numerous statements by many Soviet leaders at the 23rd Party Congress reiterated the Soviet position.[149] The escalations in Vietnam during 1965 and 1966 thus effectively ended the Kennedy-Khrushchev legacy of détente.

## Another Korea? The View from Peking

If Soviet-American relations had deteriorated because of the

American involvement in Vietnam, it was small surprise that during 1965 and 1966 China and the United States came dangerously close to war. When Dean Rusk told the U.S. House of Representatives in mid-April 1966 that there were "of course risks of war with China,"[150] he was only echoing a refrain Peking had been orchestrating for 15 months.

At the beginning of 1965, the Maoist leadership apparently expected the United States to accept the demise of South Vietnam as an independent nation. Chinese reaction to the FLAMING DART raids were strident, unlike the Soviet, and closely paralleled the previous Chinese reaction to the Gulf of Tonkin affair. After that crisis, China warned that "aggression against the D.R.V. is aggression against China" and the Peking government "would intervene" if the war in Indochina moved northward.[151] After the FLAMING DART raids, China again cautioned that "aggression against the D.R.V. is aggression against China."[152] Apparently, to the Chinese, the U.S. strikes were still retaliatory strikes and did not indicate a significant change in American policy. Therefore, the Chinese reactions could be similar after both Tonkin Gulf and FLAMING DART.

This interpretation is furthered by the Chinese attitude toward Kosygin as he passed through China on his return from North Vietnam to the Soviet Union. On his way home, he stopped in Peking for discussions with the Chinese leadership. While in Peking, Kosygin put forth the Soviet argument for "united action," which Mao summarily rejected. To Mao, Sino-Soviet unity could be achieved only in the event of an American attack on one or the other.[153] Throughout February, Soviet appeals for "socialist unity" were rejected by the Chinese. At the same time, Peking cautioned the United States that the Chinese and North Vietnamese people were "fraternal brothers."[154] Peking additionally warned that if U.S. troops attacked China, then the United States would find itself engaged with the Chinese on a front including "Indochina, Southeast Asia and the Far East."[155] Similarly, by February 19 the Chinese had moved to oppose negotiations on the Vietnamese questions. Later, the Chinese castigated the Kremlin for proposing a conference on Indochina during February despite the fact that the North Vietnamese at the time held a position almost identical to the Russians. According to Peking Review, Kosygin wanted to help the United States to "find a way out of Vietnam."[156] China had often commented that the United States' Vietnam adventure would lead to a decrease in American prestige throughout the world[157] and consequently saw nothing to gain by helping the U.S. "find a way out of Vietnam." To the Chinese, American will to maintain an independent South Vietnam was still questionable and the FLAMING DART strikes were thus viewed as merely a brief fling to shore up the U.S. position, not as a fundamental change in policy.

The Chinese did not view the beginning of the ROLLING THUNDER operations with the same degree of equanimity. Whereas the responses to both the Tonkin Gulf events and FLAMING DART in essence equated China and Vietnam, the Chinese statement condemning ROLLING THUNDER warned that "the 650 million Chinese people firmly support their brothers, the Vietnamese people." More importantly, the Chinese began to promise to send volunteers to fight in Vietnam.[158] Of more significance in underlining the changing Chinese view of the American threat was the internal policy debate that exploded in China during March and eventually led to the Great Proletarian Cultural Revolution. While it would be naive to argue that the most significant cause of the disagreements within China was the American involvement in Vietnam, it is clear that the American escalations in Vietnam during 1965 were a major factor in that disagreement.[159] Put simply, if the United States decided to stand and fight in Vietnam, then China, acting as a "reliable rear base" for the D.R.V. and NLFSV, may well have become a target of American military action. To the Chinese leadership, this was clearly an undesirable alternative. At the same time, though, Peking could not lessen its support of either the D.R.V. or the NLFSV.

This Chinese quandary was reflected in the Chinese media throughout 1965. One Chinese faction urged an improvement in Sino-Soviet relations so that China could take advantage of the Soviet nuclear umbrella, thereby decreasing the threat of U.S. retaliation on the P.R.C. as it continued to act as North Vietnam's rear area. This faction, led by Liu Shao-chi and Lo Jui-ching, perceived an increased and immediate threat from American imperialism and downplayed the dangers of Soviet revisionism. Liu and Lo therefore advocated rapprochement with the Soviet Union. The other major faction, led by Mao, Chou En-lai, and Lin Piao, viewed the Soviet and American threats as equal.[160] According to Edgar Snow, Mao eventually purged the Lo-Liu faction because of its revisionist attitudes and its search for a compromise with the Soviet Union.[161]

While disagreements within the Chinese leadership over how to respond to the American escalations in Vietnam led to purges within the Communist Party (CPC) the disagreements had little impact on Mao's line toward united action and Soviet aid to North Vietnam. Still setting the Chinese policy line, Mao best clarified his attitude toward and mistrust of the Kremlin in an unpublished letter from the CPC Central Committee to the CPSU Central Committee on July 14, 1965. According to the Maoist leadership:

> You talk glibly about united action. Why then do you incessantly distribute anti-Chinese propaganda and constantly spread lies about China...?

You also wanted to open an air corridor in China and obtain for
Soviet aeroplanes the privilege of free traffic in her air space.

In view of these moves of yours and your collusion with U.S. imperialism, we have every reason to think that you have ulterior motives
in offering such assistance.

Frankly speaking, we do not trust you.... China is not one of your
provinces. We cannot accept your control. Nor will we help you control
others....[162]

Chinese opposition to united action was further underlined by
reports that the P.R.C. was delaying Soviet aid to North Vietnam, on
occasion even relettering the boxes in which equipment was being shipped to make it appear as if the supplying nation was China.[163]
Nonetheless, if Mao feared an expansion of Soviet influence in North
Vietnam, he viewed the introduction of American combat troops to
Vietnam and their subsequent buildup as the major threat to Chinese
security. American actions had turned "this entire [Southeast Asia]
region into a battleground."[164] Mao believed that the danger of U.S. air
attacks on China existed throughout 1965 and early 1966[165] and warned
through *People's Daily* that China would not be restricted in its method
of retaliation. The United States would be "drowned in the ocean of a
people's war" if China were forced to become involved in a war.[166]
Later, Chou En-lai was even more candid, announcing that if the
United States attacked by air, China would not necessarily be restricted
in its method of response. In fact, Chou informed his listeners that
China would respond to such an attack with a land war throughout
Southeast Asia.[167] North Vietnamese leaders held similar views of both
American intentions and Chinese resolve. According to Le Duan,
speaking during the summer of 1965, if the U.S. invaded the
D.R.V., then it would be fighting not only the D.R.V. but also

the whole camp and especially China. Striking into North Vietnam
means that the U.S. had the intention of fighting with China because
North Vietnam and China are two socialist countries linked extremely
tightly with each other.[168]

Through the summer of 1965, China increasingly feared an expansion of the war. American warnings that Chinese territory would not
be considered a sanctuary added to this Chinese fear. This is not to say,
however, that the Chinese were intimidated. Following Johnson's July
announcement that the U.S. was upgrading its force commitment, Lo
warned the United States not to misjudge Chinese determination. Lo invited American troops to "come in large numbers. And the more, the
better."[169] A week later, an official Chinese government statement again
implied that volunteers would be sent to Vietnam:

We, the 650 million Chinese people, have repeatedly pledged to the
Vietnamese people our all-out support and assistance, up to and including the sending, according to their need, of our men to fight

shoulder to shoulder with them to drive out the U.S. aggressors.
warn the U.S. aggressors once more: We Chinese people mean what we
say![170]

China, then, was cognizant of an American willingness to risk
war with China as the U.S. pursued its objectives in Vietnam. It is in the
context of the Chinese view of an American willingness to risk war, the
domestic struggle for power in China, the Chinese disagreement with
the Soviet Union over united action and the ongoing insurgency in Vietnam that Lin Piao's famous "Long Live the Victory of People's War!"
must be viewed.[171]

Lin's treatise laid down the ideological framework for Mao's interpretation of Chinese foreign policy. Here, however, we are concerned
only with its applications to and implications for Vietnam. To Lin,
South Vietnam was a laboratory for people's war. On the other hand, he
also perceived it to be a laboratory for the United States' effort to suppress people's war. The "heroic people" of South Vietnam were successfully defeating American imperialism, Lin argued, and the more the
U.S. escalated the war to avoid defeat, "the heavier will be [its] fall and
the more disastrous [its] defeat." This defeat would have the same effect
as a chain reaction, with other "rural" parts of the world seeing that
"U.S. imperialism can be defeated," and "what the Vietnamese people
can do, [others] can do too." American ruling circles recognized the
threat that the purported universal philosophy of Maoism carried for
them, Lin observed, and therefore were "now clamoring for another
large-scale ground war on the Asian mainland" against the Chinese
people. The Chinese general even taunted the United States to send
troops, "the more the better," since the Chinese People's Liberation Army could "annihilate as many as you send, and even give you receipts."

For the most part, this was rather standard Chinese rhetoric.
Lin's support for revolutionary self-sufficiency under the guise of
people's war was earlier advocated by Mao himself. In essence, even
with the taunts to the United States, Lin's treatise was an appeal for
revolutionary "do-it-yourself" élan. In attempting to draw a parallel
between the Vietnamese War and the Chinese revolution, Lin warned
against "defeatism" and "blind optimism," thereby implicitly warning
Hanoi neither to be intimidated by the American military buildup nor to
ignore the tremendous difficulties presented by the American presence.
Significantly, not once in the entire article did Lin Piao threaten Chinese
intervention. According to one authoritative Rand Corporation study,
the article was marked by "a striking absence of threats of possible intervention, such as those Peking made on several occasions in the months
preceding publication of Lin's article."[172] If Hanoi adopted Peking's advice on self-sufficiency and the correct tactics in warfare, then several

Chinese objectives would have been achieved. First, the growing threat of an American attack on China would have been reduced, since the tempo of the war would have slowed. Second, the increasing Soviet influence in Hanoi would have been minimized simply because Soviet aid would have been less necessary. Third, North Vietnam would have recognized the ideological correctness of the Chinese policy line, thereby strengthening the Chinese position in the ongoing Sino-Soviet polemic. Finally, American forces would have been tied down in Vietnam with a protracted war, reducing the possibility of American action elsewhere. Unfortunately for the peace of mind of Chinese leaders, however, the D.R.V. ignored the advice.[173]

Lin Piao's article was also not taken as intended in Washington. To the Americans, the Chinese general had called for world revolution and offered Chinese support, moral if not material. This hard-line American interpretation of Lin's treatise undoubtedly reaffirmed in Mao's eyes American intentions in Vietnam. The article could now be used by the U.S. administration as another rationale to maintain and increase its presence in Southeast Asia. Increasingly through late 1965 and early 1966, American officials did exactly that.[174] China, to a degree, was caught up in events beyond its control.

Chinese policy reflected this. Beginning in the fall of 1965, Chinese engineering troops began to arrive in Vietnam, and eventually numbered 50,000. At the same time, Chinese material aid to the D.R.V. increased. These steps were obviously not designed to appease Washington, but rather were dictated by Chinese "solidarity" with Hanoi. On the other hand, incidents throughout 1965 when American planes wandered over the P.R.C.'s airspace were denounced as "provocations." On occasion, the Chinese shot down the intruding U.S. aircraft. Although the intrusions were condemned, the Chinese played down the events. To the Chinese, these may well have been American attempts at "dragon baiting."

With this Chinese perception of American intentions, it was understandable that the January Peace Offensive and bombing halt were attacked as insidious American maneuvers.[175] As the American buildup continued during the first months of 1966, China's view of a dedicated United States not afraid to risk confrontation and conflict with the P.R.C. solidified. The air war against North Vietnam moved steadily closer to the Chinese border, B-52s bombed North Vietnam, in early May the four rail lines linking China and the D.R.V. were cut and *The New York Times* reported that official United States policy had become that U.S. bombers were "free to attack the base of any planes that intercept our fliers ... even if those bases are inside Communist China."[176] Secretary Rusk again denied that the concept of sanctuary was operant.

The lack of lines of communication between Peking and Washington exacerbated the situation. Although the two countries discussed Vietnam at the February ambassadorial talks in Warsaw, there was no documented evidence that any meaningful discussion took place. One unconfirmed report indicated that China informed the U.S. that it would not directly intervene in Vietnam if it were not attacked and the U.S. reportedly took "note" of China's position, cautioning the Chinese that if Peking did intervene, the United States would consider the conflict unlimited.[177]

Following the Honolulu Conference in February, the United States continued to make seemingly threatening gestures toward China but at the same time appeared to extend the proverbial carrot with the stick. In March the U.S. Senate convened hearings on America's China policy which showed that many knowledgeable scholars of the Chinese political scene advocated at least some changes in U.S. policy.[178] On April 17 Rusk's statement on U.S.-China policy to the House Subcommittee on the Far East and the Pacific was released. For the most part, Rusk delivered an even-handed statement of American policy toward China, warning that the United States should do nothing to encourage China to believe "that it can reap gains from its aggressive behavior" but at the same time would "welcome an era of good relations" if China abandoned its strategy of world revolution. Although Rusk stressed the necessity of maintaining Asian containment, he also noted that the Chinese "acted with caution when they foresaw a collision with the United States" over Vietnam. Rusk additionally emphasized that the United States was acting "with restraint" in the Vietnamese War, and hoped the Chinese "realize[d] this" and would "guide their actions accordingly."[179]

The Chinese soon responded to Rusk. On May 10, Peking released Chou En-lai's statement of China's policy toward the United States, which Chou reportedly made on April 10.[180] In his statement, Chou emphasized that China would "not take the initiative to provoke a war with the United States." Chou confirmed that "the Chinese mean what they say" about supporting and helping anti-imperialist efforts in "Asia, Africa, and elsewhere." The conspicuous absence of a specific and explicit reference to Vietnam made Chou's corollary assertion that China would defend itself if Chinese support to these efforts brought American attacks against China appear even more cautious. Chou's third point, that China was prepared, was again paired with the inevitability of American defeat if the U.S. "imposed a war on China." Significantly, Chou declared that the "U.S. aggressor troops" would "certainly be annihilated in China," *not* Vietnam. Finally, Chou warned that a war would have no boundaries, being fought on the sea, air and land, despite the "wishful thinking" of the aggressors that it would be only an air war.[181] In the final analysis, both Rusk's statement and Chou's statement may be viewed as Sino-American efforts to establish a mutual though implicit understanding of the boundaries of the Vietnamese War.

Would the United States invade North Vietnam or attack China? Rusk said no. Would the Chinese enter the Vietnamese War? Chou said no. An understanding had not yet been reached but both sides were moving toward one and the threat of a Sino-American confrontation was diminishing.

The timing of the release of Chou's statement is also of interest. It came the day after the Chinese had exploded their third nuclear device, their first with thermonuclear materials, and two days, at least according to Peking, before the first Sino-American air skirmish. China may thus have been attempting to underline Chou's major argument, that China could defend itself if it were attacked but would itself not precipitate a confrontation.

Implicit ground rules for the conflict were being worked out. It was now the United States' turn to indicate its position. On May 18, McNamara addressed himself to the question of Sino-American communications, declaring that "the danger of potentially castastrophic misunderstandings" could be reduced by "breaching the isolation of great nations like Red China."[182] Two months later, on July 15, he made similar comments.[183] Meanwhile, on July 12, President Johnson spoke to the American Alumni Council and further underlined the American desire for peaceful relations with China by calling for "reconciliation between nations that now call themselves enemies."[184] American desires to avoid a confrontation with China were increasingly clear. While these signals were being sent to Peking, however, the war in Vietnam continued to escalate. Most significantly, on June 29, Haiphong was bombed.

The bombing of Haiphong was vociferously condemned by the Chinese government. This was not surprising, as U.S. escalations were regularly condemned. Therefore it was understandable that when Johnson called for reconciliation with China, his statement was condemned as a "fraud." Had the Chinese rejected the American proposals as insincere, and rejected the previous steps toward understanding, or were other factors operant which demanded the Chinese condemnation of Johnson's initiative?

Before this question can be answered, two other on-going chains of events must be briefly examined. The first was the expanding momentum of the Great Proletarian Cultural Revolution and the second was the Soviet criticism that China was "betraying the Vietnamese people by delaying shipments, opposing united action and colluding with the United States."

Intimations of domestic political strife had existed in China for much of 1965 and 1966 but the depth of the strife did not become apparent till May 1966. On May 9, the same day China exploded her nuclear device, the first so-called "Demons and Monsters" article was published in *People's Daily*, signaling the start of the Cultural Revolution.[185] Peng Chen, first secretary of the Peking Party apparatus, and Liu Shao-chi himself would eventually fall victims to the Revolution. But during the summer of 1966 it was not at all clear who would be purged, perhaps up to and including Mao himself. One reason for the public rejection of American overtures as fraudulent was Chinese domestic politics. No one, not even Mao, could afford to be saddled with the onus of being "soft on imperialism" during the uncertain summer of 1966.

At the same time, Soviet charges of betrayal of the Vietnamese had continually been levied against the Chinese. From January through May the Russians accused the Chinese of obstructing Soviet aid to the D.R.V. On May 3, the Chinese issued a statement, "Malinovsky is a Liar," rejecting charges of betrayal made by the Soviet Minister of Defense.[186] Peng Chen, purged in June, had been the leading Chinese advocate of united action. United action itself was decried as "a propaganda sham to deceive the revolutionary people of the world."[187] The Chinese, to counter the Soviet claim of Sino-American collusion, in turn accused the Russians of being the "number one accomplices to the U.S. gangsters."[188] Following Soviet insinuations that China and the United States had arrived at an understanding on Vietnam at the Warsaw ambassadorial talks, China responded by calling *Pravda's* implications "the height of absurdity."[189] China was clearly denying any complicity with the United States in order to protect its prestige within the world socialist system.

Thus, during the summer of 1966 when the Chinese government suddenly resumed its hard-line public stance *vis-à-vis* the United States, there were motivations other than a changed perception of the United States. The U.S. had maintained its previous stance of moderation in its position toward China and Mao undoubtedly realized it. The threat of war had been reduced. A tacit Chinese-American understanding had been reached, with ground rules for the conduct of the war having been "agreed" upon — through Mao could not acknowledge this, of course.

The same explanation may also be used to assess the motivation behind Peking's September 7, 1966, statement that "the U.S. imperialist aggression against Vietnam is aggression against China." The statement was issued after the 131st ambassadorial meeting in Warsaw, warning that Washington would be committing "a grave historical blunder" if it did not give sufficient credence to the "determination" of the Chinese people to support the Vietnamese.[190] The "aggression against Vietnam is aggression against China" formula had not appeared since the preceding fall and its appearance was therefore of some note.[191] Again, however, the Chinese domestic situation and the Sino-Soviet polemic must be considered the most likely motivations behind the Chinese statements.

By the end of 1966, Peking's perspective of American involvement had gone through several transitions, finally arriving at the view that the United States would in fact contain its presence to South Vietnam in the ground war and both Vietnams in the air war. The Chinese clearly did not want war with the United States and managed to communicate that view to Washington. According to Lyndon Johnson, "China doesn't want to get into a war and you know damned well that we don't want to get into the big war."[192]

Far more important than anything else for the future of China, however, was the on-going Great Proletarian Cultural Revolution, which would not be resolved until 1969. The Cultural Revolution, whose roots were set deep in the history of the Communist Party of China, was nonetheless precipitated in part by different perceptions of the American threat in Vietnam held by different comrades within the CPC.[193] Differing interpretations of the nature of the American threat in Vietnam also led to an exacerbation of the Sino-Soviet split and, to a lesser degree, to a decreased cordiality in Sino-Vietnamese relations.

American involvement in Vietnam had gone through a significant transformation in 1965 and 1966. Escalation had followed escalation as the war took on an increasingly American character. During the next three years, the world would view the spectacle of a rather minor military power, supporting a war near its homeland, successfully withstanding the military might that the world's most powerful nation was willing to bring against it. By the end of 1966, the perspectives from Washington, Moscow and Peking were all somewhat similar: the U.S. would be tied down in Asia, in Vietnam, for some years to come. All these powers recognized that a protracted war in Vietnam would have a major impact on the correlation of forces among the three nations. What that impact would be, however, remained to be seen.

# IV

# Continuing Commitment: 1967-1969

As 1967 opened, the Johnson administration faced growing criticism both domestically and internationally about its Vietnam policy. The specter of the immediate defeat of the South Vietnamese government had been averted but on the official level in Washington the proverbial "light at the end of the tunnel" was yet to be seen. Washington now realized the war would be long but there was no expectation that it would be futile.

During 1967, despite sporadic and uncertain successes in Vietnam and increasing isolation in the world community brought about by its Vietnam policy, the United States continued to seek a military victory in Vietnam. If anything, the Johnson administration's commitment of American might had escalated not only the war but also the *importance* of the war. Before the increased commitment of forces, an American withdrawal from Vietnam leading to the eventual possible loss of South Vietnam was a policy alternative. By 1967 that policy option had been excluded. Vietnam had simply become too much a *cause célèbre*. The United States had put its military might and prestige on the line. The American commitment, to Johnson, had a wider significance than ever before and therefore had to be continued.

## Fighting a Two Front War: Problems for Washington

During 1967, the South Vietnamese and the United States governments both pursued the so-called "two-front war" concept adopted at the Honolulu Conference in February 1966. Unfortunately for both governments, the results were inconclusive. Militarily speaking, "the mood was one of cautious optimism," with some even hoping that 1967 "would prove to be the decisive year for Vietnam."[1] On the other hand, "The political indicators ... both at home and abroad were mixed."[2] While most members of the American hierarchy recognized, in Walter Rostow's words, that it was "imperative that we mount and effectively

orchestrate a concerted military, civil, and political effort to achieve a satisfactory outcome," success in that effort remained elusive. The continued elusiveness of success was reflected in a newly emerging debate in Washington over United States policy goals in Vietnam.[3]

Militarily speaking, U.S. Commander in Chief Pacific U.S.G. Sharp pronounced the objective of the on-going Rolling Thunder attacks to be "to cause North Vietnam to cease supporting, controlling, and directing insurgencies in Southeast Asia." To Sharp, this could be achieved by attacking three different areas in North Vietnam. First, it was necessary to deny North Vietnam access to external assistance by attacking ports and rail lines. Second, the southward flow of supplies had to be curtailed. Finally, the capability of the North Vietnamese to contribute support to the insurgency had to be eliminated.[4]

Each of Sharp's concepts had proponents in Washington. Finally, in April, Rostow and McNamara agreed on Sharp's second point of attack as the basis for an expanded air war against North Vietnam's supply lines. The two advisors felt that by "closing the bottom of the funnel," the quantity of supplies reaching the South could be reduced.[5] If this could be achieved, it was argued, then the pace of pacification in the South could proceed more rapidly. Johnson accepted the Rostow-McNamara thesis.

Shortly before the stepped-up bombing began, General Westmoreland submitted his analysis of future force requirements in South Vietnam. During the March 20-21 Guam Conference, Westmoreland had presented an optimistic assessment of the military situation in Vietnam to Johnson and his advisors. In the new force requirement assessment, however, optimism was noticeably lacking. In his request, Westmoreland predicted that 201,250 more men would be needed to convince the enemy "through the vigor of our offensive and accompanying psychological operations, that he faces inevitable defeat."[6] Even with that increase, Westmoreland felt the war would continue for two years.[7]

Why was Westmoreland arguing for more troops? Lyndon Johnson and Walter Rostow elucidated what was probably the major reason. In *The Vantage Point*, Johnson admitted that by the spring of 1967, the "crossover point"—the point at which Vietcong losses exceeded capabilities to replace those losses—had not yet been reached. Although Johnson argued that there was an "unfavorable trend for the aggressors," he also cautioned that the pace of pacification in the countryside and the improvement of the South Vietnamese armed forces had

Opposite: *President Johnson, General Westmoreland, Chief of State Thieu and Premier Ky during Johnson's fall 1966 visit to Cam Ranh Bay. U.S. Air Force photograph.*

not proceeded "nearly as rapidly as it might have."[8] Rostow more optimistically assessed pacification's progress as "modest but real."[9] In other words, the U.S. policy objectives remained the preservation of an independent and sovereign South Vietnam but the method had changed. Instead of using American forces to prevent a military defeat, Johnson was now seeking a military victory. To achieve that victory, more American manpower was needed.

The pacification program itself was designed to increase the land area and number of peasants controlled by Saigon. In the first phase of pacification, U.S. units conducted search and destroy operations, which were then followed by Army of the Republic of Viet Nam (ARVN) clear and hold operations. Specially trained South Vietnamese rural pacification teams were then to enter the newly-secured territory to organize and indoctrinate the peasants. More often that not, however, the strategy failed as the ARVN units proved unable to accomplish their clearing and holding operations. Official Washington was aware of this problem, as discussed above. One of the more carefully worded but nonetheless clear criticisms of the ARVN units was provided by Admiral Sharp:

> Although the Vietnamese Armed Forces had the primary mission of supporting pacification, United States forces reinforced their efforts by direct support. Vietnamese Army units were redeployed and retrained to support these programs, but providing the motivation was difficult and progress in orienting these forces was slow.[10]

The pacification program was the core of the U.S.-South Vietnamese strategy during 1967 and 1968. There was obviously, however, disagreement within the Johnson administration about the degree of its success. An internal government memorandum circulated by John McNaughton on May 19 illustrated this disagreement, and at the same time perhaps unknowingly pointed to its cause. On the one hand, the "big war" in the South between U.S. and North Vietnamese forces was going well and there was consensus that "we are no longer in danger of losing this war militarily." On the other hand, the "other war" against the Vietcong was not going well because of "widespread" corruption in the South Vietnamese government and because "little has been done to remedy the economic and social ills of the corruption from which Vietcong support stems."[11]

The already limited success of the two front war in Vietnam was further reduced by a deteriorating consensus in the United States about the proper conduct of the war. One internal government memo after another made reference to the possible adverse domestic impact of additional troop commitments or bombing escalations. As domestic support for the war broke down, Johnson realized that more effective ways of gaining this support must be achieved.[12] Thus, in many instances, U.S. efforts on the second front in Vietnam were "attuned more to American than Vietnamese politics," with their "major purpose to make U.S. policy in Vietnam more respectable to an American audience."[13] Probably the major effort in this respect was the South Vietnamese elections of September 1967.

Throughout early 1967, the Vietnamese Constituent Assembly drafted a constitution and created laws for the election of a President, Senate and Lower House. Even with continual maneuvering and infighting among the South Vietnamese leaders for political advantage,[14] the Constituent Assembly finally succeeded in its task. Despite the efforts of the Assembly, U.S. Secretary of Defense McNamara returned from a trip to Vietnam in July 1967 and reported that the "biggest worry was on the political front."[15]

Part of the American worry emanated from the rivalry between Premier Ky and President Thieu for political predominance. Though both officers were strongly pro-American, their dual candidacy in the first half of the year threatened to undermine the entire developing electoral process and with it the stability of the South Vietnamese government as well. At the end of June, Ky had agreed to run as Thieu's vice-presidential candidate, but in July, when McNamara made his report, the alliance was still essentially untested. With the United States government as well as the South Vietnamese government clearly attempting to use the upcoming elections for propaganda purposes, it was vital for both governments that the elections be fair and minimally acrimonious.

President Johnson, aware of a feeling in the U.S. that the election would be rigged, sent a group of 22 impartial observers to Vietnam to verify the election's honesty. Their general impression was that the election was relatively legitimate, although several irregularities were in fact reported.[16] There was little doubt that Johnson was cognizant of the potential domestic political impact of the election. The American President congratulated Ky and Thieu on their electoral victory three weeks before the South Vietnamese constituent assembly validated the elections[17] and continually pointed to the almost five million votes cast in the election as proof that the United States was supporting and defending a democratically-elected regime in Saigon. Now, Johnson reasoned, there could be little disagreement with the U.S. presence in Vietnam. Following the elections, it was argued that the American military presence was necessary to buy time to give the democratically-elected Thieu-Ky government a chance to build its political and military strength so it could compete with and defeat the National Liberation Front and the Vietcong.[18]

Throughout the first nine months of 1967, the two front war in

Vietnam and the effort to maintain American domestic will were accompanied by numerous efforts to arrange negotiations. For the most part, the United States maintained the negotiating posture it adopted at the October 1966 Manila Conference. At Manila, the Johnson and Thieu governments announced that U.S. forces would be withdrawn not later than six months after North Vietnam withdrew its forces from the South and had ceased infiltration.[19] Johnson confirmed this position in a letter sent to Ho Chi Minh on February 8, 1967.[20] Johnson called his position the "Phase A Phase B plan." In Phase A, North Vietnamese infiltration would stop. In Phase B, U.S. bombing would stop. Ho's response reiterated the previous North Vietnamese position — before any steps could be taken to reverse the escalation of the war or even to negotiate, American bombing had to stop.

Other peace initiatives during 1967, including ones initiated by Pope Paul, Great Britain, Poland and the Soviet Union (see below), foundered as both sides refused to significantly alter their negotiating posture. To Johnson, the U.S. refusal to redefine its position stemmed from North Vietnamese intransigence. Commenting on the "Marigold" communications through Poland, Johnson's observations applied equally well, from his perspective, to other unsuccessful efforts:

> The North Vietnamese never gave the slightest sign that they were ready to consider reducing the Communists' half of the war or to negotiate seriously the terms of a fair peace settlement.[21]

The first significant change in the American negotiating posture since Manila was contained in the so-called San Antonio Formula, set forth by Johnson on September 29, 1967. In the San Antonio Formula, cessation of bombing was tied to guaranteed immediate productive discussions rather than to an end to infiltration.[22] However, once again, it was rejected. To Hanoi, a bombing halt remained a precondition.

Beneath the efforts to conduct a two-front military and political war and beneath the attempts to arrange negotiations, one major assumption still guided American policy — Saigon's difficulties were primarily the product of pressure applied by Hanoi. This assumption was inherent to both the two-front war concept and the U.S. negotiating position and it was the assumption under which the United States military buildup had begun in early 1965. By the end of 1967, then, the Vietnamese problem as viewed from Washington had changed in scope and tenor but not in cause. As far as Johnson was concerned, military, political, and negotiating victories had to be won in the South, but they could not be won until Hanoi's will to continue pressure on Saigon had been bent or broken. Johnson clearly felt this required concentration on military efforts. To Johnson, during 1967, it was "important that the [military] pressure be maintained and increased."[23]

Throughout the years of escalating American involvement, some U.S. officials disagreed with the major assumption on which U.S. policy was predicated. Other officials, while they accepted the assumption, rejected the conclusions and policies which were drawn and implemented. Seldom, however, had the dissenters been on a senior policymaking level. During the last months of 1967, however, this changed. A new powerful voice slowly began to be heard with those who advocated restraint. The new voice belonged to Secretary of Defense McNamara.

On October 31, 1967, McNamara, aware that the war was undermining American society and cognizant that the war could continue for years, submitted a memorandum on the conduct of the war to Lyndon Johnson. The memorandum contained, among other things, two observations and three recommendations on the war. To McNamara, an upswing in U.S. military activity would produce slow progress not "really visible to the general public." At the same time, additional military operations carried "major risks of widening the war." On the basis of these observations, McNamara advocated not expanding the air war against the North, granting a bombing halt before the end of 1967 and giving the South Vietnamese a greater responsibility for their own defense.[24] Although McNamara urged restraint, it remained to be seen what effect he would have on Johnson.

Johnson showed McNamara's memorandum to Westmoreland and Taylor, both of whom rejected it as a "pull-back" strategy. Westmoreland's opposition stemmed from his rather optimistic view of the on-going conflict. In his year-end assessment of the military situation, Westmoreland concluded that in 1967 "the enemy lost control of large sectors of the population" and now faced "significant problems in the areas of indigenous recruiting, morale, health, and resources control." The year ended, Westmoreland informed his superiors, with the enemy "increasingly resorting to desperation tactics in attempting to achieve military/psychological victory."[25] There was no reason to adopt the "pull-back" strategy, Westmoreland believed. Clark Clifford, who had also been shown the memorandum and would soon replace McNamara as Secretary of Defense, reached a similar conclusion.

Following the line of his optimistic assessment, Westmoreland sent a message to Washington on December 20 warning that his intelligence indicated that the Vietcong had decided that if they were to avoid defeat, then they "would have to make a major effort to reverse the downward trend." Westmoreland expected the Vietcong to launch a "maximum effort on all fronts," though he implied he did not know how soon to expect it.[26] Nonetheless, Westmoreland expected to enter the "third phase" of the war during 1968, a phase in which "the end begins to come into view."[27]

Other U.S. intelligence reports through the fall of 1967 indicated an increased flow of troops and equipment from the North to the South. Reports from the U.S. embassy in Saigon argued that the upcoming offensive would be the "decisive turning point" in the war, but the Washington intelligence community did not agree, although it did believe that Hanoi was contemplating a "serious risk."[28] During his December trip to Australia, Johnson informed the Australian government that he expected the Vietcong to launch a "kamikaze" attack in the near future. Johnson maintained that he also tried "to inform [his] own people," i.e., the American public, about the expected offensive, though in veiled terms since he did not want to "alert the enemy to our knowledge of his plan."[29] In retrospect, Johnson's logic appears somewhat specious, although it should be noted that Johnson later commented that he had made a mistake by not being blunt about the buildup.

The Vietcong launched its offensive on January 31, 1968, with an attack on the U.S. embassy in Saigon. Even though expected, the Tet offensive shocked the U.S. command and public. The strength, length and intensity of the offensive prolonged and intensified this shock. By February 11, the Vietcong attacks had been directed against 34 provincial towns, 64 district towns and all of the autonomous cities.[30] The American claim of "security in South Vietnamese cities" had been destroyed.

Why had the Vietcong launched such a massive offensive? The immediate assessment, both in Saigon and Washington, was that the offensive was needed to reverse the deteriorating trend in the Vietcong's fortunes.[31] Lyndon Johnson argued that the Vietcong's goals were threefold: first, to put ARVN out of action; second, to produce a popular uprising in South Vietnam; and, finally, to erode the resolve of the American people.[32] According to the Vietcong themselves, the Tet offensive sought to "overthrow the puppet regime and turn over the regime of government to the people" and to "create conditions for the pacifist movements in the U.S.A. to expand."[33] There was no doubt that to the Vietcong, the Tet offensive represented the first stage in a "prolonged strategic offensive that [will] include many military campaigns and local uprisings."[34]

In at least two respects, the Tet offensive was a disaster for the Vietcong. According to the prestigious Institute for Strategic Studies, Tet "destroyed the elite of North Vietnam's army" as well as the Vietcong.[35] Forty-five thousand Vietcong and North Vietnamese cadre had been killed by the end of February. The Vietcong had hoped to smash ARVN and lead a popular uprising but were frustrated on both accounts. High U.S. officials declared that the National Liberation Front's hope for a popular uprising was now shown to be "a myth."[36]

Nonetheless, from a political standpoint, the Tet offensive was an impressive victory. The Vietcong had proved to the American people and the world that American military might had crushed neither their will nor their capacity to fight. Even President Johnson recognized that Tet had been a "psychological" victory for the Vietcong. The actual situation in South Vietnam was reflected in the report General Earle Wheeler, chairman of the Joint Chiefs of Staff, submitted to Johnson on February 27. According to Wheeler, "the enemy failed to achieve his initial objective but is continuing his effort." At the same time, despite his losses, "he has the capability and the will to continue." Pacification of the countryside had received another severe setback as both U.S. and South Vietnamese units were moved from rural to urban areas to cope with the attacks against the cities, and therefore "the enemy [was] operating with relative freedom in the countryside." While U.S. forces retained their pre Tet capabilities and ARVN could recover theirs in "three to six months," the Tet offensive had still been "a very near thing."[37]

The seriousness of the position in South Vietnam was underlined by Wheeler's new listing of objectives in Vietnam following Tet. According to the General, the objectives had become:

> First, to counter the enemy offensive and to destory or eject the North Vietnamese invasion force in the northern part of South Vietnam.
> Second, to restore security in the cities and towns.
> Third, to restore security in the heavily populated areas of the countryside.
> Fourth, to regain the initiative through offensive operations.

To achieve these objectives, Westmoreland required 206,756 more men.[38]

To satisfy Westmoreland's request, military reserves would have to be called up, expenditures increased and political consequences accepted. To deny Westmoreland's request, or to meet it part way, would just as surely imply that a limit to the American commitment had been reached. New hard decisions had to be made and U.S. policy had to be reassessed.

Johnson chose Secretary of Defense-designate Clark Clifford to lead the reassessment effort. The reassessment group under Clifford included McNamara, Taylor, Rostow, Bundy and others. For four weeks, they undertook a detailed and painstaking examination of U.S. policy toward Vietnam, looking at what options were open to the United States in light of the Tet offensive and the Wheeler-Westmoreland request.[39] By the end of March, a degree of consensus had been reached and President Johnson had made his decision.

*Haiphong, North Vietnam, March 1968: More than 100 military trucks and tracked amphibious combat vehicles parked along safe streets in this port city, prior to U.S. bombing of Hanoi and Haiphong. Official U.S. Air Force photograph.*

On March 31, 1968, Johnson went on national television and informed the nation about his decisions. After affirming his conviction that Tet had been a military failure for the Vietcong, he informed the American people and the world that bombing attacks on North Vietnam had been suspended except for the area immediately north of the demilitarized zone; that South Vietnam would receive additional aid to strengthen its own armed forces; that 25,000 additional U.S. troops would be sent to Vietnam; and perhaps most importantly that he was not available for the Presidential nomination in 1968. Suddenly, in one swoop, in almost every respect, American involvement in Vietnam had taken on a new appearance.

What had led to Johnson's decisions? Aside from the rhetoric of many of those involved,[40] it was evident that the Tet offensive had been a massive shock to American leaders. The Vietcong did in fact fail to achieve their military objective but they had succeeded in making it abundantly clear that the United States had also failed to guarantee stability in South Vietnam. As Henry Kissinger later observed, "in a guerrilla war, purely military considerations are not decisive: psychological and political factors loom at least as large."[41] The United States government had finally accepted this. Ironically, Washington's two-front war concept had earlier recognized the importance of the psychological and political parameters but had emphasized the military. Johnson had finally reversed the order of priorities but the cost had been high.

Johnson, then, had faced a choice. He could pay the price for a military victory won by the United States for the South Vietnamese, a price that had continually increased in the past and which had once again, with Westmoreland's request, been raised considerably, or he could limit the U.S. involvement to prevent the defeat of South Vietnam, with the South Vietnamese themselves winning the struggle when they had sufficiently marshaled their strength. Johnson opted for the second choice.

Johnson had been persuaded to choose the second option for a variety of reasons. First, many of his civilian advisers, particularly Clark Clifford, believed that even 200,000 more men would not guarantee military victory. Second, as Johnson himself admitted, he gradually adopted the view that the South Vietnamese would have to win their victory themselves.[42] Finally, Johnson was moved by a conviction that unity had to be restored to the American domestic scene. In his March 31 speech, Johnson acted on these persuasions and conesquently both shocked the American public and set a new course for the U.S involvement in Vietnam.

The last ten months of the Johnson administration may best be depicted as months spent in a holding action in Vietnam while arrangements were worked out to begin negotiations with North Vietnam and the NLFSV. Hanoi, apparently impressed by the combination of the "90 percent" bombing halt and Johnson's announcement that he would not seek re-election, agreed to meet administration officials to discuss only one thing—"to determine with the American side the unconditional cessation of the U.S. bombing raids and all other acts of war against the D.R.V. so that talks may start."[43] Even with these preliminary steps toward negotiations agreed upon, the two sides almost did not meet as a mutually acceptable site for the talks could not be found. Eventually, after considerable delay, Paris was agreed upon.

Finally, on May 13, the U.S. delegation under Averell Harriman and the North Vietnamese delegation under Xuan Thuy met for the first time. At the same time, Vietcong units launched attacks on Saigon which had "no apparent military objectives but were instead mounted strictly for political and psychological gain."[44] These attacks were part of a major offensive which the U.S. Central Intelligence Agency, in mid-March, had predicted would occur. Nevertheless, the offensive was seen as "timed to coincide with the opening of negotiations in Paris."[45]

By the end of June, the Paris talks had made no progress. However, they had not been slowed by the Vietcong offensive. Rather, the major reason for the seemingly endless lack of progress was the American desire for some form of reciprocity for a total bombing halt and the accompanying North Vietnamese refusal to accept reciprocity as a legitimate issue. The primary American negotiating points throughout the Paris talks were that "prompt and serious" talks must begin if bombing were halted, that Hanoi must not violate the demilitarized zone and that neither Vietcong nor North Vietnamese forces would attack South Vietnam's major cities.[46] To the United States, North Vietnam was still the aggressor and thus reciprocity implied that the first step toward slowing down the war must be taken by North Vietnam. The D.R.V., on the other hand, totally rejected the concept and consequently the Paris talks were stalemated.[47]

If the North Vietnamese continued to reject reciprocity, why then had they agreed to negotiations? Reciprocity had long been a standard U.S. demand and Johnson's March 31 speech had not diminished its importance. In Washington, the generally accepted answer to the question was that the Vietcong and North Vietnamese realized the Tet offensive had weakened their military position in Vietnam but strengthened their political position in the United States and were acting to take advantage of both situations as best as they could. Lyndon Johnson believed that it was American "force which brought them to the table and not our eloquence on March 31."[48]

Johnson's confidence in military power led directly to the total bombing halt announced on October 31, 1968. The total halt, it must be pointed out, did not rely on or appeal to reciprocity in the least. Instead, Johnson informed the American public that "truly remarkable results" had been achieved in the South in the last several months, and that the new U.S. commander in Vietnam, Creighton Abrams, had informed Johnson that in his judgment, a bombing halt "would not result in any increase in American casualties."[49] To Johnson, military successes had achieved the possibility of negotiations. Significantly, however, military successes this time were not viewed as bringing military victory nearer but rather a negotiated settlement nearer. The perspective from Washington had truly changed.

But what had actually been the basis of the bombing halt? It was clear that no agreement had been reached on reciprocity, but rather, Johnson maintained, an "understanding." In essence, the Johnson administration by itself had concluded a bombing halt without preconditions by making clear its position on what would be expected in return. Additionally, the debate over who would be represented at the upcoming talks had been resolved. Hanoi dropped its insistence that there be four coequal sides (Hanoi, the NFLSV, Washington and Saigon) and accepted instead Washington's "our side-your side" proposal.[50] Washington and Saigon thereby managed to avert direct recognition of the NLFSV.

Throughout the period before and immediately after the bombing halt, Johnson realized that the upcoming American elections played a major role in the activities of all concerned even though Johnson had removed himself from partisan politics. Johnson was convinced that some people ardently urged a bombing halt solely to benefit Hubert Humphrey and was equally sure that others, including Thieu and Ky, opposed a slowdown in the conflict so that Richard Nixon could benefit.[51] After Nixon's victory in the election, in no small part due to his assurances that he had a "secret plan" to end the war in Vietnam, the new American leader slowly acclimatized himself to the vagaries of the Vietnam problem.

When Nixon took office, it soon became evident that his "secret plan" to end the war in Vietnam involved more than a simple withdrawal of American troops from South Vietnam. Nixon's Vietnam strategy became a complex choreography of diplomatic initiatives and military pressures designed to isolate North Vietnam from both China and the Soviet Union. According to one observer, "the efforts to end the war in Vietnam became part of a bigger package" which included improving relations with the Kremlin and abandoning twenty years of hostility toward Peking.[52] To Nixon, both communist powers had to be given a stake in improved relations with the United States so that Hanoi would feel isolated and so that the United States could use new forms of military pressure on Hanoi. Nixon, speaking to one of his supporters about his views on Soviet aid to Vietnam, made this point with regard to the Soviet Union, but may have extended it to China as well. Nixon told his listener that his approach to the Kremlin would be, "Look, if you [the Soviet Union] go on supporting North Vietnam, we will have to act dramatically.... On the other hand, we have to say 'If you are willing to give ground and help us out of this morass, it could mean lots of good things.' "[53]

Henry Kissinger, Nixon's newly-appointed assistant to the President for national security affairs, made clear the new administration's thinking on Vietnam in a January 1969 article in *Foreign Affairs*.[54] The core of the U.S. strategy had to be to find a strategy which was "sustainable with substantially reduced casualties." Kissinger believed that seeking an American military victory was futile. Tet had proved it, he argued. A negotiated settlement was the key, but it had to be delayed until South Vietnam developed confidence in its own political capabilities. Kissinger opposed a coalition government in Vietnam since it would "destabilize" South Vietnam. To Kissinger, the U.S. posture should be to seek a mutual withdrawal of forces "over a sufficiently long period so that a genuine indigenous political process had a chance to become established." In essence, a political balance of power would then have been created by U.S. military force. By adopting this strategy, the United States would gain "a reasonable time for political consolidation, it will have done the maximum possible for an ally short of permanent occupation."

The new Secretary of Defense, Melvin Laird, listed the policy options open to the Nixon government as they were viewed during the first National Security Council meeting of the new administration. According to Laird, three options were discussed. First, the U.S. could withdraw and declare Vietnam "somebody else's problem." Second, the U.S. could escalate and seek a military victory, but Laird believed that "that was impossible." Finally, Nixon could "stand firm" and develop a program "to help South Vietnam take over the war and defend itself. The President preferred to end the war by negotiations. But if the North Vietnamese refused, we had to have an alternative."[55]

From the outset of the Nixon administration, it was evident that a military victory accomplished by U.S. force had in fact been rejected as a viable policy alternative. At the same time, however, the Nixon administration rejected acceptance of defeat. In his first news conference, Nixon promised that "new tactics" would be employed which he believed would be "more successful than the tactics of the past."[56] One of these "new tactics," it later became known, was an increase in covert military pressure on the Vietcong's supply lines. Starting on March 18, 1969, a program of covert B-52 bombing raids began against supply lines and enemy forces in Cambodia. Known as OPERATION MENU, the daily raids were kept secret from the U.S. public and Congress.[57] Nixon thus illustrated his continuing resolve to the North Vietnamese. On the other hand, the "public half" of Nixon's "new tactics" was equipping and training the South Vietnamese forces to fight for themselves. This process became known as "Vietnamization."

While Vietnamization may have been a new Nixonian tactic, its intellectual underpinning had been provided by Johnson during the last year of his administration. Johnson maintained that during 1968 he had increasingly realized that the South Vietnamese would in the final analysis win or lose the war themselves. When Nixon entered the White House, he undertook a reexamination of U.S. policy toward Vietnam and concluded that Johnson's program to modernize and expand South Vietnam's army was the correct approach to the problem but was proceeding too slowly. At the same time, Nixon was not convinced that the North Vietnamese were seriously seeking a negotiated settlement. Given these conclusions, the Nixon administration "determined that a major change in policy which both complemented and provided an alternative to negotiation was in order." Vietnamization was "designed to be carried out regardless of whether North Vietnam negotiated seriously or not."[58]

During the first half of 1969, Vietnamization proceeded slowly. Nixon increased U.S. expenditures on training and equipping South Vietnamese forces in March. As these forces increased in strength, they were to assume a greater share of the military burden, thereby enabling Nixon to proceed with his phased withdrawal plan. On June 8, 1969, the President announced the first phase of withdrawals would begin.[59]

Interestingly enough, the Vietnamization program reflected the new U.S. administration's attempt to "have the best of both worlds." By withdrawing American troops, Nixon was clearly attempting to reduce the impact of the war in the United States. At the same time, by training and equipping Saigon's armed forces, the President was trying to aid Saigon in winning a final victory, a goal which had been abandoned as a policy objective for U.S. troops. To the Nixon administration, the South Vietnamese government had to be readied to achieve a military victory if negotiations failed. To Nixon, then, military power wielded by South Vietnam's armed forces rather than American armed forces remained the key to a successful resolution of the Vietnamese situation if a satisfactory and acceptable agreement could not be negotiated in Paris.

The Paris negotiations themselves did not begin until January 24, almost three months after the total bombing halt. The three-month delay was caused by South Vietnam's refusal to send representatives to Paris. Thieu delayed the talks in the hope that Nixon would be more intransigent in negotiations than Johnson and only agreed to go to Paris when Nixon publicly supported Johnson's position. Johnson himself believed that Thieu's delay was one of the few times the South Vietnamese leader had let him down.[60] Even after the negotiations began, however, they remained fruitless and hopelessly deadlocked for several months. Again, reciprocity was the central issue leading to the deadlock. Nixon demanded that North Vietnam respond to his proposed troop withdrawal program with a concommitant program but Hanoi rejected the proposal.[61] Throughout the Paris negotiations, Hanoi's representatives rejected any approach that implied American and North Vietnamese forces in South Vietnam were there on an equal footing or indicated that Vietnam was something other than the victim of "American aggression." The purpose of the peace negotiations, according to Kissinger, remained to give the people of Vietnam "an opportunity to work out their own destiny in their own way."[62] As the negotiations dragged on, it was clear that fundamentally different U.S. and North Vietnamese assumptions still precluded successful negotiations. To the United States, there were two Vietnams. To North Vietnam, there was one.

During the first half of 1969, the Nixon administration attempted to influence the Soviet Union to bring pressure on Hanoi to adopt a more conciliatory position in Paris. American representatives communicated to their Soviet counterparts that Vietnam would be linked to a wide range of issues unless the Soviets prevailed upon Hanoi. If nothing was achieved through negotiations, the U.S. maintained, then no SALT agreement could be reached. Additionally, Kissinger implied, bombing missions against the North would be resumed. On March 4, Nixon said the Soviets recognized that if the war continued, then "possibilities of escalation continued." On May 14, Nixon reaffirmed that the continuing war "will affect other decisions" with regard to Soviet-American relations. At the same time, Kissinger informed Soviet Ambassador to the United States Anatoly Dobrynin that if a settlement were not reached, then the U.S. would "escalate the war."[63]

The Nixon-Kissinger linkage policy produced limited results. Shortly before Nixon took office, U.S. Ambassador to the Soviet Union Llewellyn Thompson had warned that though the Soviets preferred a political solution, they would proceed "with caution, letting Hanoi call the signals."[64] Later, after Nixon took office, Averell Harriman maintained that the Soviets could be "very helpful in smoothing out some of the rough spots" if a basic agreement were reached but they would "take Hanoi's side in the negotiations."[65] The road to peace in Vietnam did not, then, lead through the Kremlin. Following the Soviet Union's recognition of the Provisional Revolutionary Government of South Vietnam on June 13, only one week after it was formed, Nixon realized that and no longer pursued the Moscow path.

Meanwhile, in Vietnam itself, the military situation was improving considerably for the United States and South Vietnam. Large segments of formerly-contested territory were occupied by the South Vietnamese army, ARVN expanded to over a million men, and North Vietnamese-NLFSV activity decreased. During the February to April 1969 offensive, the Vietcong committed only battalion-level forces to battle, whereas during 1968 regiment-level forces were used. Although there were different interpretations about why the military situation had improved so rapidly, the Nixon administration believed the success was due to a simple fact: U.S. policy — Vietnamization accompanied by selective application of American air power — was succeeding and had severely crippled the Vietcong and North Vietnamese.[66] Consequently, the American negotiating posture remained constant, as Nixon made clear in his May 14, 1969 speech. A negotiated peace was desired but on American terms.

In his May 14 speech, Nixon confirmed that the U.S. had "ruled out attempting to impose a purely military solution on the battlefield" and had also ruled out "a one-sided withdrawal" and a "disguised defeat." Similarly, the U.S. sought "no bases in Vietnam," insisted on "no military ties" and was willing to accept "any government in South Vietnam that results from the free choice of the South Vietnamese people themselves." Specifically, Nixon advocated "mutual withdrawal of all non-South Vietnamese forces from South Vietnam" on a staged timetable basis and "free choice for the people of South Vietnam" under fixed procedures overseen by an international body.[67]

Nixon was pulling no punches. He wanted to withdraw but would not risk the military defeat of South Vietnam if a withdrawal were undertaken. Still, a fundamental difference underlay the U.S. and North Vietnamese position. To the United States, both American and North Vietnamese troops were foreign and had to be withdrawn. To the North Vietnamese, the presence of North Vietnamese forces in South Vietnam was a domestic matter. Consequently the D.R.V. rejected Nixon's proposal.

Nixon's earlier expectation of deadlocked negotiations was thus well-founded. Both sides entered the negotiations with premises which excluded successful negotiations. Consequently, Vietnamization proceeded as had been promised. Despite Nixon's attempt to find a solution to the dilemma of American policy toward Vietnam, continuing long-term American commitment to Vietnam appeared inevitable. Nixon himself regularly confirmed this commitment. "A great nation cannot renege on its pledges," Nixon argued. The United States had to protect "other nations' confidence in our reliability."[68] If domestic political necessities forced the U.S. government to reduce the American troop commitment in Vietnam, then American pledges — and U.S. reliability — would be confirmed through aid and air power.

Nixon's view of the role of Vietnamization within the framework of the entire international situation was made clear by the Guam Doctrine, also called the Nixon Doctrine. The Doctrine set forth by Nixon on Guam in July 1969, applied to "all ... international relationships," though it had "special meaning for East Asia."[69] The Nixon Doctrine contained three precepts, and is of enough importance to be quoted at length:

> The United States will keep all its treaty commitments.
> We shall provide a shield if a nuclear power threatens the freedom of a nation allied with us or of a nation whose survival we consider vital to our security and the security of the region as a whole.
> In cases involving other types of aggression we shall furnish military and economic assistance when requested and as appropriate. But we shall look to the nation directly threatened to assume the primary responsibility of providing the manpower for its defense.[70]

Nixon and Secretary of State Rogers both stressed the new doctrine was not a rationale for American withdrawal from Asia. Rather, the Nixon Doctrine in general and Vietnamization in particular stemmed from the realization that a large U.S. presence "might inhibit development of ... indigenous strength."[71] To the American President, the South Vietnamese government had not developed enough political or military strength to "resist aggression" because it could rely on American political initiatives and military strength during time of crisis. In a way, then, Nixon argued, his doctrine was a prerequisite to the development of indigenous strength.

Although Nixon never explicitly stated it, the genesis of the Nixon Doctrine also stemmed from Nixon's perception that politically the American people preferred a decreased overseas commitment of U.S. strength. The Nixon Doctrine may thus be viewed as the President's response to domestic political imperatives as well as an international policy growing out of overseas considerations.

Throughout the remainder of 1969, American troop withdrawals proceeded at a slow but constant rate. Nixon reaffirmed his basic beliefs and policies on Vietnam in a major speech on November 3. In his speech, he defended Vietnamization, promised that American

*Saigon, July 1969: President Nixon and President Thieu meet.*

troops would be withdrawn on the basis of a secret schedule, defended the U.S. negotiating position in Paris and appealed for public support.[72] Although some Americans condemned Nixon's speech as "more of the same," the fundamental fact was that the government's perspective of the Vietnam War in November 1969 was considerably different from the one of January 1967. The President was not the same, true, but Nixon and Johnson had eventually come to the same conclusion: the United States would not seek, and possibly could not win, a military victory in Vietnam achieved by U.S. forces. In January 1967, that had been what the United States had been seeking. In November 1969, that was not the U.S. objective.

Avoiding defeat, true enough, was once again the U.S. objective, just as it had been in February 1965 when the FLAMING DART raids were launched. By the end of 1969, final victory had been relegated to a secondary position to be achieved by revitalized South Vietnamese forces if negotiations failed. To both Johnson and Nixon, the American commitment remained unquestioned but the method of fulfilling the commitment had changed. The implications of that change were still not fully understood.

## Threat and Opportunity: Moscow's Quandary

By the beginning of 1967, the Soviet Union believed that the United States had adopted a flexible policy of opposition to national liberation movements. This policy, called the "Asian Doctrine" by the Kremlin, supposedly permitted the United States to use whatever means would be successful in its opposition to the movements. In Vietnam, where limited American military strength had "bogged down," the Kremlin perceived an American attempt to increase its military successes under the "Asian Doctrine" primarily through the theory of escalation.

To the Kremlin, the theory of escalation was elementary. It was used to "build up strength" and to extend the war step by step. This buildup would be cautiously undertaken, "with an eye to the international situation, taking care not be overstep the limits beyond which a general war might be sparked off."[73]

Escalation was thus viewed as both an active and a reactive theory, on the one hand being the primary method whereby the United States implemented its "doctrines" and on the other hand being necessitated by American military defeats in Vietnam. During 1967-1968, the U.S. "theory of escalation" was seen as a three part concept. According to *International Affairs*,[74] the stages were:

(1) To strike a decisive blow at the national liberation movement in Indochina to "demonstrate to the world that the United States intended to crush it and could indeed crush it."

(2) To isolate the national liberation movement from socialist countries and to force the latter to abandon their duty to support oppressed people throughout the world.

(3) To bolster the prestige of the United States, its leaders and capitalism and to "pacify" Southeast Asia into a sphere of free activity for monopolies and for the military. Additionally, a final corollary was the reassertion of control over American allies.

As the fighting in Vietnam continued through 1967, the Soviet perception of American objectives and methods in Vietnam remained relatively constant. The flexibility of the "Asian Doctrine" permitted the United States to adopt its theory of military escalation to combat short-

*Coastal waters of South Vietnam, February 1967: military supplies originating in the Soviet Union and China were regularly offloaded to smaller craft such as these for use in South Vietnam, after transshipment through North Vietnam. Official U.S. Air Force photograph.*

term difficulties, the Soviets argued, but in the long-run U.S. policy was doomed to failure.

Soviet-American relations, meanwhile, remained relatively cool. Although progress was made on a nuclear nonproliferation treaty, other conferences and agreements achieved little. The much-touted Glassboro meeting between Johnson and Kosygin achieved little. According to Johnson, the U.S. side desired discussions on the missile race but Kosygin continually brought the conversation back to Vietnam or the Middle East. Additionally, Kosygin transmitted a North Vietnamese message to Johnson concerning a possible bombing halt. Kosygin reportedly could "not guarantee" Hanoi's reaction to Johnson's response and the issue was not examined further.[75] Aside from that, Brezhnev's promised "freeze" was still operant. The Soviet Union, perceiving a United States intent on extending its neocolonial hegemony over Southeast Asia and still sensitive to Chinese criticism that it was supplying insufficient aid to North Vietnam, could do little else.

As 1967 drew to a close, Soviet rhetoric addressed to the war had settled into a standard condemnation of U.S. actions and self-praise for aid extended. While the American intervention was continually assessed as being "doomed to failure," there was little to indicate that the Soviet Union meant other than the United States would not defeat the National Liberation Movement. There was no apparent expectation in the Kremlin that the NLFSV would militarily defeat the United States. The Soviet reaction to the Tet offensive confirmed this viewpoint.

The Soviet appraisal of the Tet offensive was at first restrained, but became increasingly vocal. *Pravda* observed only that the offensive had proven that the U.S. claim that "the forces of the National Liberation Front are exhausted" was "another U.S. fabrication"[76] but soon all Soviet media were describing Tet as "a major U.S. military defeat."[77] At the same time, *Pravda* predicted that General Westmoreland's request for 200,000 additional troops would be approved, following earlier practices of "escalation after defeat." Past U.S. policy obviously influenced Soviet expectations but this time, at least, expectation and policy did not coincide. To the Soviets, the outcome of the ongoing debate in Washington over U.S. policy was essentially predetermined. The fact that McNamara was resigning as Secretary of Defense did nothing to assuage Soviet sentiments since his replacement, Clark Clifford, was viewed as a hardliner. Even with rumors circulating in Washington that Clifford opposed additional U.S. commitment, *Izvestiia* announced that "in the political poultry coop Clark Clifford is certainly a hawk."[78]

While the Russian reaction to Tet was at first slow in coming, the same was not true of the Kremlin's reaction to Johnson's March 31 speech. This time, the Soviet's reaction was swift. *Izvestiia* immediately commented that while the bombing curtailment was a laudable step, there was no guarantee of a continuing halt. Increased troop commitments and budget expenditures were emphasized as much as the bombing cutback.[79] Four days later *Pravda* applauded North Vietnam's decision to begin negotiations, but pointed out that American bombing of the D.R.V. continued.[80] *Izvestiia*, meanwhile observed that Johnson would "probably change his mind and seek re-election."[81]

The war, the American proposal for peace talks, domestic U.S. dissent, the North Vietnamese acceptance of talks, and the decision to begin the negotiations in Paris were all combined in a May 5 *Pravda* article. Again, the impression given was that despite Clark Clifford's slowdown, despite the peace negotiations, and despite Johnson's announcement that he would not seek re-election, Soviet attitudes had not altered substantially. According to the party newspaper:

> On March 31, United States President Johnson issued an order for limiting the bombing of North Vietnam's territory and stated his desire to negotiate. The facts indicate that Washington's actions were based on an attempt to mislead public opinion by its "peace gestures." There is no other way to interpret things since the air war against North Vietnam's territory was simultaneously intensified and more American soldiers were sent to Vietnam.
>
> ... The North Vietnamese government, desiring a peaceful and just settlement of the Vietnamese problem, agreed to begin preliminary contacts on the question.
>
> Washington clearly did not expect such a turn of events and was caught unprepared. U.S. ruling circles resorted to tactics of red tape, distorting facts, and verbal juggling....
>
> The D.R.V. then took a new step and appointed its representative and stated that Paris is suitable as the site for preliminary contacts. This time the U.S.A. was compelled to agree to the time and place.[82]

Why did the Soviet Union reject these several indications that American policy toward Vietnam was changing? Two reasons are most probable. First, the Soviet rejection of American signals that the nature of U.S. involvement in Vietnam was changing may be attributed to the simple fact that the Soviet Union had long held the perception of a resolute, anticommunist, United States and that strongly held perceptions change only over time. A time lag between policy change and perception change was thus to be expected and did in fact occur. However, enough time had not yet passed and old perceptions maintained their legitimacy. Additionally, even though U.S. policy was in retrospect obviously in the midst of change, another U.S. troop increase had in fact occurred.

While the time lag phenomenon was undoubtedly important to the continuing Soviet perception of a resolute American policy, a second reason was probably of even greater significance to the maintenance of old Soviet views — the U.S. presidential election itself. To many observers throughout the world, the leading issue in the 1968 U.S. presidential campaign was Vietnam. Most Soviet observers shared this view. While the Soviet Union was hesitant to attach major importance to the antiwar positions adopted by most candidates[83] or to the immediate political significance of the new left,[84] it did recognize that "many American politicians" were changing their positions on the war because of the elections.[85] For example, both Robert Kennedy and Eugene McCarthy were accused of "supporting the first stage of escalation" and only opposing the war when they saw that "American strength has its limits."[86] Both the Republican and Democratic parties allegedly "concealed their real intentions," at least in Soviet eyes.[87] Memories of John-son's 1964 pre-election position on the Vietnamese War undoubtedly did much to increase the hesitancy of the Soviet Union to view changes of American goals in Vietnam as genuine. With it having been demon-strated in the 1964 presidential election that pre-election policy rhetoric is not necessarily identical to post-election policy, the slowed troop build-up, the suspended bombing attacks and Johnson's refusal to seek re-election were undoubtedly viewed as little more than Democratic at-tempts to influence the U.S. electorate.

Through the summer of 1968, then, the Soviet perception of American goals in Vietnam had not changed. American policy toward Vietnam was still one of "negotiations without de-escalation," and the "character of contemporary international relations" was still dominated by "the aggravation of tension throughout the world by the United States."[88]

The Soviet unwillingness to adopt a new perception of American goals in Vietnam was not destined to remain. On November 1, the United States announced that it had decided to end all hostile actions against North Vietnam. The official Soviet government statement on the bombing halt implied that the Soviet leadership was in fact finally reassessing its previous perceptions. According to the Soviet statement, the bombing halt showed

> a recognition of the fact [that only a bombing halt could lead to peace] by those circles which display political realism in their approach to the Vietnam question.... Not only the results of the coming talks in Paris, but also the prospects for an easing of international tension as a whole will depend largely on whether this had become firmly established within U.S. policy.[89]

For the first time, the Kremlin had accepted the possibility that American policy was changing and could change more. While the Soviet Union clearly did not accept changing American objectives as a foregone conclusion, the Soviets recognized that the debate and policy reassessments that surrounded U.S. policy toward Vietnam were something more than subtle subterfuge.

Why had the Soviet Union only now changed its perception? Why was the November bombing halt different than earlier bombing halts? The timing of the halt undoubtedly provided the answer to both questions. Johnson, after declaring that he wanted to begin steps toward peace before leaving office, probably would not end his political career with a bombing resumption and the new president, whoever he may be, would undoubtedly not begin his term in office with a resumption of the bombing. Therefore, the Soviet Union may have reasoned that the bomb-ing halt would be long-lasting and indeed reflected a change in policy.

The election of Richard Nixon added to the Soviet uncertainty about the eventual course of American policy. It was clear, *Izvestiia* argued, that America's preference for Nixon "could be reduced to one word — Vietnam." However, Nixon's foreign policy in general and Vietnam policy in particular were so vague that "the only thing that is really clear so far is the name of the next U.S. president."[90] This uncertainty about the course of American policy was reflected in numerous Soviet sources.[91] It was quite evident that the Soviet leadership recognized that a change was taking place in American policy toward Vietnam but did not know what course the change would take.

What motivated the change in American policy? Put simply, "the Vietnam War precipitated a movement for basic revision of American politics."[92] According to one source, the change had "little in common with the search for peace" and was prompted by "a desire to end the foreign policy deadlock."[93] *Izvestiia* speculated that

> the ruling American politicians, having burned their fingers in the Viet-
> namese War, will in the future be more cautious about unleashing a
> venture requiring the deployment of large-scale force.[94]

The Vietnamese War underlined the "bankruptcy" of "containment and the cold war" and therefore forced Nixon to develop "his own foreign policy."[95] Nonetheless, said Radio Moscow, it was still impossible

> to predict with any precision which course the Nixon government will
> choose in dealing with these problems [of Vietnam, poverty, etc.]...,
> but one must conclude that under the new administration, Washington
> does not intend to abandon the obsolete dogmas of the position of
> strength policy, although the new cabinet leaders stand for greater
> flexibility in their approach to modern international problems.[96]

The failure of the "Asian Doctrine" was thus the motivating factor behind the change in United States policy. "The grim situation in Vietnam" was "sobering up part of the American bourgeoisie" and "public pressure" in turn had "played a role in Washington's decision" to stop hostile actions against the D.R.V. The pressure itself, however, did not stop those actions. Rather the failure of those actions led to their termination. Washington had "not renounced the role of world policeman" but was simply "changing its tactics."[97] In every war," the Kremlin believed, a time came when "the future course of events are more or less clearly seen." For the American involvement in Vietnam, "such a moment [has] come."[98]

Why had the United States failed to achieve its goals? Four reasons were most often discussed, the valor of the Vietnamese people, Soviet and socialist aid to North Vietnam, poor American morale and the changing correlation of forces in the world. The first two points are self-explanatory. The third and fourth, however, require additional commentary.

Throughout the 1967-1969 period, the Soviet Union stressed the poor American morale in both the military in Vietnam and the populace

at home. The formula that Americans fighting in Vietnam were
"fighting only for money" and had "no lofty ideals worth risking their
lives for" was often repeated,[99] as was the observation, the "prime factor
of victory" is "the political essence of the objective ... above all whether
the war is just or unjust."[100] It was clearly implied that the local war in
Vietnam was "just," as were (and are) all local wars.

American morale at home was also a factor in the "failure" of
American policy. While the "new left" movement was for the most part
dismissed as a political force, the Soviet leadership realized support for
the war had steadily eroded in 1967 and 1968. Thus, politicians were
forced to try to "avoid a fate similar to Johnson's." Decreased support for
the war translated into poor morale.

The fourth and perhaps most important reason that the United
States failed to achieve its goals in Vietnam by the end of 1968 was the
so-called "changed correlation of forces." The war in Vietnam proved
that with "the changed balance of forces in today's world" even "the
strongest capitalist country cannot bring to its knees a people striving for
freedom."[101] The lack of success showed that the United States was "out
of touch with the balance of world forces."[102] An unknown member of
the Soviet hierarchy writing under the pseudonym "A. Sovetov"
illuminated the Kremlin's outlook even more. According to A. Sovetov,
the "change in the world correlation of forces" had reduced imperialist
influence. On the other hand, this reduced influence made imperialism
even more aggressive, as Vietnam showed, as imperialism tried to maintain its influence. Since the changing correlation of forces had led to a
relative decrease in strength of the capitalist world, two capitalist
methods were employed to avoid a confrontation — direct military
pressure (as shown in Vietnam) and the undermining of socialist countries from within (as shown by Johnson's concept of "bridge-building"
and the "Prague Spring" of Czechoslovakia).[103]

Soviet uncertainty over the future course of American policy in
Vietnam continued during the first several months of Nixon's administration. This uncertainty was to a great extent fostered by Nixon
himself. Although formerly identified as an intransigent anticommunist,
Nixon presented a different image during his first few months in office.
Calling for "negotiations rather than confrontation," "a profound transformation" in Soviet-American relations and "strategic sufficiency
rather than superiority," Nixon even recognized that the Soviet Union
was in "a very delicate and sensitive position as far as Vietnam [was]
concerned." The lack of significant America response to another North
Vietnamese offensive in February and March 1969 further underlined
the difference between the "new" and "old" Nixon. Nixon had called for
peaceful initiatives; what policies would be implemented?

The Soviet leadership was well aware that a significant foreign policy debate was going on within the new administration. The Nixon government was still "working out its policy for the near future" and even though it was "probably more inclined to pay attention to those who emphasize the strategic and economic importance of Southeast Asia," "changes may still occur."[104] Radio Moscow posited that Nixon's inaugural address was vague on policy toward Vietnam because he had only formulated "the general trend of future policy."[105] Washington was in a foreign policy dilemma, the Kremlin believed, and only time would tell which course the Nixon administration would follow.[106]

In a possible attempt to influence Nixon's future course, the Soviet government sent some very concrete signals to the Nixon administration that the Soviet Union was willing to end the "freeze" on Soviet-American relations. On February 17, the Soviet ambassador to the United States invited Nixon to visit the Soviet Union; in early March, the Soviet government set forth again a previous consular proposal; and on May 1, for the first time since World War II, the Soviet Union celebrated May Day without a major military parade. It is quite probable that these signals were intended to indicate that a more moderate American foreign policy in Vietnam and elsewhere would be reciprocated.

This is not to say, however, that the Soviet leadership unanimously agreed that American policy would be moderated. In the past, the United States strategic goal had not changed — a military victory to insure American hegemony in a politically, strategically and economically key area — and only tactics had been altered. The same would be true in the future, some argued. The delayed and stalemated Paris peace talks, rumors of de-escalation and even the internal American policy debate itself were all viewed as methods whereby the United States could continue its attempt to achieve its goal, according to some Soviet publications.[107]

Laird's observation that $70 million more were needed for Vietnam drew particularly heavy criticism.[108] According to one *Izvestiia* article, Nixon had "not renounced Johnson's bankrupt policy" and the "period of grace granted the new men in Washington" had come to an end.[109] Radio Moscow announced that the Nixon government had found "no road out of the impasse simply because it refused to approach the problem realistically."[110]

Clearly, during the first months of the Nixon administration the Soviet leadership held no clear perception of the future course of American policy. On the one hand, Nixon had withstood pressures to resume the bombing of North Vietnam, had planned a slow program of troop withdrawals and had opened new initiatives toward the Soviet

Union. On the other hand, American commitment to Vietnam remained massive, no new policy other than "Vietnamization" had been formulated and uncertainty remained. Thus, possibilities existed both for disagreement within the Soviet leadership over the future course of American policy toward Vietnam and for a discrepancy between Soviet polemics and its policy toward the United States. By June 1969, Nixon's policy toward Vietnam had not yet been clarified. Soviet attitudes toward that policy were similarly ill-defined. The previous unified perception of the Soviet leadership had disintegrated, giving way to several different Soviet views on Nixon's policy toward Vietnam. Within a few months, however, the Soviet perceptions would be reunified.

During June, the long-awaited International Conference of Communist and Workers' Parties met in Moscow. The Soviet government used the Conference to build a "new consensus" of progressive parties from which to attack the Chinese ideological position. At the conference, Brezhnev in particular assaulted the United States as "the main force of world reaction" and praised the "armed struggle against imperialism."[111] Numerous Soviet dignitaries as well as publications followed Brezhnev's lead. Soviet Foreign Minister Gromyko condemned the United States' "predatory goals" and "desire to win through force of arms,"[112] while the other Soviet statements stressed that the Nixon administration was "following the course begun by Lyndon Johnson."[113]

It is doubtful, however, whether great significance should be attached to this avalanche of Soviet condemnation. Nixon announced his first troop withdrawal on June 8 while the conference was in session and even though the Russians termed the withdrawal "insignificant," it still marked a reversal of previous U.S. policy. The Soviet condemnation may rather be viewed as an attempt to underline Soviet support for the D.R.V. and reaffirm that the Soviet Union was "doing its international duty" in support of national liberation movements and was therefore a "fit leader" of the socalist world. The International Congress was designed to be a forum from which the Soviet Union could reassert its preeminence in the socialist world and condemnation of the United States was to be expected.

The first American troop withdrawals were soon followed by a fundamental change in the entire framework of U.S. policy. During July, President Nixon outlined his Guam Doctrine. At first, Soviet reaction was restrained. Soon, however, Moscow decided that the new policy was yet another method through which the United States attempted to obtain its previous goals.

"The gist of the Guam Doctrine," Moscow declared, was to "make the American presence less noticeable, to shout less about the world role of the U.S.A. but to achieve the same objectives as before, only wherever possible by proxy."[114] The Guam Doctrine was a "change in tactics, a far more subtle means of achieving [Washington's] ends in Asia."[115] The Soviets interpreted the intent of the doctrine as maintaining American presence in Asia with the aid of its allies' troops. Although some cutbacks in American commitments were predicted, the Kremlin believed that the Guam Doctrine would lead to a new "Pacific Area Treaty Organization," armed with American equipment but employing Pacific and Asian area troops.[116] To the Soviet leaders, Nixon had "clearly and definitely" declared that the United States intended "to play the role of Asian policeman," except that now "the armed forces of the Asian states" would be used.[117]

What induced Nixon to proclaim a new doctrine and how would it be implemented? According to one author:

> The answer lies in the U.S. strategic concepts of the past and present. The U.S. approach to Asian problems over the past twenty years has been invariably determined by the assumption of a "communist threat" to the area.... The present U.S. administration had inherited the old policy.... In the first few months of the new administration all the sins could be on the heads of the old one, but six months later any fresh vicissitudes would be seen as inability to find a substitute policy. So it became necessary to renege on the old policy to tranquilize the public opinion....[118]

Moscow argued that the Guam Doctrine implied a policy of "global Vietnamization" intended to suppress national liberation movements throughout the world, which sought to have Asians fighting Asians, Africans fighting Africans and so on.[119] The Guam Doctrine, to the Soviets, took what in essence had been a local policy and expanded it to an Asian and then worldwide basis.

"Vietnamization" itself had been condemned by the Soviet Union even before the Guam Doctrine was formulated. At first, "Vietnamization" had been attacked because it "de-Americanized" the war rather than ended it. Following the announcement of the Guam Doctrine, Soviet condemnation of the "Vietnamization" program strengthened considerably and even occasionally invoked the specter of John Foster Dulles.[120] The Soviet media often pointed out that "Vietnamization" would lead to a longer war.[121]

The "real objectives of the United States in Vietnam," Moscow argued, were hid "behind the screen of Vietnamization."[122] These real aims included deceiving public opinion, achieving American supremacy in Asia by the hands of the Asians themselves and attaining American long-range strategic and economic objectives.[123] No less a person than Brezhnev himself attacked Vietnamization:

> Vietnamization ... is a renovation of the facade of their policy ... and
> envisages not the cessation of aggression but its transformation into a
> fratricidal war among the Vietnamese. The U.S. wants to use others to
> continue what they themselves have been doing.[124]

Supporting their claims about the Guam Doctrine and Vietnamization, the Soviets noted that as the American troop level
decreased, the Army of the Republic of Vietnam's troop level increased.
At the same time, though, the Soviets emphasized that the U.S. Air Force
and Navy were becoming more active. The Kremlin noted that from
1965 through 1968, 2.8 million tons of bombs had been dropped in Vietnam and that during the first ten months of 1969 alone, 1.2 million tons
of bombs had been dropped.[125] To the Russians, American involvement
was changing form, not substance.

The Soviet perception was further solidified by President Nixon's
November 3, 1969, speech in which he promised continued American
support for "Vietnamization" and the South Vietnamese government.
Soviet reaction was immediate. Radio Moscow trumpeted that "a year
ago, the same Richard Nixon called it Lyndon Johnson's war. Today, it
is Richard Nixon's war."[126] *Izvestiia* compared the secret timetable for
withdrawal "to repetitions of what President Johnson said about success
in the war."[127] *Pravda* condemned the "position of strength" nature of
the speech[128] and Soviet President Podgorny declared that the speech
"showed that a sober solution of this problem has not yet prevailed."[129]

By the end of 1969, the Soviet Union believed that the United
States had again adopted a hardline policy toward Vietnam. Soviet-
initiated signals showing improved Soviet-American relations to be
desired were practically terminated, the Soviet military buildup accelerated and the proposal that Nixon visit the Soviet Union had not
been followed up. For the most part, a "freeze" was again settling over
Soviet-American relations as "Vietnamization" proceeded.

## Domestic Turmoil and an External Threat: The Chinese Predicament

For China, increasing American involvement in Vietnam during
1967 and 1968 presented several difficulties. With Mao's priorities being
increasingly dominated by the exigencies of the Cultural Revolution,
Chinese material support for the North Vietnamese and the Vietcong
became increasingly difficult to render. At one time, Chou En-lai commented that in a single skirmish during the Cultural Revolution "more
than 10,000 shells" had been expended. Originally, those shells had been
intended to be given "in support of Vietnam."[130] Beyond that, the
United States had introduced a sizable military capability near the

Chinese border. *People's Daily* recognized that the United States was "very powerful; it is the strongest country in the world,"[131] but to the divided Peking leadership, a central question remained, "What did the United States intend to do with its near-by military might?"

In order to answer this question, Peking and Washington continued the subtle method of signaling their intentions in Southeast Asia that they had begun earlier. Following the 131st ambassadorial meeting between the two countries in Warsaw on September 7, 1966, both nations agreed to meet again on January 11, 1967. Even though the January meeting accomplished little, it did indicate that despite Vietnam, China did not yet believe its relations with Washington had deteriorated to the point where the ambassadorial contacts had to be terminated. The Chinese request for a delay in the next meeting to June probably was a function of China's domestic problems. Clearly, Peking desired that the only direct Peking-Washington line of communication be kept open.

This sentiment was shared in Washington. In his January 10, 1967, State of the Union message, Johnson informed the nation that he continued to "hope for reconciliation between the people of mainland China and the world community." The United States had no intention of trying to deny China its "legitimate needs for security" if China would accept peaceful relations with her neighbors.[132]

Even though it was evident that Peking and Washington desired to communicate their intentions to each other, the Cultural Revolution presented a significant barrier. One major part of the Revolution was a debate over Chinese foreign policy. Much of the debate grew from different assessments of the degree of threat to China presented by the United States presence in Vietnam.[133] To one wing of the Chinese leadership, led by Liu Shao-chi, the United States presented a significant and immediate threat to Chinese security. The other wing, identified as the Maoist faction, recognized an American threat but considered it no more significant than that presented by the Soviet Union.

Continued warnings that the Chinese government would "be ready at all times to take the necessary action ... to give all-out support to the Vietnamese people's war against U.S. aggression" must be interpreted in light of the domestic disagreement.[134] Both Chinese factions realized that they could not abandon the Vietnamese cause regardless of the immediacy of the U.S. threat. The ensuing vagueness of Chinese promises of aid probably emanated from two sources: first, the disagreement within the Chinese leadership itself and second, fear of possible American retaliation on China.

Chinese aid to North Vietnam reflected these considerations. As the Cultural Revolution proceeded and as U.S. escalations continued,

Chinese aid to the D.R.V. decreased (see chart). Nonetheless, despite the decreased quantity of aid, significant amounts continued to reach North Vietnam. Additionally, North Vietnamese aircraft on occasion used fields in southern China as staging areas.[135]

ESTIMATED MILITARY AND ECONOMIC AID TO NORTH VIETNAM[136]
*(in millions of U.S. dollars)*

|        | 1967 | 1968 | 1969 | 1970 |
|--------|------|------|------|------|
| P.R.C. | 225  | 200  | 195  | 180  |
| U.S.S.R. | 705 | 530 | 370 | 430 |

The Chinese leadership's internal disagreement did not preclude them from concluding an agreement in April with the Soviet Union on the method whereby the Soviet Union could ship aid across China to the D.R.V.[137] Although fighting in Kwangsi province just north of the D.R.V. eventually limited the effectiveness of the rail route,[138] most Soviet aid to North Vietnam through 1967 and early 1968 used this route.[139]

The conclusion of the aid shipment agreement should not be interpreted to imply that Soviet-Chinese animosity had decreased. China continued to accuse the Soviet Union of trying to "sow discord" into Sino-North Vietnamese relations[140] and the Kremlin verbally assaulted a purported Sino-American deal that if the United States did not attack China, China would not render effective aid to the D.R.V.[141] China quickly and vehemently denounced this and other claims of Sino-American collusion as "a lie"[142] and instead pointed to the Kosygin-Harold Wilson initiative to end the war and the summer Glassboro Conference as proof of Soviet-American collusion against the interests of the "Vietnamese patriots."[143] While belittling Soviet aid efforts, Chinese leaders and publications still described China as the "reliable great rear area" of the Vietnamese people.[144] Soviet support for a negotiated settlement aroused Chinese resentment more than anything else. Peking ridiculed "imperialism, modern revisionism and the reactionaries" for their support of negotiations and condemned the American "forcible occupation of South Vietnam," arguing that as long as there was an American presence there, the U.S. "remained the aggressor" regardless of whether it bombed North Vietnam. China, following the D.R.V.'s line, maintained that Vietnam was "a single entity" and dismissed the American concept of reciprocity as a "gangster principal."[145]

Why did China so vehemently oppose negotiations? Two answers are most apparent. First, the Chinese ideological line on wars of national liberation argued that protracted wars against colonial powers would inevitably be successful. Second, and perhaps most importantly, a negotiated settlement in 1967 would have further isolated China both politically and militarily. Politically, China believed that the Soviet Union and the United States were "backstage managers" of a worldwide "anti-China campaign."[146] The successful conclusion of an agreement on Vietnam would have therefore been yet another bond in the "anti-Chinese alliance." Militarily, an agreement sanctioning a divided Vietnam would have further legitimized another U.S. base near China's border. This was a genuine concern to the Chinese leadership, even divided as they were. During April and May, the Chinese repeatedly claimed that U.S. aircraft violated Chinese airspace and "provoked" the Chinese government.[147] Though the Peking leadership remained divided in its assessment of the degree of the American threat to China, all undoubtedly agreed that a continued U.S. presence in Vietnam was a more significant threat to China than a neutralized Vietnam or a Vietnam under Hanoi's rule.

Through the spring of 1967, then, it appeared that China's primary concern remained its internal problems, that it would continue to aid North Vietnam but in decreasing amounts and that it desired to maintain lines of communication with Washington. Peking's leadership was divided on Washington's intentions but had more pressing domestic matters with which to deal.

In July and August, American bombers attacked targets on the Chinese-North Vietnamese border. Not surprisingly, China condemned the stepped-up bombing.[148] The Chinese response was less vehement than in previous cases, however, probably because Chinese-D.R.V. relations themselves were deteriorating. As the stepped-up bombing continued through the fall, China viewed itself as less committed to North Vietnam even though the Chinese continued to reaffirm their pledges to "provide solid backing" to the "Indochinese people's struggle for national independence."[149]

The worsening Chinese-D.R.V. relations were directly related to North Vietnam's decision to move to limited general offensive warfare in South Vietnam. Mao and other Chinese leaders argued the D.R.V's move was both premature and dangerous and in light of the expanded American bombing, could lead to large-scale U.S. retaliation, possibly directed against China itself. The size of the disagreements between Peking and Hanoi could be gauged by a series of articles written by the D.R.V.'s Minister of Defense Vo Nguyen Giap in September 1967 on the conduct of the war in the South. Giap, the architect of the D.R.V.'s strategy in the South, not once expressed gratitude for Chinese aid or support.[150] This breach of etiquette obviously pointed to a significant disagreement.

This is not to say, however, that China abandoned the D.R.V. The Vietnamese War was still depicted as "a real people's war"[151] and Chinese-Vietnamese relations received prominent coverage on the occasion of both Vietnamese National Day (September 1) and Chinese National Day (October 1).[152] Significantly, however, Chinese leaders very seldom referred to the People's Republic as Vietnam's "reliable rear area" during the second half of 1967.[153]

Even more revealing was China's insistence on reminding Hanoi that it could be successful only if it pursued a protracted war of resistance. In his message to the NLFSV celebrating its seventh anniversary, Chou En-lai warned the Front that it would win "provided ... [you] persist in people's war and persevere in the policy of protracted war."[154] Even after the Tet offensive was launched, the Chinese media stressed the inevitability of victory if the correct method of warfare were used. To China, the Vietnamese people could "vanquish [their] ferocious enemy so long as [they] follow a correct political and military line and persevere in a protracted people's war."[155]

Although Peking opposed Hanoi's move to limited general offensive warfare and tried to dissociate herself from Hanoi's offensive, Chou En-lai hailed the beginning of the Tet offensive in January 1968 as a "great victory."[156] Again, Chou's praise was predictable. Any other response would have led to a further deterioration of Sino-North Vietnamese relations. It anything, the very success of the Tet offensive increased Chinese fears of an American attack on China.

The Chinese leadership did not accept an American escalation of the war in response to Tet as a foregone conclusion, however. Mao realized that the "U.S. ruling clique" was rent "with violent quarrels" over the future course of the war[157] and pointed to McNamara's resignation as proof of the depth of the disagreement. Nonetheless, Peking viewed McNamara as the "sacrificial wolf" in Johnson's attempt to blame others for the "Vietnam failures" so that he could "improve his own chances in the Presidential elections."[158] Despite its internal dissension the U.S. government, to Peking, was pursuing and would continue to pursue its "counter-revolutionary global strategy."[159]

China's condemnation of American policy and fear of U.S. retribution directed against China could not overcome the Chinese-North Vietnamese disagreement, however, since North Vietnamese policy itself was the cause of the increased threat to China. Perhaps surprisingly, when North Vietnam accepted Lyndon Johnson's peace talks proposal of March 31, thereby temporarily reducing the fighting in Vietnam, China opposed the talks.

Peking had long reviled the United States and the Soviet Union for their "collusion" to "force peace talks through bombing"[160] so when in early April North Vietnam accepted Johnson's offer to "go anywhere" to begin negotiations, China adamantly opposed them. To China, even with its opposition to a general offensive, the issue of Vietnam could "only be settled on the battlefield." China urged North Vietnam to forsake negotiations and fight on.[161] Johnson's bombing halt was labeled "a fraud."[162] Further underlining its opposition to any negotiations, Peking did not inform its own people of the Paris negotiations until October 19 and then still described them as "a big plot and a fraud."[163]

China's attitude toward the negotiations in particular and American policy in general were succinctly summed up by Chou in his address at the North Vietnamese embassy in Peking on Vietnamese National Day. Chou also linked Soviet revisionism and American imperialism and again stressed the propriety of protracted warfare. According to Chou,

> In fact, the peace talks scheme on Vietnam is jointly devised by U.S. imperialism and Soviet revisionism. After the invasion and occupation of Czechoslovakia by Soviet revisionism, U.S. imperialism will definitely demand a higher price on the Vietnam question.... It is high time all those who cherish illusions about Soviet revisionism and U.S. imperialism woke up....
>
> We are convinced that ... the Vietnamese people will surely be able to smash all the schemes and plots of the U.S. aggressors and win final victory in their war against U.S. aggression and for national salvation so long as they persevere in protracted war and oppose capitulation and compromise.[164]

In October, reports began emanating from Paris about an imminent breakthrough on a total bombing halt. Peking remained skeptical.[165] When the bombing finally ended in November, *People's Daily* immediately published the entire text of Johnson's speech, a highly unusual occurrence. However, this did not signify a reversal of earlier Chinese positions. Rather, during the last part of 1968 and 1969, the Chinese media for the most part suspended comment on the negotiations and further reduced its coverage of Vietnam. For example, on previous Chinese National Days, Vietnam had always occupied a prominent place. In 1968, however, it was barely mentioned.[166] Clearly, Chinese opposition to negotiations continued.[167]

If China feared American reaction to the limited general offensive, why then was the Peking leadership opposed to negotiations on Vietnam? The reasons are several. First, Mao's faction was increasingly gaining the ascendancy in the domestic power struggle and the Maoist ideological line dictated that success could be attained on the battlefield. Therefore, negotiations were not needed. Second, successful negotiations would further increase the Soviet Union's prestige in Southeast Asia since the Soviet Union had long favored a negotiated settlement. Mao dreaded this possibility. Finally, and perhaps most importantly, negotiations on the Vietnam problem presupposed that a certain degree of Soviet-American cooperation in one area could lead to cooperation in other areas, the Chinese reasoned, and those other areas could include a united front against China.

   Overshadowing the continuing poor relations between China and North Vietnam and having as much if not more of an impact on the Vietnamese War was the continued deterioration of Sino-Soviet relations. During June and July, war materiel shipments from and through China to the D.R.V. were stopped.[168] Numerous factors including the Red Guards' activities and a Chinese desire to further emphasize its differences with the D.R.V. may have led to the halt but it is similarly possible that it was designed to apply pressure to the Soviets. Following the Soviet invasion of Czechoslovakia and the Kremlin's proclamation of the "Brezhnev Doctrine" of limited socialist sovereignty, Peking's assessment of the Soviet threat to China increased. This changed Chinese assessment of the Soviet threat had tremendous impact on Vietnam—the Chinese compared the Soviet Union's invasion of Czechoslovakia to the U.S. presence in Vietnam[169] and, from Peking's perspective, reaffirmed a greater Soviet than American threat to China. Gradually the Maoist leadership began to explore the possibility of accommodation with the United States. On November 26, Peking's representatives met with those of the newly-elected Nixon administration and proposed that the two sides meet on February 20, 1969, in Warsaw to discuss "agreement on the five principles of peaceful coexistence."[170]

   This did not imply that China had come to ignore the American presence in Vietnam or considered the nature of the American involvement in Vietnam to have changed. Rather, the significance of the American threat had diminished in light of the worsening Sino-Soviet dispute. Adding to the danger of the continued existence and even possible growth of the U.S. involvement in the South, in Chinese eyes, was the election of Richard Nixon. As one of the architects of U.S. containment policy in Asia, Nixon's election was not viewed with equanimity in Peking. China's prompt suggestion of renewed ambassadorial talks following Nixon's election may be viewed as an effort to "feel out" the new administration and gauge its China policy. If Nixon maintained his anti-Chinese attitude, Peking could have been placed in an extremely uncomfortable position and Mao realized it.

   Immediately following Nixon's inauguration, China did not hesitate to criticize the new American president. Commenting on Nixon's inaugural address, Peking described Nixon as the "jittery chieftain of U.S. imperialism" who had admitted that "the imperialists are beset with difficulties both at home and abroad."[171] Throughout the course of Nixon's first months in office, similar criticisms were launched. According to Lin Piao, Nixon could not but

> continue to play the counter-revolutionary dual tactics, ostensibly assuming a "peace-loving" appearance while in fact engaging in arms expenditures and war preparations.[172]

The most important changes at this time were going on behind the scenes. Even while China was criticizing the new American president, Nixon initiated contact with Peking. According to Nixon himself, the new administration made its first approaches indicating a desire for expanding U.S.-P.R.C. relations within two weeks of his inauguration. China, still fearing a possible major U.S. escalation for the ongoing Vietcong offensive, was ill disposed to accept any American initiative. The memory of past escalations lingered and the uncertainties engendered by the Nixon administration and its formerly hardline leader were strong.

These uncertainties were undoubtedly strengthened when Nixon told his first presidential press conference listeners that he would not change American policy toward China until there was a "change of attitude" in Peking.[173] However, when Nixon failed to respond to the 1969 Tet attacks of the Vietcong, the credibility of his earlier-claimed desires to wind down the war in Vietnam and improve relations with China was strengthened.[174] Again, however, the Maoist leadership was not willing to go too fast. Ostensibly because of the defection of a Chinese diplomat in the Netherlands, China saw fit to cancel the Warsaw ambassadorial talks scheduled for February 20 since, according to the Chinese, the U.S. government "engineered the defection."[175] If the United States was waiting for a "change of attitude" in Peking, then China was similarly waiting for a "change of attitude" in Washington. Chinese policies were further complicated by the growing tension along its border with the Soviet Union. Both the Kremlin and Peking had built up their armed forces along the Sino-Soviet border during 1968. On March 2, 1969, the situation exploded as Soviet and Chinese units clashed on Damansky Island in the Ussuri River.[176] Sporadic fighting continued throughout March. To Mao, a military conflict with the Soviet Union had long been a possibility. Now, it was reality.

Following the Sino-Soviet border fighting, the United States began to signal Peking that it was in fact willing to "change its attitude" on relations with the P.R.C. The Nixon administration had apparently downgraded its assessment of the Chinese "threat" to the outside world because of a number of factors including the Cultural Revolution, the Soviet invasion of Czechoslovakia and, most importantly, the Sino-

Soviet border conflict.[177] In March 1969, U.S. Secretary of State William Rogers stated that it was in the American interest to "move toward a more constructive relationship" with China.[178] Steps were soon taken to begin this move.

In July, the United States relaxed restrictions on travel to China. Import restrictions for tourists were raised to $100 and then abandoned. Foreign subsidiaries of U.S. firms were permitted to trade with China in nonstrategic goods. During the fall, regular U.S. naval patrols in the Taiwan Strait were ended.[179] In September, Nixon spoke to the United Nations' General Assembly and stressed that the U.S. was ready to talk to representatives of the People's Republic whenever its leaders were ready.[180] Clearly, the American position had changed.

Peking did not respond directly to any of these American overtures. Nonetheless, there were indications of a reawakening Chinese interest in conciliation with the United States. On December 12, 1969, American and Chinese officials met in Warsaw and arranged the resumption of the ambassadorial talks that had been suspended since January 1968. On January 20 and February 20, 1970, the 135th and 136th meeting in the series were finally held. Earlier, on December 17, China released two American yachtsmen who had been detained for ten months for violating Chinese territorial waters. Even more interestingly, China's New Year's Day editorial advocated peaceful coexistence among all nations — capitalist and socialist included — for the first time since 1966.[181]

The changing Chinese posture reflected a number of things. First, China was increasingly threatened on its north by the Soviets and consequently wanted to minimize the possibility of a two-front conflict. Second, Mao was cognizant of the changing U.S. position toward China and probably wished to indicate to Nixon that the U.S. initiatives were noticed and appreciated. Finally, the Chinese leaders perceived a reduced U.S. threat from the south. This perception in turn was the product of two factors. First, Hanoi, had again opted for protracted warfare, thereby reducing pressure on Nixon to escalate. Second, the United States had begun withdrawing troops from South Vietnam and clearly was not considering an invasion of North Vietnam or China.

Hanoi's return to protracted warfare was a gradual process. Between the beginning of the Tet offensive in January 1968 and the spring of 1969, North Vietnamese and Vietcong forces had lost 250,000 men. Although the limited general offensive had destroyed America's political credibility in Vietnam, it had also led to the destruction of the Vietcong's infrastructure in South Vietnam. Because of these losses, Vo Nguyen Giap, North Vietnam's defense minister, felt that he had no choice but to revert to protracted warfare. Ho Chi Minh's final testament eloquently pointed up Hanoi's return to lower level warfare. Ho promised to "fight against the U.S. aggression till total victory" was achieved and at the same time admitted that "the war against U.S. aggression may drag out."[182]

It was not until the second half of 1969 that Chinese-Vietnamese relations began to improve noticeably. During March and April, the Sino-Soviet border dispute delayed the transit of Soviet supplies to North Vietnam for months, a fact which Hanoi's leadership did not overlook.[183] Also, sometime during 1969, China withdrew the 50,000 railroad construction troops it had sent to the D.R.V. in 1964 and 1965. Finally when the Provisional Revolutionary Government was created in South Vietnam in June, China extended "only belated and unenthusiastic recognition," in the words of one observer.[184] Despite Hanoi's return to protracted warfare, then, Peking only slowly renewed its old close ties with the D.R.V. and the NLFSV.

Not until Vietnamese National Day, September 1, was it evident that Sino-Vietnamese relations had improved considerably. In their National Day message to Ho, Mao and the other Chinese leaders stressed that the D.R.V. would be victorious "by persevering in protracted war, persevering in maintaining independence in [its] own hands and persevering in self-reliance." This, of course, was the standard Chinese line of the preceding year. Significantly, however, the Chinese leaders pledged that their people stood "firmly on the side of the Vietnamese people" and supported them "to the end until final victory."[185]

Ho's death followed closely on the heels of Vietnamese National Day. The improving relations between Hanoi and Peking were accentuated during the transition of power. Immediately upon Ho's death, Chou En-lai flew to Hanoi, arriving on September 4. For the first time in several months, Chou described China as Vietnam's "reliable rear area." Additionally, he assured the D.R.V.'s new leaders that China would continue to support them.[186] Chou left Hanoi the morning of September 5 to avoid Soviet Premier Kosygin, who was scheduled to arrive the next day. China sent a lower delegation for Ho's actual burial.

China's National Day served as yet another forum from which improving Sino-Vietnamese relations could be viewed. The communiqués released at the conclusion of the visits of the delegations from the D.R.V. and the NLFSV both stressed Chinese calls for protracted warfare and Chinese references to itself as Vietnam's "reliable rear area." The outstanding feature of both documents, though, was the agreement among all three concerned parties that "the sole correct road to a settlement" in Vietnam was a total and complete U.S. withdrawal.[187] There could be no doubt that Peking and Hanoi were once again drawing closer.

There could similarly be no doubt that China was aware of the decreasing American troop commitment in South Vietnam. China criticized the withdrawals as "too slow" and as a means to disguise "continued American aggression" but was nonetheless aware of the reduction in manpower. To be sure, Chinese condemnation of the American presence in Vietnam continued on a regular basis but as much out of duty as conviction. Two American policies in particular, Vietnamization and the Nixon Doctrine, drew particularly heavy fire. Vietnamization was condemned as a policy of "having Asians kill Asians." Peking noted that the American phased withdrawal had been more than compensated for by the increase in manpower in ARVN and concluded that the entire Vietnamization program was a "flim-flam" designed with three objectives in mind: to drag out the war, to "preserve the puppet Thieu," and to enable U.S. military strength to "dig in in South Vietnam."[188]

The Nixon Doctrine was similarly decried. Attacking it as a "nonwithdrawal policy," the Chinese argued that the new concept in reality meant American "noninvolvement" only in that the United States would no longer "send its own aggressive troops," opting instead for surrogate forces. Under the Nixon Doctrine, according to the Chinese, "nonwithdrawal is the real thing while noninvolvement is a fake."[189] Vestiges of American control and influence would remain throughout Southeast Asia and the Pacific despite the Nixon Doctrine, the Chinese reasoned, but now under a more subtle disguise.

Nonetheless, by the beginning of 1970, Mao was well aware that the United States desired accommodation with China.[190] Mao still viewed the U.S. involvement in Vietnam as one manifestation of American imperialism but considered its threat to have become pale by comparison to the Soviet threat. In Moscow, meanwhile, the Soviet leadership believed that the U.S. involvement in Vietnam and its conceptual framework had changed in style but not substance. Old aims were being pursued through new methods, the Kremlin argued.

In retrospect, it is evident that the character of American involvement in Vietnam had undergone a series of significant changes between 1966 and 1969. Perceptive Americans, even in 1969, realized that the era of the "American world policeman" was drawing to a close and hoped that a new era, one of "negotiation rather than confrontation," had set in. Even with this hope, however, the conflict in Vietnam raged on.

# V
# Steps to Withdrawal: 1970-1972

If the preceding two periods of the Vietnamese War may be characterized as periods in which the North Vietnamese-NLFSV side and the American-South Vietnamese side both futilely sought military victory, then the 1970-1972 period must be characterized as one during which each side realized that neither could achieve that victory. As long as American military might could be brought to bear in Vietnam, South Vietnam's survival was assured. Consequently, the D.R.V. and NLFSV could not realistically expect victory. On the other hand, Washington and Saigon could not develop the indigenous South Vietnamese political-military structure sufficiently to achieve security in many of the territories nominally under Saigon's control. While Hanoi and the NLFSV could not hope to defeat the United States, they enjoyed enough support in the South so that they themselves could not be defeated. In Washington, though, one question increasingly was asked: how long could the United States continue to apply its military power?

This question had special significance for Hanoi. By 1972, Nixon's and Kissinger's skillful maneuvering had succeeded in isolating Hanoi from both the Soviet Union and China. Each Communist giant had been given a stake in improved relations with the United States, relations which the American President did not hesitate to assert would be directly linked with the Soviet and Chinese attitudes and policies toward the Vietnamese conflict. While it would be an overstatement bordering on the ludicrous to assert that the Soviet Union and China courted American favor, it cannot be denied that Nixon's détente with Moscow and "open door" with China not only improved U.S. relations with those countries but also coopted them to such an extent that American policy toward Vietnam enjoyed a degree of latitude unlike any it had previously experienced, at least in regard to Soviet or Chinese reaction.

This new latitude was limited only by domestic American opposition to the war. Although its ground involvement in Vietnam had been reduced considerably, U.S. air attacks on suspected Vietcong

123

positions in the South intensified. This in itself guaranteed continuing antiwar sentiment in the United States. When Nixon decided to use his new-found international freedom of action to invade Cambodia, mine Haiphong and finally bomb Hanoi, the antiwar movement in the United States regained much of the fervor it had had during the Johnson years.

The 1970-1972 period may thus be viewed as one during which several different tendencies conflicted. Washington no longer sought a military victory, but still hoped to apply military strength to achieve the best political settlement possible. Washington's freedom of action *vis-à-vis* the Soviet Union and China was offset by domestic opposition to increased exercise of that latitude. The race was on. Could Vietnamization succeed in creating a viable South Vietnamese political-military structure before domestic political considerations forced the Nixon administration to terminate the application of U.S. air power to Vietnam, or could North Vietnam and the National Liberation Front, despite their isolation, succeed in outlasting the U.S. military presence, and emerge again after an American withdrawal?

## The View from Washington: Vietnamization Triumphant — with Help

As the Nixon administration ended its first full year in office, Nixon and Kissinger's objectives in Southeast Asia in general and Vietnam in particular were becoming increasingly clear. First in both their minds was avoiding a direct Soviet-American or Chinese-American clash over Southeast Asia or Vietnam. However, American defense alliances had to be honored, as did American promises to help allied governments through military assistance programs. The military assistance programs themselves were to be carried out in conjunction with economic assistance programs. Where needed, the United States would use its air and naval might to achieve the desired objectives. The use of American troops for major ground combat operations would be shunned.[1]

In conjunction with the Nixon-Kissinger program for Southeast Asia, U.S. troop strength dropped considerably. Lower weekly casualty counts reflected both the reduced number of U.S. troops in Vietnam and the takeover of more ground operations by ARVN (see chart). At the same time, by 1970, the number of men at arms in the South Vietnamese military had grown to 1.1 million. Correspondingly the territory controlled by the South Vietnamese government grew. To the Nixon administration, then, the two-pronged policy of Vietnamization was succeeding. The modernization and improvement of the South Vietnamese armed forces was going forward as planned, and the simultaneous withdrawal of American troops was proceeding without delay. During 1971, the U.S. offensive ground combat role "virtually ended."[2]

INDICATORS OF DECREASED U.S. COMBAT ROLE[3]

|        | Soldiers in Vietnam (December of Year) | Average Battle Deaths per Week |
|--------|------------------|------------------|
| 1968   | 549,000          | 278              |
| 1969   | *(not available)* | 181             |
| 1970   | 344,000          | 81               |
| 1971   | 159,000          | 26               |
| 1972   | 24,000           | 6                |

This is not to argue, however, that Washington was satisfied with the progress of Vietnamization. Washington had not abandoned the option of escalating the fighting in Vietnam again if, in the eyes of the President, it was necessary to do so. In January 1970, Nixon showed his uncertainty about the success of Vietnamization and at the same time showed his willingness to exact retribution from the North Vietnamese if the necessity arose. According to Nixon, if the D.R.V.

> took advantage of our troop withdrawal to jeopardize the remainder of our forces by escalating the fighting, then we have the means—and I will be prepared to use those means strongly—to deal with that situation more strongly than we have dealt with it in the past.[4]

Why did Nixon feel he was able to deal with possible escalations "more strongly" than in the past? One reason was the increased hostility between China and the Soviet Union. With both nations increasingly concerned with the threat presented by the other, the stage was set for a transformation in international relations. Kissinger realized this, explicitly pointing it out in August 1970:

> The deepest international conflict in the world today is not between us and the Soviet Union, but between the Soviet Union and Communist China.... Therefore, one of the positive prospects in the current situation is that whatever the basic intentions of Soviet leaders, confronted with the prospect of a China growing in strength and not lessening in hostility, they may want a period of detente in the West, not because they necessarily have changed ideologically, but because they do not want to be in a position in which they have to confront major crises on both sides of their huge country over an indefinite period of time.[5]

Nixon and Kissinger believed that the time was ripe for improved relations with the Soviet Union. If in fact Kissinger was correct and the Soviet leaders desired improved relations with the United States, then the United States could demand a price for the improvement of relations. Nixon clearly felt part of the price tag was more freedom of action in Vietnam.

China found itself in much the same predicament as the Soviet Union. A potential two-front crisis would tremendously endanger Chinese security. Just as in the Soviet case, Nixon held out the carrot of improved relations with the United States. During 1970, Washington informed Peking that it was "determined to withdraw from Vietnam as speedily as possible, to seek a negotiated international guarantee of the independence of Southeast Asia, to end the impasse in Sino-American relations by clearing up the Taiwan question and to bring the People's Republic into the United Nations and into diplomatic relations with the United States."[6] Even though it was not explicitly stated, Nixon linked successful resolution of the Vietnamese problem with improved Sino-American relations. If Vietnam could be "solved," then Sino-American relations could be improved.

Nixon's preferred "solution" to the problem of Vietnam was a political settlement on terms favorable to the Thieu-Ky regime. Nixon continued to deny the validity of the principle of "complete and total withdrawal" of U.S. troops that the North Vietnamese put forth throughout 1970 and at the same time rejected Hanoi's demand that the Thieu-Ky regime be removed from power. Kissinger and Le Duc Tho, special advisor to the D.R.V. delegation to Paris, met four times during February and March, 1970, and each time the meeting foundered on the issues of unconditional American withdrawal and the legitimacy of the Thieu-Ky government.[7] Increasingly, the U.S. position that the Thieu-Ky government was the only legitimate government in South Vietnam and the North Vietnamese rejection of that position became the central issue preventing any progress toward a compromise agreement on Vietnam. Since the U.S. firmly supported Thieu, only an agreement favorable to him was acceptable to the Nixon administration.

Nixon's April 20 speech on troop withdrawals illustrated this. Nixon posited that a "fair political solution should reflect the existing relationship of political forces within South Vietnam." Additionally, the U.S. President declared that he was willing to accept a political solution that "fairly apportioned political power" in South Vietnam.[8] Nixon thereby implied that as far as he was concerned, the NLFSV and the Provisional Revolutionary Government (PRG) could maintain control of the areas of South Vietnam which they held at the time.[9] Not coincidentally, the territory controlled by the NLFSV and PRG had been considerably reduced during the preceding year as North Vietnamese forces in the South were reduced. The territory controlled by the PRG did not include any of the larger cities. Nixon's April 20 proposal consequently would have kept the Thieu government in effective political control of South Vietnam and would have asked the PRG to accept both the legitimacy and superiority of the Thieu government. American military power would have thus given the South Vietnamese government a new lease on life and in a perverse sort of way confirmed the old Maoist dictum that "political power grows out of the barrel of a gun." Not surprisingly, the PRG rejected Nixon's proposal, just as the United States and South Vietnam had previously rejected their opponents' proposals for accommodation when Saigon controlled limited territory in South Vietnam.

Thus Vietnamization continued. Although Nixon changed the emphasis of the rationale for the continuing United States involvement from one of preventing the expansion of North Vietnamese communism to one of attaining an "honorable conclusion" to the original U.S. commitment, it was nonetheless evident that the United States still placed great importance on a successful resolution of the conflict. Secretary of Defense Melvin Laird pointed this out in December 1969. Speaking behind closed doors in Congress, Laird asserted that "if Vietnamization fails in South Vietnam, then the Nixon Doctrine for all Asia goes down the drain."[10] Secretary of State William Rogers made a similar point before Congress in April 1970. According to Rogers, the United States' Vietnamization program had to be successful in Vietnam itself without permitting an expansion of the war. To Rogers, "if U.S. troops go into Cambodia, our whole [Vietnamization] program is defeated."[11]

Even with the Nixon administration's claims that Vietnamization was progressing satisfactorily, it was clearly evident that the Vietnam conflict was far from over. If anything, there were some indications that it was expanding throughout Indochina. On March 6, Nixon informed the American public that over 13,000 North Vietnamese troops had entered Laos during late 1969 and early 1970 and that he had asked Soviet Premier Kosygin for assistance in improving that deteriorating situation.[12] The Cambodian Assembly overthrew Prince Sihanouk in March and the following month leaders of North Vietnam, the Provisional Revolutionary Government of South Vietnam, Prince Souphanouvong of Laos and Sihanouk met and declared that the Indochinese War was "one war" which could not be restricted to a single geographical area within Indochina or divided into several smaller wars. In early May, the accuracy of the conference's observation was confirmed as the United States attacked Vietcong positions and supply lines within Cambodia.

To the decision makers in Washington, the Cambodian invasion served a dual purpose. Nixon's original rationalization for the action was to "protect our men who are in Vietnam and to guarantee the continued success of our withdrawal and Vietnamization program."[13] Nixon reasoned that if Vietcong bases and supplies in Cambodia could be destroyed, then both withdrawal and Vietnamization could continue unimpeded. The invasion may thus be considered an attempt to buy time for the further strengthening of the South Vietnamese armed forces. Washington had come to the conclusion that the South Vietnamese military could not yet function at a level sufficient to offset the withdrawal of U.S. ground forces and needed more time to develop that capability. This interpretation was further supported by Nixon's later observation that the United States had to take action in Cambodia if it were to "escape the probability of total and humiliating defeat."[14]

Even to the most ardent advocates of Nixon's policy, it was evident that Nixon's admission implied that Vietnamization was proceeding less satisfactorily than desired. While the government of South Vietnam was reducing the territory controled by the NLFSV, particulary in the Mekong Delta area, results of the pacification program were less satisfactory. Part of the dissatisfaction may be attributed to the Thieu government's unwillingness to adopt and then carry through many much-needed domestic reforms such as extensive land redistribution and the removal of corrupt government officials. Another part of the dissatisfaction was due to the inability of either South Vietnamese or American forces to remove the threat to the Saigon government posed by the Vietcong. They were "down but not out," according to one U.S. official, and Hanoi was busily sending men and supplies southward to sanctuary bases in Cambodia.

Nixon's second rationale for the Cambodian invasion was therefore "to put the enemy on warning that if it escalates [by building up its force levels and supplies] while we are trying to deescalate, we will move decisively and not step-by-step."[15] In essence, Nixon's second rationale for moving into Cambodia was to increase the credibility of American air attacks on and ground invasion of North Vietnam.

There were some in Washington who in fact advocated an invasion of North Vietnam rather than Cambodia. The Joint Chiefs of Staff, according to Admiral Thomas Moorer, argued for a ground assault against the D.R.V., but Nixon overruled them.[16] Despite the tremendous public outcry against the invasion, Nixon probably viewed the Cambodian invasion as a victory for constraint. Something had to be done to protect Vietnamization and to signal continued American resolve and Nixon believed he had taken the minimum step possible to do both.

By the summer of 1970, then, both the United States and North Vietnam were in essence "buying time." The United States, still trying to preserve an independent South Vietnam under Thieu, needed more time to strengthen the political and military structure of the South Vietnamese state. The strengthening was needed to compensate for the ongoing American military withdrawal. The D.R.V., still intent on reunifying Vietnam, needed more time to strengthen its own armed for-

*Washington, November 1970: South Vietnamese Vice President Nguyen Cao Ky in the midst of a two-week visit with President Richard Nixon. Courtesy The White House.*

ces and those of the Vietcong. The D.R.V.'s earlier decision to return to protracted warfare was consequently in the short term interests of both nations. To the North Vietnamese, the change was a conscious policy leading to future victory. To the United States, the change was a result of U.S. military power, Vietnamization and pacification. Even though the Nixon administration was dissatisfied with the pace of Vietnamization, it still viewed the policy as a success since the Saigon government increasingly expanded the territory under its control.

That both sides viewed the conflict in Vietnam as an exercise in buying time was confirmed by the peace proposals which each side brought forward during the fall of 1970. On September 17, the Provisional Revolutionary Government made a proposal which for the first time defined the coalition government it had previously advocated. The coalition was to have three segments: one representing the PRG, one representing those who stood for "peace, independence and neutrality" in the Saigon regime, and a third for those with "various political and religious ... tendencies standing for peace, independence, neutrality and democracy." The Saigon segment specifically could include neither Thieu nor Ky. Additionally, the proposal supported a prisoner-of-war exchange and guaranteed safe passage out of Vietnam for American troops if they agreed to leave Vietnam by June 30, 1971.[17]

The United States had long rejected any proposal which required the exclusion of Thieu or Ky from the government. The PRG knew this and consequently expected the United States to reject its proposal. Similarly, Nixon's "Peace Initiative for All Indochina," first enunciated on October 7, was preordained to fail since it contained a specific reference to a position long-known to be anathema to the PRG. Nixon proposed an immediate in-place ceasefire in Vietnam to be followed by negotiations leading to a timetable for the withdrawal of all non-South Vietnamese forces. Nixon also supported an all-Indochina ceasefire, a political solution in South Vietnam reflecting the will of "all the people," and unconditional release of all prisoners.[18]

The PRG had earlier rejected the principal of conditional withdrawal of U.S. forces, so the PRG's rejection of Nixon's proposal surprised no one. The two major disagreements which had stalemated negotiations since 1968 — the North Vietnamese demand for unilateral unconditional withdrawal of American troops and the American demand for Thieu and Ky to participate in any new government — continued to frustrate hopes for a negotiated settlement. Although numerous secret proposals and negotiations were carried out throughout 1970,[19] these two issues remained unresolved.

Neither side undertook any new initiatives to eliminate the impasse until May 31, 1971, when Kissinger presented the D.R.V. with a significantly different American proposal. In the May proposal, Kissinger offered a ceasefire throughout Indochina on the basis of territorial control. The ceasefire was to be tied to a deadline for a complete withdrawal of American troops in exchange for U.S. prisoners. For the first time, there was no call for the reciprocal withdrawal of North Vietnamese troops from the South. However, it did imply that Thieu would still participate in the government.[20]

North Vietnam rejected the proposal and countered with one of its own. On June 26, Le Duc Tho met with Kissinger and offered to release American prisoners simultaneously with American troop withdrawal. For all practical purposes, then, the two sides had resolved the issue of reciprocity. The issue of Thieu and Ky's participation in a future coalition government, however, remained unsettled. Le Duc Tho continued to demand that the United States end its support for Thieu and Ky so a new government could be formed. Additionally, Hanoi maintained that an Indochinese ceasefire had to be arranged by the parties in each country, not by the United States and North Vietnam.[21]

Thieu now became the single central issue blocking the consummation of an agreement. American support for Thieu and North Vietnamese opposition to him prevented any additional progress on the negotiations for over a year. Hanoi's suggestion that the United States withdraw its political support from Thieu in the scheduled October 1971 South Vietnamese Presidential election brought Kissinger's response that the United States had been and would remain neutral in the campaign and election.[22] To Hanoi, an American repudiation of the Thieu candidacy presented a way out of the impasse in negotiations. To the United States, repudiating Thieu undermined the creation of a democratic state.

The creation of a democratic state in South Vietnam was at least in part impeded by the electoral process in South Vietnam itself. Following Kissinger's rejection of the North Vietnamese proposal, the "peace candidate," former South Vietnamese Chief of State Duong Van Minh, withdrew from the campaign. Thieu now ran unopposed and won the election with 82 percent of the vote. To the United States, the election was a disaster. While the result was undoubtedly the desired one in Washington, the process was less than satisfactory. The one-candidate election did not add any legitimacy to Thieu's claim to the presidency, and the United States realized this. Secretary of State Rogers' year-end report on U.S. foreign policy illustrated the American dissatisfaction in a classic instance of understatement—"in terms of political development, the Presidential election was disappointing."[23]

After the election, and possibly because of the questionable appearance of the election, the United States put forward another proposal in Paris for a reorganized South Vietnamese government, the so-called "eight point position." The new U.S. proposal had two key provisions: Thieu would resign one month before the election was held, and an "independent body representing all political forces in South Vietnam" would organize and conduct the elections.[24] The first provision was totally new and the second marked a significant departure from the concept put forth in 1969 by the United States in which an international commission would merely oversee elections.

Even so, the D.R.V.-PRG side rejected the proposal and, again, the reason was the "lackey of American imperialism Thieu." Under the

U.S. proposal, Thieu could both participate in the organization of the election and even run in the election. To Hanoi, this was unacceptable.

While negotiations on the political front remained deadlocked throughout 1971, on the military front, at least in Washington's eyes, the situation improved considerably. In February 1971, South Vietnamese forces invaded Laos to cut the Ho Chi Minh Trail, with the United States providing "considerable air and back-up support."[25] The entire operation, though limited in time and area, produced mixed results. Although the trail was never put out of operation and some ARVN units proved inept under combat conditions, others performed admirably. The success of Vietnamization was viewed, at the time, as uncertain. Gradually, though, both Saigon and Washington took a more optimistic outlook, as the Saigon government adopted a "Community Defense and Local Development Plan" which symbolized "the virtual completion of military pacification and the concentration on local self-defense, self-government, and self-development."[26] Throughout 1971, the number of people and area of territory under Saigon's control increased dramatically. According to U.S. Secretary of State Rogers, Vietnamization had proceeded so well that ARVN would assume all ground combat missions during 1972.[27]

In Washington, then, it was believed that military success was just around the corner even though the political front remained deadlocked. There was, however, an alternative explanation to the new military successes of 1971, but Nixon and his advisors apparently overlooked it: the North Vietnamese had temporarily withdrawn their forces from the South. One knowledgeable observer reported only a single Northern division in South Vietnam at the close of 1971.[28]

In North Vietnam, Laos, and Cambodia, however, a massive North Vietnamese military buildup was taking place. From the late spring of 1971 onward, Soviet military supplies began arriving in North Vietnam in quantities greater than ever before. By early 1972, the entire area around Hanoi and Haiphong was described as "a full-fledged arsenal" with great quantities of tanks, missiles, artillery, and supplies.[29] Moscow may have hoped the munitions would be used as part of an offensive designed to embarrass Nixon's forthcoming trip to Peking; Washington was positive that this was the intent.

During the fall and winter, United States intelligence began reporting the concentration of arms. Nixon authorized limited bombing of arms concentrations within North Vietnam. By February 1972, official Washington believed that the raids had disrupted the build-up sufficiently so that no attack could be made.[30]

Nixon's visit to China occurred without incident. Within

two months, however, North Vietnam had again built up its stocks of war equipment, supplies, and munitions.

In late March, North Vietnamese and Vietcong units attacked across the demilitarized zone and routed ARVN's Third Division.[31] The People's Liberation Armed Forces (PLAF) also then launched assaults on An Loc and the central highlands, where ARVN forces reportedly "got scared and ran."[32] On May 1, Quang Tri fell. Rioting broke out in Hue as the PLAF rolled into the outskirts of the city and stopped. In Washington, U.S. leaders for the first time "faced the grim prospect that Saigon could actually lose the war." U.S. intelligence agencies informed certain Senators that "the demoralization of the South Vietnamese soldiers could proceed to the point where they would no longer fight."[33] In short, Vietnamization had not succeeded, and its total failure was a distinct possibility.

To stop the PLAF offensive, Saigon committed its strategic reserves. This strategy succeeded in slowing the offensive, but at the same time it left previously pacified areas open to guerrilla actions by the PLAF. In Quang Ngai province alone, it was estimated that Saigon lost control of 365,000 people.[34] Before the offensive began, Saigon officially conceded only seven hamlets to the Provisional Revolutionary Government. By October, 1400 hamlets were conceded. Although the PRG zone had not reached its pre-1969 dimensions, Saigon's territorial losses were considerable. Militarily, ARVN and the local militia units lost 140,000 men, while PLAF losses were estimated at only 70,000.[35]

It was obvious that the North Vietnamese offensive was much more than a "most desperate effort" to avoid defeat.[36] Since Nixon and Westmoreland were aware that Hanoi had committed 12 of its 13 operational divisions to the assault on the South, both men considered it a "go-for-broke offensive."[37] On April 6, U.S. B-52s stepped up bombing attacks on the North. As raids were launched deeper into North Vietnam, Chairman of the Joint Chiefs of Staff Thomas Moorer warned that the bombing would continue until the offensive in the South ended.[38] On April 15, B-52s hit Haiphong. At the height of the raids against the North, 100 B-52s, several hundred fighter bombers, and planes from six aircraft carriers flew against the D.R.V.

Even this massive air armada did not stop the offensive. As Quang Tri fell and Hue was threatened, Nixon realized that stronger steps were necessary. On May 8, Nixon appeared on national television and informed the world that there was "only one way to stop the killing ... to keep the weapons of war out of the hands of the international outlaws of North Vietnam." In order to do this, Nixon disclosed that he had ordered the mining of all North Vietnamese ports and the interdiction of rail and communications networks "to the maximum extent possible." Air and naval strikes against other military targets were to continue.[39] Nixon had now undertaken actions against the North long-proposed but never implemented; mining Northern harbors had been advocated as early as 1964 and B-52 raids on Hanoi and Haiphong had been suggested shortly thereafter. The American air war against the North had reached a level not earlier seen.

Why were these extreme steps taken? The most obvious and immediate answer was the success of the North Vietnamese offensive. As previously seen, by early May, Washington realized that Saigon could actually lose the war. With less than 100,000 American troops in Vietnam, the burden of South Vietnamese defense fell on marginally effective ARVN units. Extreme measures were needed to stop the offensive, and the only effective ones available were bombing raids and mining operations against the North. In short, Nixon believed he was forced to opt for a policy rejected by Johnson — closing the top of the funnel sending supplies, men, and munitions to the South.

Skillful diplomatic maneuvering by Nixon and Kissinger had further increased the effectiveness of the air raids and mining. Chinese and Soviet reaction to the raids was exceedingly mild (see below) and may be explained by Nixon's détente diplomacy. In previous instances of escalation, both communist nations had threatened to retaliate with their own unspecified escalations. Following the raids and mining in 1972, Chinese and Soviet statements condemned the American actions but made no threats.

This is not to say that either Peking or Moscow had abandoned Hanoi. Peking and Moscow simply had more important considerations. At the end of Nixon's February trip to Peking, the Sino-American Shanghai Communiqué affirmed both sides' previous positions on Vietnam. The People's Republic continued to support the PRG's Seven Point Proposal and the United States defended its own Eight Point Proposal.[40] Nonetheless, Washington believed a "correction of misperceptions on both sides" had been achieved on many issues, quite probably including Vietnam, and the "potential for misunderstanding [had] been lessened."[41]

If the Maoist government had been given a stake in improved Sino-American relations, a similar process was underway in Moscow. Even while the first American B-52s were striking the Haiphong area, preparations for Nixon's upcoming visit to Moscow were being worked out. None of the subsequent escalations, including mining, slowed these preparations.

Washington expected to encounter some difficulties with Moscow but, again, the lack of Russian reaction supported Nixon's observation that Brezhnev had too great a political stake in improving Soviet-American relations to jeopardize it over even such a celebrated issue as Vietnam. Nonetheless, Nixon kept Brezhnev informed of the general intent of U.S. policy, probably realizing and intending that the outline would be transmitted to Hanoi. Thus, on April 20, Kissinger traveled to Moscow for four days of discussion with Brezhnev on a variety of topics, but most importantly, Vietnam. Kissinger pressured Brezhnev on Soviet arms shipments to the D.R.V. and warned the Soviet leader that the United States would take "whatever steps are necessary" to halt the offensive. The Secretary of State clearly implied the United States would step up its bombing.[42]

Brezhnev responded that there was no choice but to continue negotiations and added he was convinced the D.R.V. was ready for "serious" talks. Nonetheless, K. F. Katushev, an aide to Brezhnev, immediately flew to Hanoi to tell the D.R.V. leadership about Kissinger's threat.

The accuracy of Nixon's assessment of Brezhnev's position was further underlined by the lack of Soviet reaction to damage done to Soviet vessels in Haiphong. The April 15 B-52 raids sank a Soviet ship, but the Kremlin did not even lodge a protest.[43] Four other Soviet vessels were subsequently damaged. When Moscow protested that the raids had damaged these ships, Washington responded that "countries which supply offensive equipment to the North Vietnamese and enable them to mount an invasion of South Vietnam share responsibility."[44] The issue was dropped.

Despite the increased tempo of the war in Vietnam, Nixon was cordially received in Moscow for his first summit meeting with Brezhnev. Nixon and Brezhnev discussed Vietnam in detail twice during the eight-day summit meeting (May 22-30), once for three hours at Brezhnev's dacha and again after Kissinger and Soviet Foreign Minister Gromyko had discussed it.[45] The U.S. President insisted that the Soviet leader persuade the North Vietnamese to accept the U.S. peace plan, but Brezhnev responded that the only possible path to peace was to end all American acts of war and to establish a coalition government without Thieu.[46] In the Moscow Communiqué issued at the close of the summit, the mining of the North was not even mentioned.

Hanoi was isolated. Nixon had played his hand masterfully, influencing both Peking and Moscow to consider their improved relations with Washington more important than reacting to the stepped-up American war effort against the D.R.V. With China and the Soviet Union coopted, and with the domestic U.S. reaction to the mining surprisingly restrained, Nixon for all practical purposes enjoyed a free hand. Hanoi realized this. Sometime during the spring offensive,

probably as the D.R.V. assessed its diplomatic isolation and the impact of the bombing, the North Vietnamese decided that one of three basic agreements should be sought during 1972 depending on the outcome of the offensive: the war could continue by tacit agreement following the withdrawal of U.S. forces; Thieu's government could be replaced by a transitional coalition government; or Thieu could stay in power but must recognize the Provisional Revolutionary Government as an equal.[47]

During the summer of 1972, Hanoi continued to prefer a three-part coalition government. The D.R.V. still maintained that the "segment belonging to Saigon" could include anyone except Thieu,[48] but even this marked a radical departure from the D.R.V.'s earlier position that all segments of the coalition must renounce an anticommunist position. The United States, however, chose to ignore this change. Kissinger and the other American negotiators refused to accept the concept of a coalition government throughout the summer and fall. For all practical purposes, it appeared as if Kissinger was seeking a military settlement divorced from a political settlement. To Kissinger, a political solution was desirable but only after a military solution — including an immediate ceasefire, the withdrawal of American troops, and an exchange of prisoners — had been negotiated.

Why did the United States ignore the changed North Vietnamese position? Two reasons are most apparent. In the first place, Nixon's détente diplomacy had already demonstratively given the United States a new military freedom of action in Vietnam. If neither the Chinese nor the Russians responded to the mining of Haiphong or the resumption of large-scale air attacks on the North, then, to Washington, it was plausible they would not respond to other stepped-up pressures. Nixon was thus presented with the opportunity to push the North Vietnamese to accept his political terms of settlement. With the Red River nearing flood stage, the North Vietnamese flood control system provided an ideal potential pressure point.

U.S. officials continually denied that the dike system on the Red River was targeted, but did admit that "stray weaponry" occasionally struck the dikes.[49] Regardless of whether the bombing of the dikes was intentional or not, when viewed in light of Nixon's repeated threats to do "whatever necessary" to bring North Vietnam to a settlement, the damage to the dike system provided Nixon with a very real tool with which to pressure Hanoi. This tool was rendered even more useful in

*Opposite: Moscow, May 1972: President Nixon, an interpreter, Soviet President Nikolai Podgorny, and Party Chief Leonid Brezhnev toast the signing of science and space cooperation agreements. Courtesy The White House.*

early July when U.S. Department of State officials predicted a "strong likelihood" of flooding in North Vietnam because of poor dike construction.[50] From the Vietnamese viewpoint, this statement was ominous. Washington had moved to protect itself from blame in the events of flooding in the North, regardless of the cause of flooding. Flooding resulting from bomb damage to the dikes could be dismissed as resulting from faulty dike construction.[51] Nixon thus had another avenue through which to apply military pressure to achieve diplomatic results.

A second major reason why the changed North Vietnamese position was ignored by Washington was Nixon's increasing political popularity in the United States. Nixon's summit successes coupled with his Haiphong mining coup had raised the popularity of his Vietnamese policy considerably.[52] By mid-summer, most political observers agreed that Nixon would win a second term. During the summer of 1972, then, Nixon enjoyed considerable latitude of action and could search for his own preferred solutions to the Vietnam question.

Hanoi was well aware of Nixon's new freedom of action and did not look forward to the events implied by it.[53] At the same time, the D.R.V.'s leadership was disappointed by the results of its 1972 spring offensive.[54] Consequently the D.R.V., acting under the influence of these various pressures, advanced yet another proposal designed to achieve an acceptable settlement. Hanoi decided to drop its demand that Thieu be excluded from the South Vietnamese government, but only if his government proved willing to abandon its claim to sole sovereignty in South Vietnam.

According to U.S. sources, North Vietnam proposed several formulas designed to create an influential National Council of Reconciliation and Concord during July and August. The United States, meanwhile, made several proposals for a tripartite election commission with limited powers. Gradually, during July, August, and September, a mutually acceptable formula on a National Council became a possibility.[55] By September 26, the D.R.V. had dropped its demand for Thieu's removal. On October 8, Le Duc Tho gave Kissinger a document proposing a National Council whose sole duty was to administer elections in South Vietnam and promote the implementation of any agreement.[56] For the most part, with the exception of several minor matters, Kissinger found this document acceptable.[57] By October 12, the two sides disagreed over only replacement of war matériel and the release of civilian prisoners.[58] Kissinger returned to Washington to present the tentative agreement to Nixon.

In Washington, the general assessment of the draft agreement was that it was "basically acceptable" although there were some areas that needed to be "tightened"[59] There were isolated instances of outright opposition to the draft, most notably from Alexander Haig, who felt that large sections of the draft needed to be renegotiated since, to him, they were more the result of Kissinger's desire to achieve a pre-election peace than self-interested bargaining.[60] Additionally, doubts were raised about the wisdom of signing the draft before the election.[61] Nixon himself felt that too much had been negotiated away, particularly since he believed the North Vietnamese leadership desperately desired an immediate settlement.

These objections in Washington were not the only instances of opposition to the agreement. On October 19, Kissinger traveled to Saigon to present the draft to Thieu. Thieu termed the draft "a sell-out" and a "surrender" to the communists.[62] Specifically, Thieu objected that the draft agreement implied the acceptance of North Vietnamese troops in South Vietnam; that it did not mention the demilitarized zone as an international boundary; and that it implied that the National Council would become South Vietnam's government.[63] To Thieu, the agreement was totally unacceptable.

The United States, of course, had the means to pressure Thieu into accepting the draft since fully 85 percent of his military supplies and economic aid came from the United States. The central question in Washington was whether or not the Nixon administration was sufficiently committed to acceptance of the agreement. If the U.S. used its leverage on Thieu, Thieu could have maintained that the U.S. was blackmailing him. On the other hand, if leverage were not applied, then the agreement, viewed in Hanoi as having already been accepted, would die, and negotiations would again be deadlocked. If these had been the only factors to be considered, the outcome of the debate in Washington would have been uncertain.

In Washington, however, there was one additional major consideration. The Nixon administration had planned to give large quantities of aid to Saigon during 1973 to further the Vietnamization program. An early conclusion of a ceasefire agreement would prevent the shipment of this aid. To Nixon, the decision was clear. If Vietnamization were to succeed, additional arms had to be sent — and Vietnamization had to succeed.

In essence, then, Thieu was given veto power over the October draft agreement. Nixon opted for what one administration official called "the lesser hazard" of North Vietnamese charges of negotiations in bad faith, thereby avoiding the charge that he had rushed into an "unworkable ceasefire" for political purposes.[64] Nonetheless, it is clear that with the election well in hand, the shipment of major amounts of war matériel to South Vietnam before the signing of a ceasefire agreement played the major role in Nixon's decision.

Nixon felt that the agreement had to be delayed. At the same time, though, too obvious a delay would guarantee North Vietnam's rejection of the agreement. Thieu's opposition was thus a welcome diversion to Nixon. If the agreement was not signed, it would be Thieu's fault. Nixon was well-protected.

Still, Nixon felt it necessary to buy time and reassure the D.R.V. that the United States would not renege on the October text. On October 20, Nixon reportedly sent a secret message to Prime Minister Pham Van Dong of the Democratic Republic of Vietnam and assured him that "the text of the agreement can now be considered complete."[65] Two days later, the President again assured Hanoi that the agreement would be signed on October 31. On October 23, Kissinger informed Hanoi that the United States was having some difficulty gaining Thieu's approval for the agreement, but the American Secretary of State did not request a delay in the signing.[66]

Almost immediately, Hanoi realized what was happening. On October 26, the D.R.V. released a public statement charging that Nixon, not Thieu, was delaying the signing of the agreement. Nixon, facing an election in two weeks, now had to face a charge that he was using the draft agreement for political purposes.

Kissinger was placed in the delicate position of trying to maneuver out of the charges of delaying the agreement and negotiating in bad faith. On October 26, he held a press conference and proclaimed that peace was "at hand" and could be achieved within a few days since only a few additional points needed to be negotiated. In the United States, North Vietnam's charges were quickly forgotten and Nixon's reelection proved to be the previously anticipated landslide. Pressure for a ceasefire agreement had once again decreased.

Following the American election, then, the last significant constraint had been removed from Nixon's actions. On November 20, Kissinger submitted a list of demands to the North Vietnamese for alternatives to the October text. These revisions were substantial and included the reestablishment of the demilitarized zone, the limitation of civilian traffic across the DMZ, the withdrawal of some North Vietnamese troops,[67] a reduction in the power of the proposed National Council, a change from an election for a new Constitutent Assembly in South Vietnam to an election for a new President only and not necessarily within six months, an expansion of the ceasefire to Cambodia and Laos, the elimination of all references to the PRG, and the insertion of specific references to the "sovereignty of South Vietnam."[68]

Le Duc Tho, on behalf of his government, quickly accepted the revision of the demilitarized zone, so long as it was recognized as only provisional. He also acquiesced to the demand for references to the "sovereignty of South Vietnam" and dropped the six-month election deadline. On the other issues, however, North Vietnam would not bend.

Throughout the remainder of November and early December, the two sides haggled over the terms of the agreement. By December 14, three major issues remained — the movement of civilians across the demilitarized zone, the status of the Provisional Revolutionary Government and the areas under its control, and the nature of the National Council. Negotiations were deadlocked over all these issues, each of which was regarded as major by both sides. Kissinger returned to Washington for consultation.

By mid-December, then, the imminent peace that had been proclaimed at the end of October had not yet materialized. The "minor disagreements" Kissinger had noted in his "Peace Is at Hand" speech had grown considerably, and the American side itself has resurrected questions that had been apparently solved in October. While "almost all question of substance had been solved," as Washington later maintained, the outstanding issues themselves remained substantial. There appeared to be little to support Washington's claims that Hanoi was blocking the settlement "for tactical reasons unrelated to the substance of the negotiations."[69] Washington had agreed to a basic settlement in October, except for minor provisions. During November and December, it was Washington that demanded significant alterations in the settlement. The war went on and American supplies flowed into Saigon. By the end of 1972, South Vietnam's Air Force alone was the fourth largest in the world, with over 2000 planes.

What had led Nixon to adopt a more intransigent position and reopen issues that had apparently been settled? One of the more obvious reasons was Nixon's election landslide. Shortly after his resounding victory, reports began filtering from Washington that the American President believed that his landslide had tremendously strengthened his hand in negotiations.[70] This belief, when viewed in conjunction with Nixon's earlier attitudes that the October settlement had negotiated away too much and that the North Vietnamese were desperate for an agreement, led directly to only one conclusion. Better cease-fire terms could be reached if renewed pressure was threatened and perhaps used.

On December 13, 1972, Kissinger warned the North Vietnamese that unless they accepted Washington's peace terms, they would suffer greater destruction than ever before.[71] Such a threat was not new to Hanoi. Earlier, Nixon had threatened heavy bombing of the North to deter Hanoi's effort to upset Vietnamization and to warn Hanoi to call off its 1972 spring offensive. The December threat, however, went one step further. After Kissinger returned to Washington and briefed Nixon that his choices were either to back down or have the North Vietnamese

refuse to continue negotiations, Nixon himself sent an ultimatum to the
D.R.V.[72] The North Vietnamese had 72 hours to accept American terms,
or Hanoi and Haiphong would face indiscriminate bombing.[73]

The North Vietnamese refused to be pressured. Consequently, at
7 p.m. on December 18, American bombers attacked Hanoi and
Haiphong. Over 200 B-52s, as well as some F-111s and F4s, participated
in the wave of attacks, dubbed LINEBACKER II. The raids went on for 12
days. During that time, the United States lost 34 B-52s, a statistic that
shocked U.S. strategists.[74] Five thousand North Vietnamese were killed.
Political, social, economic, and military targets were all attacked.[75] In
the United States, a total news blackout was clamped on both the
specific targets bombed and the results of the bombing.[76] Later reports
from Hanoi indicated that the North Vietnamese government believed
the U.S. was levying an "air blockade," cutting off all land, air, sea, and
radio communication to and from Hanoi.[77]

When the bombing first began, Nixon declared that it would
continue until a settlement was reached.[78] This position soon changed,
however, quite possibly because of the high toll of B-52s the North Vietnamese air defense system was exacting. Within a week, Nixon altered
his position and declared that the bombing would end when Hanoi indicated it would negotiate "in a spirit of good will and in a constructive
attitude.[79] On December 30, the bombing ended.

It is still unclear exactly what specific indication (if any) Hanoi
sent to Washington to guarantee "good will" and a "constructive attitude" in negotiations. There is considerable room for speculation that
the termination of bombing was more the product of political pressure
on Nixon than a changed attitude in Hanoi. Foreign governments almost
universally decried the bombing and domestic American opposition was
considerable from the public, Congress, and even the military itself.
Nixon had played his trump card, and the results were questionable.
The American strategic bomber fleet had been crippled, and while
Hanoi and Haiphong had suffered monumental damage, the government of North Vietnam as well as factories and schools still functioned
since they had earlier been moved to the countryside.[80] North Vietnam
had survived the penultimate sanction.

Nixon realized this. With his political support eroding at home
and abroad in the wake of his abortive bombing effort, and with the
strategic bomber ploy having been used and turned back, Nixon had
reached a crossroads. In the words of Le Duc Tho, the American government could either "resolve the Vietnamese problem and sign the treaty
that was agreed upon or else continue the war. The American administration must make a definite choice." Even more directly, as a
secret letter Nixon sent to Thieu later revealed, Nixon himself realized he

stood at a crossroads. By mid-January, Nixon believed that his own political future required the signing of a peace agreement. According to Nixon himself:

> Your [Thieu's] rejection of [the newly negotiated] agreement would now irretrievably destroy our ability to assist you. Congress and public opinion would force my hand.[81]

On January 2, technical negotiations between the American and North Vietnamese delegations resumed. When Kissinger and Le Duc Tho met on January 8, it soon became apparent that the bombings had not influenced the D.R.V. to alter its position. On all three of the major outstanding issues — the demilitarized zone, the status of the Provisional Revolutionary Government, and the National Council — Tho was adamant. The D.R.V. would stand by the positions it had advocated, and which the United States had accepted, in October. The U.S. must change its stance.

The issue of the demilitarized zone and civilian transit across it was significant to the D.R.V. since the United States proposal that civilian movement across the DMZ be strictly regulated appeared to be a subtle maneuver to keep Vietnam divided despite the American acceptance of the principle that the DMZ was only temporary and military. Washington, on the other hand, feared that Hanoi would continue military infiltration under civilian cover if civilian transit were not closely monitored. The solution to the problem turned out to be simple. The United States agreed that "North and South Vietnam" would negotiate the terms of civilian transit. Since the PRG controlled the South Vietnamese territory abutting the DMZ, the U.S. agreement in essence indicated acceptance of unrestricted civilian transit. Hanoi had won on Issue One.

Issue Two, the status of the PRG, was less easily settled, but North Vietnam again emerged predominant. The U.S., going along with Thieu, had demanded that all mention of the Provisional Revolutionary Government be dropped from the October text. North Vietnam rejected this position since it implied that the PRG was not a coequal party. After a week of disagreement, the two sides agreed to prepare two documents, one signed by the United States and North Vietnam with Saigon and the PRG "concurring" and the other signed by all four parties. The first document specifically mentioned the PRG. The second did not. The United States in essence had "recognized" the PRG as a legitimate government even though Saigon had not. For the most part, Hanoi had won on Issue Two.

Issue Three, the scope and function of the National Council of Reconciliation and Concord, was the last major problem area. American and South Vietnamese demands were several: the Council's function to "promote" the agreement was to be reduced, lower level regional and local councils were to be eliminated, the word "National" was to be excluded from its title, the nonaligned element of the Council was to be restructured, and wording implying the Council was "administrative" rather than "governmental" was to be used. These changes would have effectively emasculated the Council, thereby permitting Saigon to be politically predominant. Hanoi and the PRG, of course, opposed these changes, and in four of the five instances, again won their points. Only on the last point did the United States obtain its objective, and even then the wording remained ambiguous. Once again, Hanoi had emerged victorious.[82]

On January 13, both sides agreed on the main text of a ceasefire agreement once again, and Kissinger returned to Washington to brief Nixon. This time Nixon had little choice. The military pressure of the December bombings had not obtained any significant concession from the North and no other means of military pressure were available. On January 27, 1973, the United States and the Democratic Republic of Vietnam signed the "Agreement on Ending the War and Restoring Peace in Vietnam."[83] America's longest war had officially ended.

Several protocols were signed at the same time as the major agreement. These protocols included statements on prisoners and detainees, on an International Commission of Control and Supervision, on a Joint Military Commission, and on mine-clearing in North Vietnam. In most instances, the United States again acquiesced to the North Vietnamese position or substantially altered its own preferred position. The protocols, as did the major agreement, implied American acceptance of much less than American objectives.

After all is said and done, what may be concluded about American policy toward Vietnam in the last three months of 1972? On the basis of available evidence, it appears that Nixon and Kissinger had not substantially altered their earlier conviction that a political settlement satisfactory to the United States could be achieved through the application of military force. At worst, the late 1972 period was viewed by Washington as a period during which vast quantities of military supplies and equipment could be funneled to the Saigon government before an agreement was signed. At best, Washington hoped that North Vietnam could be pummeled into accepting the revised American terms. Either interpretation, or any interpretation between the two extremes, still revolves around the fact that Washington considered a militarily imposed political settlement to the Vietnamese question a distinct and preferred possibility. Since the Nixon administration finally signed an agreement which was little changed from the October text, it would appear that the Nixon administration was as much in error in its assessment of the Vietnamese situation as the Johnson administration had been before it. In the final analysis, both American Presidents had seriously underestimated the North Vietnamese.

## Moscow, Hanoi, and Détente

While American decision-makers had misread the North Vietnamese during the years of overt American involvement in the war, Soviet leaders had apparently made the same mistake in their assessment of both North Vietnamese and American decision-makers. During the 1970 to 1972 period, the Soviet Union had become so involved in other international efforts, specifically détente and the Sino-Soviet conflict, that one prominent international observer was led to describe Soviet influence in Hanoi as "irrelevant" despite the sizable Soviet aid to the D.R.V. (a total of $845 million during 1970 and 1971).[84] The Kremlin's underestimation of Hanoi and Washington contributed tremendously to Moscow's irrelevance.

To the Soviet Union, American foreign policy had changed form but not substance during the first year of the Nixon presidency. The Nixon Doctrine was dismissed as little more than a method to find new ways to permit American meddling in Vietnamese affairs.[85] *International Affairs* observed that the formulation of new "doctrines of armed struggle against the national liberation movement" had become "a White House ... tradition," and Nixon was no exception. This "tradition," put simply, was caused by "the fiasco of the previous principles and the inability to understand that the crux of the matter is ... the unrealistic reckless nature of American imperialist strategy."[86] The Nixon Doctrine, then, remained a part of the general United States imperialist line.[87] The only difference between it and previous doctrines was that it was more subtle. The additional subtlety was necessary, Moscow argued, since it was formulated during a period "marked by a steady decline of the role of the U.S. as leader of the capitalist world."[88]

Vietnamization, as the leading example of the Nixon Doctrine, was similarly denounced.[89] Under Vietnamization, the Kremlin rightfully observed that electronic warfare, a buildup of ARVN, increased use of the U.S. Air Force, and a rural pacification program were all being used to strengthen Saigon's hand.[90] The on-going U.S. troop withdrawal program was designed to "cut the expenditures of intervention" and to mislead world public opinion.[91] The American President had changed, and the name of his policy had changed, but objectives remained constant — defeat of the national liberation movement and maintenance of American neocolonial hegemony in Southeast Asia.

There were instances of sentiment in some Soviet circles that U.S. policy had in fact changed, but this was distinctly a minority view. The chief practitioner of this position was Georgi Arbatov, director of the prestigious Soviet Institute for the Study of the U.S.A. and Canada. Arbatov dismissed speculation that Nixon's foreign policy was identical to Johnson's, and instead posited that a "felt need for change" existed and would continue to influence U.S. policy. Arbatov was still uncertain which direction the change would take. On the one hand, there was a trend to alter "primarily method and form," of which the Nixon Doctrine was a leading example. On the other hand, Arbatov envisaged "a certain correction in policy itself."[92] The American experience in Vietnam had:

> laid bare the flagrant gap between goals and means, between desires and possibilities, between a policy put together over the years and the realities of the international situation today.[93]

On occasion, even *Kommunist*, the leading theoretical organ of the CPSU, implied support for Arbatov, maintaining that "the firmness of America's international position" could be questioned.[94] These views were, however, distinctly in the minority. On April 5, 1970, Brezhnev delivered a major foreign policy address and vehemently condemned American policy. The Soviet leader argued that "Vietnamization" was only the "renovation of the facade of U.S. policy."[95] To Brezhnev, American objectives remained constant, and U.S. policymakers were now only using foreign troops to seek their objectives. To the Russians, military victory remained the objective of Nixon just as it had been the objective of Johnson.

Events in Cambodia during early 1970 served to confirm this Soviet viewpoint. On March 19, Prince Sihanouk was overthrown and replaced as head of state by the pro-American Lon Nol. Within two days, the Soviet Union and China had granted Sihanouk the right to live in exile in either country. Unlike China and North Vietnam, however, the Soviet Union continued diplomatic relations with the Lon Nol regime despite the fact that, to the Kremlin, the coup was a product of U.S. aggression."[96]

While Soviet reaction to the Cambodian coup was quite restrained and presented a rather confused picture, the Kremlin's response to the military incursion into Cambodia of first ARVN and then American units in late April and early May 1970 was a different story. The incursion illustrated the "insidiousness" of the Guam Doctrine, the Soviet Union believed, and showed that "Vietnamization" was merely an effort to quiet U.S. opposition to the war.[97] By far the most significant Soviet reaction to the Cambodian incursion was a press conference given by Kosygin on May 4. The press conference was the first given by a Soviet premier since Khrushchev had done so in 1960. In part, Kosygin's statement read as follows:

> President Nixon's practiced steps in the field of foreign policy are fundamentally at variance with those declarations and assurances that he repeatedly made both before assuming the presidency and when he was already in the White House.
>
> ...the real meaning of the President's statement and indeed of the entire policy of the United States in Southeast Asia, is to eliminate progressive regimes in the countries of the region, to stifle the national liberation movement, to hamper social programs, and through colonial methods, to subordinate the foreign policy and domestic policy of the states of Indochina in its military blocs.[98]

Even though the Soviet perception of American objectives in Southeast Asia had undeniably reverted to that of the Johnson era, it cannot be argued that Soviet foreign policy toward the area maintained its old pattern, that is, following the North Vietnamese lead. As has already been seen, the Soviet Union maintained diplomatic relations with the Lon Nol regime following the Cambodian coup while North Vietnam did not. Shortly thereafter, the Soviet representative to the United Nation, Yakob Malik, told a news conference that "only a new Geneva Conference could bring a new solution" to the Indochina situation.[99] This was a position long anathema to Hanoi. Even though Malik altered his position the following day by declaring that such a conference was "unrealistic" as long as American forces remained in Indochina, it was evident that Moscow and Hanoi no longer saw eye to eye on this and other issues. Throughout the spring and summer of 1970, the Kremlin decried a Geneva Conference on Indochina as unrealistic,[100] but the damage had already been done. While Soviet-North Vietnamese relations grew cool, North Vietnamese-Chinese relations steadily improved.

The Soviet Union realized that this discord was apparent to Washington, and consequently moved to caution Washington that the differences, though existent, were not serious. In his mid-June election speech, Brezhnev warned Washington that no one in the American capital should "have doubts about our [Soviet] firmness," and promised that the Soviet Union could continue to give "resolute rebuff to the efforts of aggressive circles."[101] By the fall, the momentary crisis in the Kremlin's relationship with Hanoi had passed.

What had been the genesis of the deteriorated relations? The ambivalent Soviet reaction to the Cambodian coup and the Malik statement on negotiations were undoubtedly partial explanations, but the primary cause may well have been the Chinese-sponsored summit conference of Indochinese peoples, held somewhere in southern China in late April. The conference proclaimed the unity of the wars against

American imperialism in Indochina, and was quite clearly carried out under the tutelage of the Chinese. Soviet Premier Kosygin sent the conferees a rather nondescript message of support on April 29, but this did little to offset the presence of Chou En-lai at the Conference or the location of the conference itself. To the Soviet leadership, supporting an effort to reunify Vietnam was one thing, but supporting an effort to eliminate the American presence in Vietnam, Laos, Cambodia, and Thailand was quite another, especially when viewed in light of the perceived American intention to change the form but not the substance of intervention. Put simply, the Kremlin may well have expected the Vietnamese war to become a much larger Indochinese war, and was consequently laying the groundwork to limit the boundaries of its own involvement. By the summer, the fear of a larger war had been reduced, and the Soviet Union was mending its fences with Hanoi. When the PRG put forth its September peace proposal, Soviet support for it was immediate and strong.[102] The Soviet departure from support for Hanoi on major policy matters had been brief and rather ineffective. It would not happen again before the fall of Saigon five years later.

As if to underline the Kremlin's return to support for D.R.V.-PRG initiatives, Soviet criticism of Nixon's counterproposal to the PRG offer was unusually strong. Brezhnev himself dismissed the proposal as "nothing new" and other Soviet sources termed Nixon's offer "a gigantic fraud" and a "mere political maneuver."[103] American actions in the next several months served to confirm the legitimacy of this assessment, at least in Soviet eyes. On November 21 and 22, American planes raided North Vietnam in response to the downing of American reconnaisance planes and launched an abortive raid against prisoner of war camps in the D.R.V. These actions were viewed as proof that the United States had "in no way abandoned its policy of resolving the Vietnamese question militarily."[104] Nixon's December 10 warning that the U.S. would reinstitute regular raids against the D.R.V. if North Vietnamese infiltration "threatened remaining [American] forces" was decried as an effort to "justify any armed provocation beforehand so as to impose a solution of Indochina's problems satisfactory to the imperialist desires of the United States."[105] Later Soviet commentaries on the November-December escalations attributed them to the failure of Vietnamization and warned that they were "bound to have an effect on Soviet-American relations."[106] Such warnings had limited impact, however, since with the exception of the soon-to-be-begun strategic arms talks in Vienna, Soviet-American relations remained substantially frozen.

By January 1971, after two years of the Nixon Presidency, the Soviet perception of American involvement in Vietnam had changed little. Over 200,000 American troops had been withdrawn, reducing U.S.

force levels in the South to 336,000, but increased application of U.S. air power in the South and strengthened ARVN forces more than made up for this reduction, at least in Soviet eyes. The Laotian incursion of February and March, 1971 fit well within this pattern as far as the Kremlin was concerned. Even though American troops were not used in the bulk of the operation, Moscow viewed the sweep as designed by and run from Washington.

The incursion itself was greeted with the standard Soviet rhetoric about American imperialism and aggressiveness. The immediate military purpose of the sweep was to cut D.R.V.-PLAF supply lines in Laos, one source recognized, but also observed that it served as a test for ARVN.[107] Another source went so far as to speculate that the previous drive into Cambodia and the ongoing drive into Laos were "in preparation of more extensive operations against the D.R.V."[108] The official Soviet government statement on the invasion merely promised continued Soviet aid, and argued that U.S. public claims about the necessity of the action were designed "to mislead world opinion."[109] *Izvestiia* once again warned that "American actions in Indochina cannot but affect Soviet-American relations."[110]

With the Laotian invasion occurring just before the Twenty-Fourth Congress of the Communist Party of the Soviet Union, it may have been expected that the Congress would deal with the Southeast Asian situation in some detail. Such was not the case. Except for occasional mention in various speeches and a single appeal for freedom in the area, Vietnam, Cambodia, and Laos were virtually ignored. This may have been due simply to concern with matters considered to be more pressing. By April 1971, the Soviet leaders had long realized that the D.R.V. was operating independently, accepting aid from all but directions from none. Thus, Brezhnev emphasized Soviet-North Vietnamese cooperation, aid, and solidarity during his speech, and refrained from commenting on over all American policy in Vietnam. Other addresses to the Congress followed Brezhnev's lead.[111]

Two other factors undoubtedly played a role in the Kremlin's restrained commentary on Southeast Asia during the Twenty-Fourth Congress. First, the American peace movement was once again gathering momentum in the wake of the Laotian incursion, and the Kremlin undoubtedly wanted to minimize the possibility that charges could be made that the peace movement paralleled Soviet foreign policy objectives. Second, and perhaps more importantly, there were indications shortly before the Congress that major changes would soon take place in Chinese-American relations, and the Soviets undoubtedly wanted an opportunity to assess these rumored changes.

Before 1970, Soviet commentary on American domestic opposition to the Vietnamese War had been very limited. According to *New Times*, this was because the American peace movement had been indecisive, confused, and divided.[112] Shortly before the Cambodian incursion, however, Soviet sources began to reassess the potential impact of the peace movement. Georgi Arbatov argued that:

> one should not underestimate the importance of the activization of the opposition which is coming out for a re-examination of American foreign policy.... Even more important is the fact that the line of the opposition expresses the objective requirements of the situation and finds a response among broad public opinion. This converts it into a political factor which can affect the formation of Washington's foreign policy.[113]

Though Arbatov was in the minority on the issue of change in American foreign policy, powerful voices soon supported his position on American dissent. Kosygin "welcome[d] this struggle" against the war in the U.S. since he believe[d] ... it [was] of significant assistance to the people of Indochina."[114] A month earlier, Brezhnev had noted that "the aggressor's situation has sharply deteriorated not only militarily but also politically" because of domestic dissent.[115] Throughout the remainder of 1970 and 1971, Soviet sources continued to emphasize the importance of the antiwar movement as an input to U.S. foreign policy. Nixon's stress on troop withdrawal, the publication of the Pentagon Papers, and the whole concept of Vietnamization increasingly were interpreted as events and actions intended to stifle the antiwar movement.[116] With this Soviet view of the importance of dissent, it may well be argued that the Kremlin preferred not to use the Twenty-Fourth Congress as a platform from which to stress its condemnation of U.S. policy in Vietnam. If such an action had been taken, Nixon could have used the inevitable similarity of viewpoint between the Twenty-Fourth Congress and the antiwar movement as a pretext to silence dissent.

Evolving Chinese-American relations also added to the Kremlin's reticence. Although the Soviet Union had earlier told China that there was "no place left" for a third major force in the world,[117] the Soviet leaders clearly feared such an eventuality. Even while the Twenty-Fourth Party Congress was taking place, the long-time freeze in Chinese-American relations was thawing rapidly. "Ping pong diplomacy" ushered in a new era in Chinese-American relations. The potential significance of the "rebirth of American-Chinese friendship," as Chou En-lai termed it, was not lost on the Russians. Whereas previously the Soviet Union had nothing to fear from Sino-American cooperation, now such collaboration could in fact be inimical to Soviet interests.

Immediately after the early April announcement that the American table tennis team would visit China, *Pravda* began close coverage of the on-going events.[118] The entire affair was made possible, the newspaper argued, because of the restrained Chinese reaction to both the Cambodian and Laotian incursions. At the same time, and here *Pravda* quoted the *New York Times*, the success of the Nixon Doctrine and Vietnamization depended "in large measure on at least the tacit cooperation of the Chinese People's Republic." From the Kremlin's perspective, then, the incipient rapprochement had a definite import to the Vietnamese situation. The United States' Chinese gambit did not imply that the United States had altered its goals in southeast Asia. Rather, "building bridges to Peking" was simply "a devious method for the achievement of its [neocolonial] goals" since no less a person than Mao himself had "tacitly guaranteed" that China would not intervene.[119] While it was possible to consider the normalization of Sino-American relations an indication of "realism on the part of the United States," such an interpretation was "erroneous" because of "the context in which the new policy has been institutcd." That context was to take advantage of "difficulties" between Moscow and Peking.[120]

If the Soviet Union felt uneasy because of the diplomacy begun over ping pong tables, then the July 15 announcement that Nixon would visit Peking in early 1972 left the Kremlin appalled. Western officials in Moscow described Russian leaders as "stunned." The Soviet media published terse reports on the announcement without commentary.[121] After several days, Moscow apparently decided to make the best of a bad situation, observing that while there were no indications that either nation had undertaken a "critical reassessment" of basic foreign policy positions, the Soviet Union supported normalization of relations if they were not anti-Soviet or antisocialist in nature.[122] The ever-equivocating Arbatov argued that the Kremlin had to beware of whether the changed relationship was of policies or of appearance of policies.[123] Brezhnev launched a veiled criticism against Nixon's trip at a state dinner for French President Pompidou several months later, when he denounced "attempts to impose a foreign will in Vietnam by force or by backstage intrigues."[124]

To Soviet eyes, the emerging Sino-American rapprochement thus had both strategic implications and theater implications for Southeast Asia. The Soviet leadership clearly feared that its interests in Vietnam could be compromised by a Chinese-American understanding on the situation, especially in light of the fact that Soviet-North Vietnamese relations were less than satisfactory. Two main factors consequently influenced the Soviet Union to pursue closer relations with the D.R.V. during the fall: first, as discussed above, the Soviet desire to mend the damage caused by its zig-zag diplomacy of the spring, and second, fear of the effects of the Sino-American rapprochement on the Vietnamese situation itself.

In its effort to improve relations with the D.R.V. the Kremlin had already reverted to its earlier policy of echoing D.R.V.-PRG pronouncements. In early October, the Soviet Union further underlined its commitment to closer relations as Soviet President Podgorny headed a government and military delegation to Hanoi. Arriving on October 3, the Soviet President quickly promised Soviet aid to the Vietnamese people and, in a clear allusion to the Sino-American rapprochement, stressed that "the facts show that Washington has not given up its aggressive neocolonialist designs." Podgorny further gave his own estimation of the state of Soviet-D.R.V. relations:

> If one were to give an overall evaluation of the relations between the Soviet Union and Vietnam, between the Communist Party of the Soviet Union and the Vietnamese Workers Party, and between the Soviet and Vietnamese peoples, they would be described as being in complete mutual agreement and complete mutual understanding on all the most important question.[125]

One of these "most important questions" was Sino-American relations. North Vietnam mistrusted the motives of both nations, and consequently was quite receptive to improved relations with the Kremlin.[126] By the end of 1971, then, much of the former amity in Soviet-North Vietnamese relations had been restored.[127]

North Vietnamese mistrust of China was further accentuated by the lack of Chinese response to the series of "protective reaction" raids the United States launched against the D.R.V. beginning on December 23. The Soviet Union, cognizant of the low-keyed Chinese reaction and seeking to cement its new closeness with Hanoi, immediately pounced on the American raids and Chinese reaction as proof that no good could come of the rapprochement. *Pravda* condemned both the American raids and the Chinese reaction, saying that China was keeping silent since it "evidently did not wish in any way to darken President Nixon's forth-coming visit to Peking."[128] As the protective reaction raids continued, Peking was berated for betraying the national liberation movement since Nixon's visit was not postponed.[129] The Kremlin maintained that the bombing proved Washington still sought a military solution to the Viet-namese conflict.[130] The United States had stepped up its bombing since it knew China would not react, according to the Soviet line, and Nixon's visit served as further proof of this collusion.[131] Following Nixon's visit, Soviet leaders, Brezhnev included, often conjectured that "something more happened in these talks than is stated in the communiqué."[132]

By February 1972, then, the Soviet Union believed that American policy toward Vietnam still had not changed. The Nixon Doc-trine and Vietnamization were still condemned as aggressive, and the im-proving relations between China and the United States simply disguised American efforts to "exploit" Peking's desires for improved relations.[133]

The Vietnamese situation as it stood in early 1972 gave the Soviet leadership grounds for both reservations and temptations. The Kremlin realized that it could not control the situation in Southeast Asia, and the possibility that the war could explode to cover all Indochina and beyond still existed. Such a possibility had caused the Soviet Union to edge away from Hanoi the preceding spring, and the likelihood of an expanded conflict, though it had decreased, had not disappeared. These reservations were matched by the temptation to take advantage of the upcoming election in the United States and North Vietnamese disenchantment with China over its relations with the U.S. Additionally, any event that served to hamper the Sino-American rapprochement would have been welcomed by both Moscow and Hanoi.

It would be naive to argue that the 1972 spring offensive, carried out by the D.R.V. and the People's Liberation Armed Forces (PLAF), was designed to worsen Chinese-American relations. Rather, it was designed to change the military-political balance in South Vietnam and to damage ARVN main force divisions.[134] Nonetheless, it also served to strain the new Peking-Washington accommodation as well as to jeopardize the upcoming Soviet-American summit. If, as American sources claimed, 80 percent of the arms and equipment used by the PLAF in the offensive were Soviet provided,[135] why did the Soviet Union provide the equipment? Even more centrally, did the Soviet Union know the spring offensive was to occur?

Although Michel Tatu has cited unspecified "overwhelming evidence" to support the claim that Soviet leaders were not informed or consulted before the North Vietnamese offensive,[136] other evidence implies the opposite. Some American sources described the Hanoi-Haiphong area as an "armed camp" by December 1971. Since the Soviet military mission that accompanied Podgorny to Hanoi in October remained there until late March,[137] it is highly unlikely they could have missed the developing concentration of military equipment. Immediately after the original delegation left, a second one under Marshal P.F. Batitsky arrived.[138] Additionally, "highly important negotiations" in Moscow during December resulted in an agreement on "additional nonrepayable Soviet assistance" to "strengthen the D.R.V.'s defense capabilities."[139] A consignment of 60 SA-2 missiles which arrived in the D.R.V. during February may well have been part of the result of the December agreement. On the basis of this information, then, it appears highly unlikely the Kremlin did *not* know that the spring offensive was to be launched.

Why, then, did the Russians supply the equipment if it jeopardized the Moscow summit? Perhaps the immediate answer is that, if things had gone as planned, the Moscow summit would not have been jeopardized. Rather, the Peking summit would have been. It must be remembered that the original American estimation was that the offensive was planned to precede or coincide with Nixon's trip to Peking, and the protective reaction strikes of December and January were intended to prevent this occurrence. If the Russians and/or Chinese were privy to the timing of the offensive and Washington was correct in its estimation, then not only the reason behind Russian aid but also a further clarification of Russian and Chinese reaction to the U.S. strikes became obvious. Russian aid was designed to embarrass and undermine the Peking summit.

Why was the offensive not launched until the end of March? Again, either of two answers is possible. First, the American bombing may have effectively disrupted the timing of the offensive. Second, the North Vietnamese may have been no more confident of Soviet assurances that the Moscow summit would not arrive at a secret agreement to end the war than they were of earlier Chinese assurances. On May 20, *Nhan Dan* issued a veiled warning against the Moscow summit that "a few signs of weakness will encourage American truculence."[140]

Again, if this reasoning is correct, why did the Russians continue arms deliveries even after it became apparent the offensive would not embarrass the Chinese? Put simply, the Russians had been trapped by their own rhetoric. Too much had been promised for too long, and if shipment had been stopped or drastically curtailed, then the Russian machinations would have become painfully transparent. As it turned out, there was still an indication of Soviet restraint. North Vietnam never received weapons that threatened the U.S. carriers in the Gulf of Tonkin.

Soviet coverage of the D.R.V.-PLAF offensive was extensive, at times overly optimistic. At one time, the fall of Quang Tri was seen as the "prelude" to final victory.[141] Soviet commentary noted rightfully that Washington "viewed the situation with alarm," and remarked that there was a growing feeling in Washington that "the South Vietnamese puppet troops" could not successfully resist the PLAF.[142] Only on rare occasions did the Soviet media acknowledge that D.R.V.-PLAF successes were made possible through Soviet aid.[143] Soviet and North Vietnamese officials remained in rather close contact during the first several weeks of the offensive. Secretary of the Central Committee of the Vietnam Workers Party To Huu traveled to Moscow and engaged in "ideological, cultural, and other" talks from March 22 through April 7. The talks were conducted "in an atmosphere of cordiality and complete mutual understanding."[144] On April 12, Brezhnev and the North Vietnamese ambassador to the Soviet Union met to discuss "questions concerning Soviet-Vietnamese cooperation." This meeting proceeded in an "atmosphere of cordiality and fraternal friendship," Soviet catchwords which implied some disagreement existed.[145] One may well imagine the disagreement centered on continued Soviet aid in light of the upcoming American summit.

As has already been seen, the success of the PLAF offensive clearly shocked Washington. Moscow was similarly affected. Washington laid the blame for the offensive on Moscow, so it was no surprise that when Kissinger flew to Moscow in late April to discuss plans for the upcoming summit, much of the discussion centered on Vietnam. Kissinger reportedly warned the Russians that increased retribution would be exacted from the North if the offensive continued. *Pravda* merely reported that the Kissinger visit touched on "questions of bilateral relations and on important international problems."[146] Four days later, Party Secretary K.F. Katushev flew to Hanoi, presumably carrying Kissinger's warning.

Even before this, the United States had begun an aerial assault on North Vietnam to slow the offensive. On April 6, B-52s stepped up bombing of the D.R.V., and on April 15, Haiphong was attacked. In the B-52 raids on the 15th, a Soviet freighter was sunk, but not even a mild protest was lodged.[147] Why not? Obviously, the Russians wanted to protect the summit. Consequently they found themselves in the same position the Chinese had been in a few months earlier.

On May 8, while the PLAF offensive rolled onward, Nixon announced that North Vietnamese ports would be mined to keep weapons "out of the hands of the international outlaws of North Vietnam." The TASS news agency immediately issued a statement condemning this "overt act of aggression," and the official Soviet government statement issued three days later promised only continued Soviet aid, although it did warn that the Soviets would "draw the appropriate conclusions" from the U.S. actions.[148] All in all, the statement was quite weak. Despite the statement's claim that the mining was "fraught with serious consequences," Soviet Ambassador to the United States Dobrynin and Minister of Foreign Trade N.S. Patolichev met with Nixon as scheduled on May 11.

The Soviet media approach to Vietnam in the weeks immediately before, during, and after the summit presented a picture closely paralleling China's response to the December-January bombings. Before the summit, *Pravda* and *Izvestiia* extensively covered the D.R.V.-PLAF offensive, but as the summit approached, coverage fell off sharply. Following the summit, coverage remained limited for several weeks.[149] Clearly, the summit had to be protected. References to discussions between Brezhnev and Nixon on "questions of Soviet-American relations, as well as on certain international problems" appeared in the Soviet press, but there was nothing more specific.[150] In actuality, Vietnam was the one centrally discussed issue. Nothing, however, was resolved as Brezhnev, Kosygin, and Podgorny all backed Hanoi's demand for a coalition government without Thieu and demanded that the U.S. end its aggression against the D.R.V. The communiqué issued at the conclusion of the summit offered separate Soviet and American statements on Vietnam, with the Soviets maintaining that peace could come only after the "complete and unequivocal withdrawal of the troops of the U.S. and its allies from South Vietnam" and the U.S. positing that the "political future of South Vietnam should be left for the South Vietnamese people to decide for themselves, free from outside interference." Shortly thereafter, the Soviet Union confirmed its intention to continue tendering support to national liberation movements.[151] The summit had been held, but despite later claims to the contrary by both sides,[152] nothing concrete had been accomplished or agreed to on the Vietnam issue.

In mid-June, Podgorny once again traveled to Hanoi carrying news from the summit and about a new Kissinger diplomatic initiative on Vietnam.[153] During his three-day visit, the Soviet President offered the D.R.V. sophisticated new antiaircraft missiles if North Vietnam accepted Soviet missile operators. The Vietnamese refused the offer, supposedly because it insulted national pride to have foreigners run their air defenses.[154] The final communiqué declared the Soviets would still extend "necessary assistance," and said the talks proceeded in an atmosphere of "frankness, friendship, and comradeship."[155] Once again, disagreement had cropped up.

These disagreements did not imply, however, that Soviet aid had stopped. U.S. Chairman of the Joint Chiefs of Staff Thomas Moorer told a congressional subcommittee that the Soviet Union and China had both given North Vietnam "heavy resupply of war matériel" during the summer,[156] and a French correspondent observed "endless convoys" of new Soviet and Chinese trucks laden with all types of munitions and equipment moving southward in North Vietnam.[157] Exigencies of détente may have forced the Soviet leadership to limit its criticism of the United States and adopt a two-sided policy, but there was nothing to indicate that the Kremlin intended to curtail its supply of equipment and munitions to the D.R.V. in order to pressure Hanoi into changing its position on negotiations or policy on the war. Moscow may have had influence in Hanoi, but it clearly felt its interest lay in not using it.

Consequently the Soviet Union continued to follow the diplomatic lead of Hanoi on questions of negotiation. When the Provisional Revolutionary Government and the D.R.V. issued a statement on September 11 calling for a three-part coalition government without Thieu in the South, Moscow quickly called on the United States to recognize that two governments and two armies existed in South Vietnam. Continuing, Moscow supported the PRG proposal for a tripartite government without Thieu and demanded the cessation of American aggression.[158]

By the fall of 1972, Moscow was again resigned to a continuation of the war. There were no indications that the Kremlin expected the 1972 presidential election to act as a constraint on American policy, and if anything, the Soviet leadership favored the re-election of Nixon. Moscow believed that the timing of the "false peace" of October was an election ploy, and observed that while the U.S. administration admitted that the "conditions for peace [were] at hand," peace would not be forthcoming. *Pravda* observed that the American public was "gradually being prepared" for the failure of the latest breakthrough.[159] Thieu's obstinacy did not serve as a convincing rationale for the breakdown of the October text in Moscow's eyes since Thieu received almost all his military aid from the United States. If the United States wanted peace, the Soviets reasoned, then it had the means to pressure Thieu. Since Nixon refused to do so, peace was not his primary objective; rather, the maintenance of Thieu as the U.S. puppet in South Vietnam, and the extension of his political influence, were the central objectives.[160]

Since all the prerequisites for a peace settlement that the United States had previously demanded were at hand, why then, according to Moscow, did the United States delay the agreement? Two reasons were immediately discerned. First, the United States hoped to improve the Republic of Vietnam's military position before a ceasefire was signed. Second, the United States hoped to further build up the South Vietnamese military before an agreement was finalized.[161]

Nonetheless, the Soviet Union remained cautious in its assessment of the possibility for peace. On October 27, Kosygin offered his hope that further negotiations would "soon lead to an agreement ending the war."[162] Gradually, as hopes for consummation of the October text faded and disappeared, other Soviet leaders began to speak out more strongly in support of the D.R.V. On November 5, First Deputy Premier Mazurov called on the United States to sign the agreement "as soon as possible," and on November 16, Suslov confirmed Soviet support for the D.R.V.'s stance in a conversation with Le Duc Tho.[163] Events in Vietnam had settled back into their pre-October pattern.

Did any of these occurrences witness an alteration in the Soviet perception of U.S. objectives in Vietnam? Not necessarily. The American explanation for the failure of negotiations, as has been seen, carried little weight in Moscow. The "false peace" of October, at least in Soviet eyes, was simply a continuation of previous patterns of American behavior. They saw "improving the Republic of Vietnam's military position" and "further strengthening the South Vietnamese military" as simply two manifestations of Vietnamization that did not indicate any change in American objectives. In Soviet eyes, Nixon had designed the "false peace" to obtain political advantages in the United States.

The massive bombing raids that came in late December served to confirm this Soviet view once again. The TASS statement issued at the commencement of the bombing called the raids an effort to "blackmail" the D.R.V.-PRG side into "accepting the American terms of settlement." Continuing, the statement warned that the governing circles of the Soviet Union were "giving the most serious consideration to the situation."[164] During the bombing, Soviet and North Vietnamese officials met several times. Kosygin met the D.R.V. ambassador to the Soviet Union twice, and Suslov met Truong Chinh once.

The United States, meanwhile, had been in contact with the Soviet and Chinese governments both before and during the bombing, informing the Communist powers that the objective of the raids was to force North Vietnam to negotiate seriously.[165] The Soviet Union did not take this explanation seriously. Brezhnev, addressing a meeting honoring the fiftieth anniversary of the formation of the Soviet Union, cautioned that the course of Soviet-American détente would "depend on the course of events in the immediate future and, in particular, on what kind of turn is taken on the issue of terminating the war in Vietnam."[166]

Brezhnev's warning, mistakenly interpreted by some Western observers as a significant threat against détente, was almost identical to Soviet warnings following the Laotian and Cambodian incursions. Similarly, the Soviet revelation that "the latest weapons — antiaircraft missiles, guns, and fighter planes" — had been shipped to the D.R.V. during the height of the bombing[167] was misconstrued as a new Soviet dedication to the North Vietnamese cause. Rather, it must be realized that the resupply of weapons to the D.R.V. was a longstanding Soviet practice, and in the instances of the December resupply, perhaps a product of the "nonrepayable technical and military aid agreement" finalized between the two countries on December 9.[168] To the Soviets, the December bombings changed little, though they did serve to reconfirm the Soviet perception that the United States still sought to achieve a victory through military force of arms.

The cessation of bombing, meanwhile, was interpreted as a "victory for the patriotic forces" of South Vietnam. Nixon had been forced to end the bombing, *Pravda* informed its readers, because the bombing had proved ineffective in isolating the D.R.V. and stopping the functioning of society.[169] While the "logic of events continued to be on the side of negotiations and a political settlement," the United States "still sought a military victory."[170] American proposals for "fundamental changes" in the October text illustrated the "insidiousness" of Nixon's claims that he wanted peace.

The sudden culmination and signing of the ceasefire agreement and accompanying protocols in late January was, to the Soviets, unexpected though not undesired. With the Soviet view that the United States sought a political settlement attained by military force in Vietnam up to the very moment of the signing of the agreement, it was perhaps to be expected that the Soviet Union declared the United States had been "forced" to sign the agreement.[171] Noting that the final text "satisfied most of the demands of the D.R.V. and PRG," the agreement was declared "a major victory" for the people of Vietnam and of "tremendous historical significance" for both the worldwide national liberation movement and the "normalization" of the international situation.[172]

How, exactly, had the United States been "forced" into signing the agreement? For the most part, the Soviets identified three factors, linking all with the "changing international correlation of forces." These three factors included the PLAF, which had stalemated American and South Vietnamese military might in the field; "socialist solidarity," which included not only Soviet and socialist support for the D.R.V. but also North Vietnamese resilience in the face of American air raids; and finally "the antiwar movement in the United States," which played "an important part in the world-wide struggle to halt the U.S. aggression."[173] In some Soviet sources, it was implied that the last factor had perhaps the most importance in forcing the American government to accept the ceasefire agreement.[174] It must be stressed, however, that this was an *ex post facto* Soviet realization. To the end, the agreement was unexpected.

With the signing of the agreement, a major potential obstacle to Soviet-American relations and the Brezhnev-Nixon détente was removed. The Vietnamese War had threatened the rapprochement not once, but several times. The mining of Haiphong and the December 1972 bombings were the most critical instances. One may well imagine Brezhnev's relief upon the finalization of the agreement. The Soviet leader, having built much of his stature on the policy of détente, was indeed pleased. On January 30, hosting a dinner party for Le Duc Tho, Brezhnev categorized the cease-fire agreement as "a victory for realism and sanity." Looking toward the future, Brezhnev waxed optimistic:

> It can be expected that the political settlement in Vietnam will have a positive effect on the relations among states that were involved in one way or another in the events in Indochina.[175]

## Peking's Change in Policy and Its Impact on Vietnam

The gradual improvement in Soviet-American relations was not the only transformation taking place in the international arena that had a significant impact on the Vietnamese situation. Between 1970 and 1973, it became evident that the People's Republic of China itself sought an accommodation with the United States (and vice versa). Uncertainty remains even today about the factors immediately precipitating the change,[176] but most sinologists agree that the Chinese had in fact reevaluated the international balance of forces. By 1970, Peking had begun to view the Soviet Union as the main threat to its security.[177] This implied, to the Chinese leadership, that a tacit alliance should be sought with the United States for the purpose of improving Chinese security.

This by no means implied that Chinese opposition to American "imperialist" activity ceased. Rather, in the words of one prominent observer, the Soviet Union and United States were linked by the Chinese leadership as a "single dangerous pair" with the United States "subjected to attack only a few decibels in intensity below those directed against the Soviet Union."[178] Chou En-lai, appearing on French television during 1970, made this point exceedingly clear:

> There exists in the world one or two superpowers that continually seek to oppress others through force, and to treat the weak and the small badly while fighting among themselves for world hegemony.[179]

It was therefore no surprise that even while the Chinese and American leaders were quietly signaling each other their desire to explore the possibility of improving relations between the two countries, the Chinese continued to condemn U.S. policies in Vietnam. Vietnamization was labeled a "gangster" policy and the troop withdrawal program was castigated as a "smokescreen." The Nixon Doctrine drew its share of condemnation as a policy of having "Asians kill Asians."[180] Speculation that the United States would reduce the number of military bases it had in Asia was summarily dismissed by Mao himself, who described the bases as "so many nooses around the neck of U.S. imperialism."[181]

The slow movement toward improved Sino-American relations that had occurred in late 1969 and early 1970 came to a temporary halt because of the Cambodian crisis of spring 1970. Cambodia's Prince Norodom Sihanouk had kept his country publicly out of the conflict in Vietnam by walking a tightrope between North Vietnam, China, the Soviet Union and the United States, but in March 1970, his balancing act came to an end.[182] While Sihanouk was in Moscow the Cambodian Assembly deposed him as head of state. The Prince continued on his planned journey to Peking. Upon arriving in the Chinese capital, according to Sihanouk himself, Chou gave him "formal assurance of complete support in all fields."[183] The first public support for the deposed Cambodian leader was not given until April 7, again by Chou.[184]

Meanwhile, in Cambodia itself, the Lon Nol government had moved to end its tacit acceptance of North Vietnamese-Vietcong operations within Cambodia. On March 23, the Cambodian-Vietnamese border was proclaimed closed. Two days later, Sihanoukville was closed to ships bearing arms for Communist forces in Cambodia. The same day Lon Nol expressed a desire to negotiate the withdrawal of D.R.V. forces from Cambodia. On March 29 and again on April 3, North Vietnamese forces engaged Cambodian forces in fire fights. Throughout April, the situation in Cambodia worsened. Finally, on May 5, Sihanouk set up a government-in-exile in Peking. The P.R.C. immediately broke relations with Lon Nol and recognized Sihanouk's new Royal Government of National Unity.

While the Chinese condemned the Cambodian coup itself as an American plot to expand the war into Cambodia so that Washington could extricate itself from the "quagmire of Vietnamization,"[185] the change of government in the Khmer state presented little threat in and of itself to China. The American and South Vietnamese invasion of Cambodia in early May did little to change this assessment despite American acknowledgments that the threat of possible Chinese intervention was an "acceptable risk."[186] The invasion served to confirm the Chinese thesis that Indochina was embroiled in "one war." Peking condemned the incursion[187] and withdrew its tentative feelers for improved relations with the United States. China informed the United States that because of the Cambodian invasion, the Warsaw ambassadorial talks scheduled for May 20 would not be held.

While the Cambodian situation halted the Sino-American discussions, it is doubtful whether the May talks could have accomplished much to begin with. The United States was clearly displeased with Chinese sponsorship of the summit meeting of Indochinese revolutionary movements held in south China during late April. The Chinese, on the other hand, hailed the summit as a "tremendous victory" for the "peaceloving forces" of Indochina. The conference met under the tutelage of Chou, and was attended by Sihanouk, Souphanouvong of Laos, Pham Van Dong for the D.R.V., and representatives from the PRC. The Chinese considered the meeting of sufficient importance to devote a special issue of *Peking Review* to it.[188] During the conference, the Indochinese representatives pledged "mutual support" for each other's efforts. China, for its part, promised to provide a "reliable rear area" and "powerful backing" for the "war against U.S. aggression." The wars in Indochina had been united, at least in Chinese eyes, and Chinese influence with the various movements had been reconfirmed.

For China, even with the termination of the movement toward improved relations with the United States, events were proceeding favorably. On April 24, the first day of the summit, China had launched its first ICBM. The U.S.-South Vietnamese invasion of Cambodia had confirmed the Chinese argument that all the Indochinese peoples were united in their struggle against American imperialism. Soviet influence in the area was again declining. Additionally, Cambodia was distant and the invasion presented no immediate threat to China. On May 20, Mao issued a rare foreign policy statement, read by Lin Piao at a large mass rally, that condemned the U.S. as a "paper tiger." Although the statement warned that the "danger of a new world war still existed," it for the most part was an optimistic assessment of the state of world affairs through Chinese eyes.[189]

Following the withdrawal of American troops from Cambodia and throughout the remainder of 1970, the Chinese media praised the "excellent situation" in Indochina brought about by the "infinite power of guerrilla warfare."[190] Chinese-North Vietnamese relations remained cordial, with China extending additional economic and military aid regularly.[191] The American bombing raids against North Vietnam in November brought the expected Chinese recriminations. By the end of 1970, then, China's overall international position had improved tremendously, with the sole exception of its northern border with the Soviet Union. The American invasion of Cambodia had served the Peking leadership excellently.

The Laotian incursion of South Vietnamese troops during February 1971 stood in marked contrast to Cambodia. Laos eventually disrupted Chinese relations with the D.R.V., provided a threat to China and probably exacerbated dealings among the Chinese leaders themselves.

Chinese concern over the Laotian invasion was to be expected. Between 1969 and 1971, Chinese construction troops built a major road from China almost to the Laotian border with Thailand. As many as 395 radar directed antiaircraft guns and 20,000 Chinese troops protected this road.[192] A number of factors explained this Chinese interest in Laos. First, during the period from 1969 through 1971 American involvement in Laos was increasing. The Chinese effort may thus have been in response to the United States. Second, the road itself may have been constructed to facilitate the transport of supplies into either northeast Thailand or South Vietnam. Finally, the genesis of the increased Chinese interest may have been simply a product of Peking's desire to expand its influence. When South Vietnamese troops invaded Laos, Peking consequently saw an increased possibility of its own involvement in the Indochinese conflict. Laos was not only geographically contiguous to China; Chinese army units were actually in a potential zone of fighting.

Unlike that following the Cambodian invasion, Chinese reaction was immediate and intense.[193] Chinese fears of a major action were further strengthened as the North Vietnamese leadership decided to test the mettle of the invading ARVN force. To meet the ARVN troops, the D.R.V. withdrew troops from its southern province along the demilitarized zone and introduced them to Laos, thereby opening itself to attack from South Vietnam itself. China recognized this possibility and its implications for China. Chinese military leaders began to caution that the United States was once again "plotting to attack North Vietnam."[194]

Chinese fears went beyond a mere American or South Vietnamese attack on the D.R.V. Throughout the duration of the Laotian incursion, China warned that the South Vietnamese and American actions in Laos represented a "grave menace to Chinese security."[195] One of the more grandiloquent statements declared that Laos and China were

> linked by the same mountains and rivers and have a common boundary of several hundred kilometers.... By spreading the flames of aggressive war to the door of China U.S. imperialism poses a grave threat to China.[196]

Assurances by Nixon that the incursion was not intended to jeopardize Chinese security failed to quiet Chinese fears. Rather, amid reports from Washington that certain of Nixon's advisors were privately advocating use of tactical nuclear weapons, Chinese trepidation increased. Indeed, shortly after the invasion, the Chinese media printed a barrage of articles about the increased possibility of nuclear war.[197]

Even with this discomfiting perspective, Chinese support for the D.R.V. never wavered. On February 15, the two countries signed a supplementary economic and military aid agreement for 1971, and in early March, Chou En-lai made a dramatic three-day trip to Hanoi. In addition to the usual rhetoric that China would make "the greatest national sacrifice" to honor its commitments to the D.R.V. and that China would "never allow U.S. imperialism to do whatever it pleases" in Indochina, Chou promised the North Vietnamese leaders that the P.R.C. was "prepared ideologically and militarily to eliminate any enemy that endangers its territories."[198] The closeness of Peking-Hanoi relations was shown during the Twenty-Fourth Communist Party Congress in Moscow where, on April 1, Le Duan thanked both the Soviet Union and China for their "tremendous aid."[199] To say the least, this was a highly unusual occurrence.

Since even Western observers termed the ARVN Laotian operation disappointing at best and humiliating at worst, it was not surprising that China labeled it a "catastrophic defeat" for American efforts in Indochina. On March 26, the Chinese leadership threw a "victory banquet" for the North Vietnamese, and three days later, Mao, Chou, and Lin Piao all signed a message congratulating the Indochinese people for their victory in Laos.[200] This Chinese show of unity was as deceiving as the impression that the Laotian events had finally cemented Chinese-North Vietnamese relations. Immediately following the South Vietnamese withdrawal it became clear that fundamental differences divided Peking and Hanoi, and perhaps even more significantly, the leaders in Peking itself.

In Hanoi, North Vietnam's military hierarchy viewed the results of the Laotian events as the doom of Vietnamization. Following this line of thought, both *Nhan Dan* and *Hoc Tap* began stressing "battles of annihilation" as the next step in the war. This of course implied that the D.R.V. was again considering main force warfare. Indeed, it may well be argued that the failure of the Laotian invasion spurred Giap to begin planning his 1972 offensive. To China, such a course of action was foolhardy and presented an unacceptable increase in the likelihood of confrontation with the United States.

Mao Tse-tung and Chou En-lai had drawn different conclusions from Giap about the Laotian experience. The continued withdrawal of American forces from Vietnam after the Laotian debacle impressed the Chinese leaders. At the same time, their confidence in manpower over airpower similarly influenced the Chinese to downplay American air-strength as a replacement for ground troops. These factors, when viewed in conjunction with the obvious American eagerness for a *modus vivendi* with China, forced Mao and Chou to conclude that the United States' days in Vietnam were numbered. To China, escalating to main force warfare was needless. Indeed, it was highly significant that China's renowned "ping pong diplomacy" was undertaken in the wake of the American "defeat" in Laos and the accompanying American failure to do much to save face there. The New Year's editorial for 1972 in *People's Daily* went so far as to say that the outstanding characteristic in the world was "global upheaval," in part caused by the "rapid decay" of American imperialism.

With this perspective, the Chinese not surprisingly opposed "battles of annihilation." The D.R.V. merely had to continue applying pressure as it had been doing, Mao and Chou reasoned, and South Vietnam could be taken. Increased pressure was senseless since it could provoke an American response and a corresponding change in American heart. Different interpretations of the meaning of the Laotian events consequently led to a slowly widening split between Hanoi and Peking.

The incipient disagreement on the conduct of the war was further underlined by an episode during July concerning the Chinese attitude toward a Geneva Conference on Indochina. On July 14, 1971,

Australian Labor Party leader Gough Whitlam returned to Australia from Peking and informed an astounded world that China now supported a Conference on Indochina that would include non-Asian nations. *Nhan Dan* reacted immediately. According to the North Vietnamese paper, "decisive voices belong only to those who are defeating" American aggression; and the "most important cause of our victories is our correct and creative independent and sovereign line." North Vietnam had long opposed a new Conference on Indochina, and it was making it exceedingly clear to the P.R.C. — and everyone else — that its position had not changed. Although *People's Daily* quickly backpedaled, opposing a conference and calling for an "immediate withdrawal" of American troops from Indochina,[201] Peking and Hanoi obviously did not see eye to eye.

Mao's and Chou's disagreements went beyond those with foreign leaders. Even within the Chinese leadership, there was division over the correct policy option. As the Second Plenum of the Ninth Congress of the Communist Party of China, held during August and September 1970, Lin Piao opposed the decision taken by the plenum to gradually improve relations with the United States. To Lin, the United States was still the primary enemy, while the rest of the Chinese leaders, Mao and Chou included, considered the Soviet Union to be.[202] Events immediately following the plenum conformed to the plenum's decision. By December 1970, the radical Chen Po-ta had been purged; rehabilitation of some military and government personnel purged during the Cultural Revolution had begun; and the Chinese military had split into pro-Lin and anti-Lin factions. Also by this time, according to American sources, Peking had privately informed Nixon of its interest in improving relations. In January 1971, the United States responded and inquired how a high-level envoy would be received by Peking.[203]

These steps toward improved relations, as we have already seen, were frozen by the invasion of Laos. Lin Piao undoubtedly viewed the invasion as confirmation of the correctness of his assessment of the degree of threat presented by the United States, and argued that the movement toward improved relations should be reversed. Instead, accommodation should be sought with the Soviet Union.

Obviously, the invasion of Laos gave Mao and Chou several bad moments. Had Lin been correct? Had Mao and Chou miscalculated and underestimated the American threat? These thoughts undoubtedly entered the Great Steersman's mind, but as the Laotian invasion sputtered and then failed, Mao's self-confidence returned. The United States was still dangerous, but as the Laotian failure had revealed, the danger was limited. Steps toward improved relations with the United States designed to counter the primary Soviet danger could once again be undertaken. In April, Peking issued an invitation for an American ping-pong team to visit Peking. Lin was shocked, and reportedly began plotting against Mao. As Sino-American relations grew steadily warmer, Lin's machinations were uncovered. On September 13, Lin Piao fled toward the Soviet Union only to be killed when his plane crashed en route.[204]

The Laotian incursion thus proved to be the factor which led to a rapid transformation in world affairs. China's table tennis invitation was reciprocated by a number of U.S. actions. In March, the U.S. State Department terminated passport restrictions for travel to China. In April, currency controls were relaxed, nonstrategic goods were permitted to be exported to the People's Republic, and imports from the P.R.C. were authorized. The following month controls on dollar transactions with China were removed.[205] Both *Red Flag* and *People's Daily* expressed a desire for improved relations with other nations so China could "learn from others" while others "learned from China."[206] Even more strikingly, on July 4, Peking supported a North Vietnamese plan proposed in June calling for an all-Indochinese ceasefire. This marked the first time since 1965 that Peking had publicly called for peace in Indochina.

It was obvious that Sino-American relations were warming considerably, but no one outside the two governments' inner circles was prepared for the bombshell that exploded in mid-July. On July 15, Nixon announced that he would visit Peking during early 1972. Chou En-lai reasonably explained the Chinese invitation, asking, "If you do not talk to the leader, who else should you talk with?"[207] Shortly thereafter, on July 28, the United States terminated its SR-71 and drone aircraft spy overflights of the P.R.C. and on August 2 Secretary of State Rogers proposed that both the P.R.C. and the Republic of China hold United Nations seats.

This sudden improvement in relations did not imply that all areas of disagreement had been overcome or put aside. Chou En-lai made this exceedingly clear during Henry Kissinger's July trip to Peking to arrange the Nixon visit. Chou told Kissinger that Vietnam, not Taiwan, was the primary obstacle to improved Sino-American relations, and later reiterated that the Chinese demand for an American withdrawal from Indochina was "even stronger than the demand to restore the relations between the Chinese and American people."[208]

Nonetheless, Hanoi was aghast. Xuan Thuy, the D.R.V.'s chief negotiator at the Paris talks categorized Nixon's upcoming visit as a "perfidious maneuver" and a "false peace offensive," the real objective of which was to divide the socialist world.[209] In the months after the July announcement, Hanoi's anger and mistrust did not abate despite

Peking's assurances that the Nixon trip would not lead to any steps detrimental to Hanoi's interest.[210] A steady stream of North Vietnamese dignitaries traveled through Peking following the announcement, but none was convinced by the Chinese argument. On July 31, Le Duc Tho traveled through Peking as he returned from Paris, to be followed by Nguyen Thi Binh on September 16 and a larger government and party delegation in late September. Pham Van Dong followed in their footsteps on November 20 and was greeted by a crowd of 500,000 cheering Chinese in Peking.[211] Despite this, the communiqué issued at the end of his week-long visit had the usual "complete agreement" clause conspicuously absent.[212] Sino-North Vietnamese disagreement remained so significant that shortly thereafter *Nhan Dan* castigated Nixon's trip as "dark plotting to carry out continued U.S. neocolonialism," while the NLFSV radio labeled it an attempt to "capitalize on the internal disagreements of the socialist camp."[213]

While Nixon's visit in particular and the Sino-American rapprochement in general were the most immediate public causes of the P.R.C.-D.R.V. disagreements, there was a deeper underlying cause. By late 1971, the North Vietnamese had decided to move back to main force warfare, a move which not only challenged the Chinese perception of the tactical situation in Indochina, but also threatened to undermine Peking's maneuvering in the Sino-Soviet-American triangle. If the North Vietnamese main force threatened to bring about a rapid and humiliating defeat for the United States in Vietnam, then Peking fully expected American escalations in Vietnam. This undoubtedly would have forced the cancelation of Nixon's trip and prevented Peking from playing its American card against the Soviet threat to the north. It is highly unlikely, then, that the obvious Sino-North Vietnamese disagreement was as much the product of dispute over the correct tactics to apply in Vietnam as over the Sino-American rapprochement.

The low-key Chinese reaction to the American bombing raids of December consequently reflected not only Chinese restraint in light of the upcoming Nixon visit, but also Chinese relief over the fact that the bombing would undoubtedly delay the timetable of the offensive, thereby removing it as a threat to the visit. The P.R.C. called the raids "ineffective" and expressed the "utmost indignation at the U.S. imperialists' crimes of aggression,"[214] but wording of the Chinese response was obviously restrained.

By the beginning of 1972, the Chinese leadership favored a settlement in Indochina. Improved relations with the United States were the order of the day and, to Peking, the Indochinese War threatened this policy. With Lin Piao and his supporters having been removed from power, with Nixon soon to visit Peking, and with Mao and Chou believing the United States was seeking to end its Vietnamese adventure, the Chinese saw no reason to continue the conflict. From Peking's viewpoint, only the Soviet Union could benefit if the war continued.

This did not mean that China was willing or able to initiate a settlement of the Vietnamese conflict. The Shanghai Communiqué signed by both sides at the conclusion of Nixon's February visit stated that "neither side" was willing to negotiate for a third party.[215] Chou En-lai reportedly told Nixon during this visit, in response to Nixon's request that the P.R.C. act as an intermediary, that it was "China's duty to support these resistance movements until total victory" and that if American forces stayed in Indochina then "tensions will be lasting."[216] The Shanghai Communiqué itself made it apparent that despite the P.R.C.'s desire for a resolution of the conflict, support for the D.R.V.-PRG was still an integral part of Chinese foreign policy.[217]

Further proof that Peking had by no means abandoned Hanoi came shortly after Nixon left the P.R.C. A week after the President's departure, Chou En-lai traveled to the D.R.V.'s capital, presumably to brief North Vietnam's leaders on the course of the discussions with Nixon. Neither side announced the visit.[218] Then, on March 10, China verbally assaulted Washington for the renewed "protective reaction" strikes against the D.R.V.[219]

The North Vietnamese offensive which the Chinese had opposed just a few months earlier was finally launched at the end of March, and instead of jeopardizing Sino-American relations, it threatened to undermine Soviet-American relations. Little wonder, then, that the Chinese Foreign Ministry could declare,

> The Vietnam Nation is a whole. It is fully legitimate for the Vietnamese compatriots in the North and South parts of the country to support each other and jointly combat the aggressors.[220]

The Chinese media gave accurate coverage to the progress of the North Vietnamese army as it swept through the I Corp area of South Vietnam. Stepped-up American bombing received the usual Chinese condemnation, but it was somewhat surprising, in light of the new cordiality in Sino-American relations, that it should come from Chou himself.[221]

What explained the Chinese attitude? The most apparent cause was that the United States, though bombing North Vietnam during April, was still sending signals indicating its desire to maintain good relations with Peking. Even while North Vietnam was being bombed, Senators Hugh Scott and Mike Mansfield were en route to Peking. From Peking's perspective, the Soviet Union, not China, now stood to lose the most because of the continued success of the D.R.V.'s offensive. China could afford to offer relatively strong verbal public support to the

D.R.V. Now, unlike the time of the December bombings, it was Moscow, not Peking, that was coopted.

This Chinese perspective was further confirmed when the United States mined Haiphong and other North Vietnamese ports on May 8. While some accounts reported that Washington had privately informed Peking and Moscow of its intentions even before the mining occurred,[222] it escaped no one's notice that when Nixon delivered his speech informing the world of his actions, he admonished Hanoi and Moscow, and said nothing against Peking. No clearer message could have been sent, and Peking realized it. Despite the success of the offensive, the U.S. wanted to maintain good relations with China.

The mining itself was condemned by an official Chinese government statement on May 12, which labeled the action a "new aggression" and promised Chinese support of the Vietnamese until "final victory" was won.[223] In light of the significant nature of the American action, the Chinese response was very restrained. Peking was seeking to play both ends against the middle. Public rhetoric attacking the United States created the image of strong support for the D.R.V., but the rhetoric was not too strong, thereby protecting the young rapprochement with the United States.

By June 1972, it was evident that the United States had received a significant setback in Vietnam but was not in danger of absorbing the humiliating defeat earlier feared by the Chinese. Further, it was evident that the success of the offensive had not substantially harmed Sino-American relations. Only now, after the offensive had begun to recede, did China begin to funnel supplies and equipment to the D.R.V. In May, China had rejected a Soviet request to permit Soviet ships into Chinese ports to offload goods, and (at least in part because of the U.S. bombing), over 1000 freight cars with war materials were backed up in China.[224] During the summer, China reversed its position on the use of ports, and diverted trains to transport the materials. A four-inch petroleum pipeline was constructed between China and North Vietnam,[225] and truck convoys streamed southward across the Sino-Vietnamese border.[226] Chinese minesweepers appeared in Haiphong, and in June, the two countries concluded a supplementary military aid agreement.

What accounted for this sudden increase in aid? One consideration was that, in the eyes of the Chinese leaders, the United States no longer linked Sino-American relations and the Vietnamese conflict. Nixon's May 8 speech had made its point well. Since the United States was in no danger, by June, of losing its position in Vietnam, and since the D.R.V. was slowly moving away from its main force offensive, the Maoist leadership undoubtedly reasoned that an increase in aid was both justified and safe. American air strikes near the Sino-Vietnamese border occurred on June 7 and August 24, and underlined the fact that Washington was aware of the increased aid and would stop it if it was deemed necessary. The Chinese foreign ministry declared that the raids "threatened the security" of the P.R.C.,[227] but following a June 13 U.S. Department of State denial that the raids imperiled China, the issue was dropped. This was in marked contrast to similar accusations during the Laotian events 16 months earlier. Sino-American relations had come a long way, and the Chinese perception of the American involvement in Vietnam had altered considerably.

A second major reason for the increased Chinese aid may well have been a Chinese effort to take advantage of North Vietnamese mistrust of the Soviet Union engendered by Nixon's May trip to Moscow. Remembering that the Soviet Union had used worsened Sino-Vietnamese relations following the announcement of Nixon's Peking visit during July 1971 to increase its prestige and influence in Hanoi, the Chinese leadership simply took a page from the Kremlin's book — if one mistrusts a rival, move to improve one's own position.

Even while the Chinese were increasing their aid to North Vietnam, American leaders were traveling to China to discuss the Vietnamese and other situations. Kissinger arrived in Peking for a four-day visit on June 19 and engaged in "extensive, earnest, and frank" discussions with Chou. Upon his return from Peking, Kissinger described the P.R.C.'s leaders as "men of principle." Consequently, according to Kissinger, final resolution of the Vietnamese conflict depended on Hanoi.[228] A month later, House Minority Leader Gerald Ford traveled to Peking. Following his trip, Ford announced that he was "convinced" that China did not want an American withdrawal from the Pacific following Vietnam. Chou quickly denied Ford's statement, asserting that he had complained to Ford that while the U.S. was withdrawing from Vietnam, it was strengthening its forces in Thailand and its navy off Indochina.[229] Nonetheless, Chou had made a fundamental admission. As far as he was concerned, the United States was in fact leaving Vietnam.

With the changed Chinese perspective on world affairs in general and Vietnam in particular, it would not have been at all surprising if there was more fact than fiction in Ford's statement. By the fall of 1972, Soviet-Chinese relations had deteriorated so much that in its National Day editorial on October 1 *People's Daily* described the Soviet Union as "even more deceitful than old-line imperialist countries, and therefore even more dangerous." A month earlier, the Peking media argued that China had to "ally with and struggle against" those who opposed the "main imperialist enemy."[230] Viewed in light of Chinese policy, the implication was that the Soviet Union was the "main imperialist enemy." With Soviet military might expanding, and with the United States retrenching following its foreseen withdrawal from Vietnam, Chou may well have wanted to signal that a precipitous withdrawal from the Pacific would serve neither Peking's interest not Washington's interest.

Vietnam itself, however, was another story. Ever since July 1971, China had advocated a negotiated settlement in Vietnam. This settlement, to China, had to include an American acceptance of the Seven Point Proposal of the PRG, an end to all aggressive action, and withdrawal of American troops from Vietnam.[231] Consequently, it surprised no one that China lauded the news from Paris that an agreement was imminent. When the "false peace" of October fell through, the Chinese response was a mixture of anger and hope. The official government statement issued on October 31 criticized the United States for not signing the accord, and argued that the United States must "keep its promise" and "sign the accord" or "accept all the consequences."[232] Less than a month later, on November 29, Chinese Foreign Minister Chi Peng-fei made an "important statement" in which he posited his government still hoped that the United States would "through negotiations sign the agreement."[233] The American assertion that the agreement had fallen through because of Thieu's opposition, *People's Daily* maintained, was "ridiculous."[234]

While China reacted to the false peace with relative equanimity it clearly was not pleased. Much the same may be said for its response to the December bombing raids. The Chinese Foreign Ministry condemned the massive bombings as "barbarous crimes"[235] and in Peking, the first anti-American rally in over a year was held.[236] The P.R.C. privately informed Washington that no negotiations would take place while the bombings continued, and one unidentified U.S. official declared that Sino-American relations were "frozen as hard as before the President went to China."[237] Nonetheless, the Chinese response was the minimum support that China could be expected to tender the D.R.V. in the light of the American escalation. The public condemnations were severe but well within the past pattern of Chinese response. The Peking rally was an isolated incident, and the halt in negotiations was communicated privately. Indeed, following the first day of bombing, the Chinese foreign minister cautioned merely that the bombing "threatened to wreck a peace agreement which is close at hand."[238]

The conclusion of the peace agreement in late January was greeted in Peking with an audible sigh of relief. The agreement was termed a "great victory" for the Vietnamese people. The P.R.C. believed the struggle had entered a "new stage," implying the time for military conflict had passed and protracted political struggle had come.[239] This,

of course, was in keeping with Peking's strategic interest of reducing potential areas of conflict with the United States. Once again, the Chinese
Foreign Minister made the Chinese position clear. The agreement, Chi
said, was "not only in conformity with the interests of the Vietnamese
and American people," but also was "conducive to the relaxation of tension in the Far East and Asia."[240]

By early 1973, then, the United States' active involvement in
Vietnam was officially at an end. There was no evidence to suggest that
the policy-making elite in Washington, however, had altered its objective of maintaining the Saigon regime as a juridically independent
government. Rather, domestic and international pressures had convinced the U.S. leadership, and Richard Nixon in particular, that American
participation in the conflict was no longer politically feasible. The outcry over the December bombing and the questionable success of that
bombing had been Nixon's last major card. Support for the South Vietnamese was still a mandatory tenet of American policy toward Vietnam
since independence for the Thieu regime remained the objective, but
neither American ground capabilities nor air power could be directly
applied. United States support for the Thieu regime consequently rested
on supplies and diplomacy.

Meanwhile, in Moscow, the Soviet leadership was pleased by the
conclusion of overt American involvement, but not convinced that the
agreement signaled a legitimate change in U.S. objectives in Indochina.
The agreement removed a potential obstacle for the development of
Soviet-American détente, but again, from Moscow's perspective, the
changing international correlation of forces had "forced" Washington
into its course of action. Washington's objectives had not changed, only
its ability to carry them out.

Peking's leaders were probably the most pleased by the
agreement. The Mao-Chou line on foreign policy had been vindicated,
and with the conclusion of the ceasefire, one of the last major stumbling
blocks in Sino-American relations had been removed. China clearly
believed that now the United States could pay more attention to its other
commitments throughout the world, thereby forcing the Soviet Union to
follow suit and reducing the Kremlin's freedom to act against the P.R.C.
In Indochina itself, the Peking leadership believed that by the beginning
of 1973 the United States had moved from an offensive to a defensive
posture, and of its own volition. Doubtless, none of the leaders of the
three powers believed that the peace agreement meant the end of the
military struggle in Vietnam, but all realized they could now afford to
devote less public comment and concern to it. The American war had
ended, and the ceasefire war was about to begin.

# VI

# The Ceasefire War

Following the signing of the 1973 peace agreement, the conflict in Vietnam lost much of its immediacy and newsworthiness. The American public had long wanted to forget the war, and the agreement provided it with such an opportunity. To the Nixon administration, the war had become a political liability. The peace agreement offered a method through which Washington could maintain that its war objectives had been successfully attained. Much the same was true as far as both the Soviet and Chinese governments were concerned. With both nations seeking accommodations with the United States, the vaguely worded peace agreement removed a major area of long-standing contention that jeopardized improved relations and at the same time permitted them to claim a "victory" for the D.R.V.-PRG side. As far as the three major powers were concerned, then, the agreement provided convincing proof that the war had ended. The Vietnamese War, the war that everyone wanted to forget, was relegated to the background.

A number of observers adopted a more cynical view. To the cynics, the agreement was simply a face-saving device under which the United States could proclaim that it had achieved its objectives, thereby permitting it to withdraw from Vietnam. After a "decent interval" of peace, fighting would resume between the PLAF and ARVN. Estimates of the length of the expected pause in fighting ranged from a few months to a year or longer.[1]

The ceasefire itself was to take effect at 8 a.m. Saigon time, January 28. In the several days immediately preceding the ceasefire, the People's Liberation Armed Forces launched an extensive final offensive designed to expand the area under its control before the ceasefire took effect. Saigon's armed forces counter-attacked, and the ensuing fighting continued past the ceasefire deadline.[2] In many instances, Saigon's military effort after the ceasefire was directed not only against hamlets captured by the PLAF immediately before the ceasefire, but also against hamlets long held by the PRG.[3]

The Vietnamese ceasefire consequently had a greater impact outside Vietnam than in the unfortunate nation itself. In fact, the conflict still raged. According to one prominent observer, the ceasefire war could be divided into three distinct periods.[4] The first period extended throughout 1973, and was characterized by ARVN units moving against smaller PLAF concentrations. This period of "nibbling operations" was intended to gradually reduce the size of the territory controlled by the Provisional Revolutionary Government. The second period opened on January 4, 1974 when Thieu called on Saigon's forces to attack the PRG concentrations "in their base areas." This period ended in late March, 1974. On March 22, North Vietnam called on the PRG to "regain its lost territory." The third period covered the time from this North Vietnamese appeal to the fall of South Vietnam.

Why did the war continue even after the ceasefire and peace agreement? While there is no simple and definitive answer to this question, at least part of the explanation centers on the Nixon administration's view of the ongoing conflict. Even though the United States had officially terminated its involvement in the war on the public level, it was still very much encouraging and supporting the military activities of the Thieu regime.

## Washington and the Ceasefire: Ignoring the Peace

Assessing blame for the continuation of hostilities past the ceasefire is a nearly impossible task, and requires accepting one piece of documented evidence and rejecting an equally documented piece. Both sides clearly violated the truce in numerous instances. The Saigon government clearly wished to frustrate the operation of the Joint Military Commissions provided for under the auspices of the Peace Agreement[5] and at the same time attempted to abrogate the concept of free movement of people the agreement promised. During the months immediately after the agreement was concluded, Saigon's propaganda units told the South Vietnamese people that the peace was "nothing more than a ceasefire in place, and the people are supposed to stay in place."[6] The ARVN military operations meanwhile increased in intensity. By the end of 1973, South Vietnam controlled 15 percent of the land and 779 hamlets which were under PRG control at the time of the ceasefire.[7]

Hanoi similarly saw fit to ignore provisions of the peace it found unfavorable. During the months immediately before the ceasefire, the North Vietnamese poured as many supplies and military personnel into the South as it could[8] and this infiltration continued after the ceasefire.[9] By the end of 1973, 184,000 North Vietnamese troops reportedly were in South Vietnam, 30,000 more than at the time of the ceasefire.[10] The reason for this infiltration was clear. According to one PRG source:

> this very "leopard skin" [of PRG base areas in South Vietnam surrounded by R.V.N. territory] must disappear within the shortest time. The existence of two zones ... is not intended to last indefinitely.
>
> ...As shown by the events since January 1973, the situation "half-war, half-peace" will be a backcloth for a multi-sided struggle on the ground in South Vietnam with its political, economic, and also its military aspects.[11]

The fundamental reason for the continued fighting in South Vietnam was thus that neither side accepted the legitimacy of the other. Despite the fact that the agreement recognized "two South Vietnamese parties" each with their own "areas of control," the parties themselves mutually rejected each other's legitimacy. The same primary cause of the Vietnamese War still existed, and the fighting went on.

The United States, for its part, adopted a position closely supporting that of the Thieu regime. Nixon made this clear in his January 23 address to the nation on Vietnam. In it Nixon promised that despite the provisions of the agreement, the United States would "continue to recognize the government of the Republic of Vietnam as the sole legitimate government of South Vietnam."[12]

With such encouragement from his ally and provider, it is understandable why Thieu felt he could ignore terms of the agreement which he disliked. American commentary on ARVN post-ceasefire operations provided the South Vietnamese President with additional encouragement. U.S. Secretary of Defense Elliot Richardson called the South Vietnamese post-ceasefire counter-attacks "encouraging"[13] and Kissinger gave his approval by asking, "After all, how are the two sides going to establish areas of control except by testing each other?"[14]

The United States did not limit its support for abrogation of the agreement to mere words. Despite the agreement provisions ending fighting in Laos and Cambodia, the United States continued air attacks into Cambodia through March. Additionally, the spirit if not the letter of the agreement was violated by the United States by bringing into Vietnam several thousand "civilians" to do jobs formerly done by military personnel. In many instances, these "civilians" were recently retired military personnel who arrived in South Vietnam just as the last American troops were being withdrawn.[15] At the same time, while direct military activity was decreasing, indirect activity was increasing. Air America, the CIA airline in Southeast Asia, increased the dollar value of its contracts from $17.7 million in 1972 to $41.4 million in 1973. Washington similarly made sure that Thieu's armed forces were well supplied and well equipped. Between October 1972 and January 1973, the United States shipped over $1.2 billion in arms to the Saigon government.

As if the public encouragements and continued high level of military support were not enough to convince Thieu that he could ignore the peace agreement with impunity and still be guaranteed Washington's backing, Nixon had privately assured Thieu that if North Vietnam violated the peace accord, the United States would "react very strongly and rapidly," take "swift and severe retaliatory action," and "respond with full force."[16] These vague though unmistakable promises of support, when viewed in conjunction with the other American statements and actions, undoubtedly convinced Thieu that he had carte blanche from Nixon to ignore provisions of the agreement unfavorable to or disliked by Saigon.

Nixon's private assurances to Thieu were lent additional credibility by public statements by Nixon and Kissinger during February and March. At a February 1 news conference held before his visit to Hanoi, Kissinger was asked what the American response would be if Saigon requested U.S. bombing support. The Secretary of State coyly responded that it would be "unwise for a responsible American official at this stage ... to give a checklist about what the U.S. will or will not do."[17] Nixon was much more forthright a month later. After minimizing the significance of the on-going fighting in the South and acknowledging that the continuing infiltration from the North to the South "could be simply replacement personnel," Nixon scarcely veiled his threat:

> Our concern [over the infiltration] has also been expressed to other interested parties and I would only suggest that based on my actions over the past four years, that the North Vietnamese should not lightly disregard such expressions of concern, when they are made, with regard to a violation.[18]

In subsequent weeks, administration "leaks" to the American press revealed that high level strategy sessions at the White House were discussing the possibility of U.S. air attacks on SAM sites, the PLAF base at Khe Sanh, and even renewed bombing and mining of the D.R.V.[19] As if to underline the sincerity of the "leaks," the United States stopped its mine clearing operations of North Vietnamese harbors and rivers on April 17 in response to the continued infiltration.

Through the first several months of 1973, then, American policy toward Vietnam was multifaceted. None of the facets indicated that American objectives in Vietnam had been substantially altered by the signing of the agreement. Rather, as far as Washington was concerned, the new political realities of the post-ceasefire period necessitated changed methods of operation. To the United States, South Vietnam had to remain an independent nation under the Thieu government. To achieve this, South Vietnamese forces needed to retain the military initiative. At the same time, North Vietnamese resupply and infiltration to the South had to be limited. All this had to be achieved without overt American military aid and without overwhelming the political fiction that peace had come to Vietnam. Consequently Nixon downplayed the level of fighting, tacitly supported Thieu's military policies, and warned the North Vietnamese that the United States would resume its involvement if the D.R.V. did not reduce its infiltration. In essence, then, Washington was attempting to permit Saigon's breaches of the agreement to continue while curtailing those of Hanoi.

This policy might have been successful but for the reduced credibility of American threats of reintervention. Hanoi had long believed that final victory would be achieved by victory on the political front in Washington, and from the spring of 1973 onward, this point of view became increasingly correct. The December 1972 bombing had undermined much of Nixon's own domestic political support, and there was almost no political support for a resumption of bombing. Indeed, on May 10, the House of Representatives voted to cut off funds for continued bombing of Cambodia. Ten days earlier, the Nixon White House was shattered by the forced resignations of two key members of the senior White House staff, H. R. Haldeman and John Ehrlichman. The revelations of Watergate increasingly reduced Nixon's political freedom of action from this time on. Thus, by mid-May, the threat of renewed bombing was simply not credible, primarily because of the President's relations with Congress and the specter of Watergate. With Congress voting on June 31 to end all bombing in Indochina and to prohibit future military operations there without Congressional approval, and with the House and Senate voting four months later to override Nixon's veto of the War Powers Act, possibilities for American action undertaken only on the initiative of the President were further reduced. Nixon's multifaceted Vietnam policy had consequently been rendered inoperative.

Events in Vietnam itself reflected this. While "nibbling operations" by the ARVN continued with some success throughout the year, by the fall, South Vietnam was rife with speculation that the PLAF would soon launch a major offensive. When fighting escalated in October following several PLAF attacks on ARVN camps, it was widely assumed that the offensive had begun.[20] Though the offensive never materialized, the fear of one remained, and was sufficient enough to influence Kissinger to present Le Duc Tho with a demand on December 20 that Hanoi suspend its impending offensive.[21]

If the military front presented little hope for peace, the same was true for the diplomatic front. On March 19, 1973, PRG and R.V.N. delegates met outside Paris at La Celle St. Cloud to begin negotiations on "internal South Vietnamese matters." The objective of these negotiations was to produce an agreement providing for election of a new government in South Vietnam which would then integrate the two zones of South Vietnam. By April 25, both sides had presented proposals that were totally unacceptable to the other. Saigon demanded the removal of all North Vietnamese troops and control over most aspects of the hypothetical electoral process, while the Provisional Revolutionary Government demanded a full ceasefire, the beginning of demobilization, and freedom of political propaganda. The political talks were deadlocked, and remained so until they were broken off for good in May 1974.

Meanwhile, in the United States, the political deadlock that had existed between the Legislative and the Executive branches was disintegrating as Watergate exacted an ever-increasing toll from the Nixon administration. The changing congressional-presidential power balance had tremendous impact on the ceasefire war, for it was often over the issue of the level of support to be extended to South Vietnam (as well as Cambodia) that Congress and Nixon fought. In 1973, Congressional opposition to Nixon as well as the Watergate affair itself had destroyed the credibility of Nixon's threats against North Vietnam. In the first half of 1974, the same two factors cast doubt on the continued viability of American support to Saigon.

During fiscal 1974 (July 1, 1973 to June 30, 1974), the United States budgeted $1.126 billion in military and economic aid to the Thieu government. On March 18, 1974, the Pentagon admitted that it had "miscalculated" and "overspent" in the first half of the fiscal year. According to the Pentagon, funds originally budgeted for South Vietnam would run out well before the end of the fiscal year, and operations of the South Vietnamese military would have to be "severely curtailed" by mid-April. Consequently the Pentagon, with Nixon's approval, requested $474 million in supplemental military aid appropriations for the remainder of the year. On April 4, the House of Representatives rejected the request, 177-154. Most observers termed the rejection "unexpected." Senator Barry Goldwater, long a supporter of administration policy, commented on his own change of heart in explaining his opposition to supplemental appropriations.

> For all intents and purposes, we can scratch Vietnam. I think it's evident that the South will fall into the hands of ... North [Vietnam].[22]

The change of heart in Congress was made even more apparent in the debate over aid to South Vietnam contained in the budget for fiscal 1975. The original budget requested $1.5 billion in aid to Saigon. Secretary of Defense James Schlesinger argued for it, maintaining that "if we continue to give them support and they fail to survive, that's a different issue than pulling the support out from under them."[23] Congress was not convinced. On May 22, the House accepted a $1.126 billion ceiling for aid, the same level as in the preceding fiscal year. In essence, with inflation, this figure represented a decrease. The Senate version of the same bill, passed on June 11, was even less generous, extending only $900 million in military aid. A bill sponsored by Senator Edward M. Kennedy that would have limited aid to $750 million was defeated by one vote, 46-45.[24] The compromise bill set a ceiling of $1 billion on military aid to South Vietnam for fiscal 1975. On August 5, in one of his final acts as President, Nixon signed the bill with "certain reservations."[25] After Nixon's resignation, erosion of support for high levels of aid accelerated. On September 23 and 24, the House and Senate respectively passed bills setting defense appropriations for Vietnam for fiscal 1975 at $700 million.[26] In addition, Saigon was to receive $450 million in economic aid and $125 million in food. Beleaguered Cambodia received only $377 million in total aid, $275 million of which was military aid. (Gerald Ford, now President, had requested $551 million in total aid for Cambodia.)[27] In December, the assault on high levels of aid to South Vietnam continued when it was proposed that military aid to South Vietnam be transferred from the sacrosanct Department of Defense budget to the highly vulnerable foreign aid budget by mid-1976.

The difficulties encountered by the aid requests should not be interpreted to imply that official U.S. government policy toward Vietnam had changed. Rather, the executive branch was no longer capable of following its preferred course of action. Even the August 8 change of administration in Washington did little to alter preferred American policy. In his August 12 address to a joint session of Congress, Ford asserted that he was "determined to see the observance of the Paris Agreement on Vietnam."[28] By this time, however, there was little possibility of that.

The change in administrations if anything strengthened the resolve of the D.R.V. and the PRG to fight on. Generally speaking, Ford was considered "a political lightweight" in Asia.[29] Radio Hanoi declared that Ford must "prove" he was different from the departed Nixon, who had committed "countless ... horrible crimes" in Indochina.[30] The D.R.V. leadership simply expected "more of the same" from Ford.[31]

There were indications, moreover, that Hanoi fully intended to take advantage of the Legislative-Executive confrontation and the turmoil of Watergate. In early August, PLAF units attacked ARVN posts near Danang, and American officials in Vietnam reported that North Vietnam alerted its troops in South Vietnam as well as six home divisions on August 7-8. Following the alert, speculation rose that communist forces were finally about to launch the long awaited offensive. According to some sources, 4000 trucks, tanks, and artillery pieces had been moved to forward positions during the alert, and a total of 650,000 troops had been placed at combat readiness.[32]

Indeed, according to one prominent observer in Hanoi, the D.R.V. leadership believed an "entirely new political situation" had evolved in South Vietnam. Nixon's resignation, the economic crisis in the United States, the uncertainty of the new Ford administration, and the deteriorating political, economic, and military situations in South Vietnam had combined to make the Thieu regime "increasingly unstable."[33]

The situation in South Vietnam had in fact deteriorated. An authoritative *Foreign Affairs* article declared that

> In the 23 months since the ceasefire, it has become clear that all three American achievements in South Vietnam — political, economic, and military — have begun to erode and are now in danger.[34]

Political unrest in South Vietnam had grown throughout 1974, starting on January 19 when Thieu arranged for the National Assembly to vote through a constitutional amendment permitting him to run for a third time. Throughout 1974, political liberties were increasingly repressed, particularly after anti-Thieu demonstrations broke out in South Vietnam's larger cities during September and October.[35]

The nation's economic problems heightened its political instability. The South Vietnamese economy, long dependent on foreign aid for sustenance, could not survive the twin shocks of reduced U.S. economic assistance and the withdrawal of a half million American troops without contracting tremendously. Unemployment and inflation ran rampant during 1974.

Militarily, from May onward, D.R.V.-PLAF forces had been on the offensive. In late March, Hanoi called on the PLAF to liberate territories it had lost to the Saigon government, and by late summer, the border areas near Cambodia, Laos, and the demilitarized zone were all once again under PRG control.[36] By the fall, the balance of military forces in the South had shifted to the PLAF as it developed both logistics areas and high-speed roads in its zone of control. During mid-December, fighting flared to the highest level since the Paris Agreement was signed.[37] In most of these encounters, ARVN forces were defeated.

The United States, aware of the dire straits the Thieu government was in, attempted to remedy the situation. The policy the Ford administration put forth was in many respects a reflection of that advocated by Nixon in earlier years. North Vietnam would be intimidated into ending aid to the PLAF/PRG, while at the same time massive quantities of aid would be injected to the South. Unfortunately for Ford, the factors that had frustrated Nixon were still operant. Threats had no credibility, and Congress questioned the wisdom of continued high levels of aid.

On January 11, 1975, the United States sent a note to the seven guarantors of the Peace Agreement — the Soviet Union, China, Great Britain, France, Hungary, Poland, and Indonesia — which stated that the upsurge in fighting reflected "a decision by Hanoi to seek once again to impose a military solution in Vietnam." The note warned that Hanoi must accept the full consequences of its actions.[38] Such a veiled threat was deemed insufficient. Three days later, on January 14, Schlesinger declared that despite the law barring a resumption of U.S. military activities in Indochina, a major North Vietnamese offensive could impel the President and Congress to "authorize the use of American force."[39] A week later, Ford commented that he did not foresee any circumstances in which the United States might reenter the Vietnamese War, but when asked whether he ruled out the possibility of a resumption of either bombing or naval action, he responded that it was not "appropriate for me to forecast any specific actions that might be taken."[40] Ford and his administration were trying to leave all options open, while at the same time attempting to restore the credibility of military intervention as a viable policy alternative.

This effort was rendered ineffective by Congressional reaction to Ford's January 28 request for an additional $522 million in supplementary military and economic assistance for South Vietnam and Cambodia, $300 million of which was for the Thieu regime. Making the request in a special message to Congress, Ford betrayed the seriousness of the South Vietnamese and Cambodian positions by declaring that with "adequate U.S. material assistance," the two countries could "hold their own." According to Ford, U.S. Ambassador to Saigon Graham Martin believed that with adequate assistance, "within two or three years, the South Vietnamese would be over the hump militarily."[41] Additionally, Ford's 1976 fiscal year budget requested $1.3 billion in military aid for South Vietnam.[42]

Congress responded with shock and disbelief. The Martin argument was the same one that had rationalized the preceding decade of American support for one Saigon regime after another. After some debate and delay, eight Congressmen finally left for the two Indochinese countries on February 24 to assess the need for the requested $522 million. The Congressmen left Southeast Asia on March 2, but supported only a $75 million grant to the two countries in emergency economic assistance.[43]

By this time, however, events in Vietnam were proceeding faster than the newly cumbersome American governmental bureaucracy could react to them. On March 5, the North Vietnamese launched a series of attacks in the Central Highlands and rapidly succeeded in cutting Route 19, going from Pleiku to the coast. On March 10, the U.S. Department of State revealed that 50,000 additional North Vietnamese troops had in-filtrated the South since January 15.[44] The long awaited offensive had begun.

The 1975 PLAF offensive as originally planned had rather limited objectives. Taking advantage of the deteriorating fabric of South Viet-nam society, the PLAF at first sought only to create stronger pressures for Thieu's removal by pushing the extent of PRG control and destroying parts of ARVN. A win-the-war offensive was envisioned for 1976.[45] The rapid and complete collapse of ARVN was totally unexpected.

On March 10, after five days of fighting, the central highlands capital of Ban Me Thuot capitulated. Thieu suddenly concluded that the remaining highlands provinces of Pleiku and Kontum were in-defensible, and ordered an unexpected strategic withdrawal from those provinces. At the same time, Thieu ordered a withdrawal from the nor-thern provinces of Quang Tri and Thau Thien. Although Thieu later told his forces to stand and fight for Hue, the rout had begun. The ARVN 1st Division refused to turn back to defend Hue, and poured pell-mell in-to Danang. Disorder and chaos swept the city as the soldiers' terror in-fected the city's population. On March 30, PLAF troops captured Danang without a fight.[46]

The rout continued down the coast. One province after another fell as the joint D.R.V.-PLAF forces swept southward. Phu Cat, Tuy An, Ninh Hao, Dalat, Phan Rang, and Phan Thiet were under their control by April 2. With two-thirds of the country lost, ARVN had disintegrated as an effective fighting force and Saigon itself appeared virtually indefen-sible.

What had happened to ARVN? After the years of American training and billions of dollars of expenditures, why had the South Viet-namese army disintegrated so rapidly and completely? The reasons are numerous, and of course cannot be viewed individually. However, in retrospect, it is evident that ARVN had become both psychologically and militarily dependent on American air power to extricate it from difficult situations — and now that air power could not be employed. Ad-ditionally, ARVN morale was nonexistent. According to the United States defense attaché's office, ARVN pay was inadequate to provide basic necessities of life for the soldiers' families, and this had led to a "deterioration of performance, which cannot be permitted … if [ARVN] is to be considered a viable military force."[47] Throughout 1974, low morale led to desertion or defection. In one instance, a 600-man bat-talion of local militiamen reassigned to the regional forces was reduced to three men after a few weeks in the field.[48]

President Thieu had yet another explanation for the demise of ARVN as an effective fighting force. According to Thieu, reductions in

American aid had undermined South Vietnam's armed forces. On April 4, Thieu condemned the United States for its decreased aid commitment, declaring that the United States was earning for itself the "label of traitor."[49] Thieu claimed that decreased American aid had "seriously affected the morale of our troops as well as the faith of the Vietnamese people in American promises."

The Ford administration, to a great degree, agreed with Thieu. On March 20, Ford himself maintained that uncertainty about continued U.S. aid had caused the ARVN pullback. Secretary of Defense Schlesinger castigated Congress' "niggardly" approach to aid for South Vietnam the same day.[50] Kissinger added his voice to the cry on March 26, asking whether the U.S. would "deliberately destroy an ally by witholding aid from it in its moment of extremity."[51] Other statements by Ford and Kissinger in early April reaffirmed their position, although neither explicitly blamed Congress for the aid reduction.[52] Finally, on April 15, Kissinger appeared before the Senate Appropriations Committee and argued that the reduction of U.S. aid not only led to the dire situation in South Vietnam, but also contributed to the wave of anti-Americanism in the country.[53]

With both Ford and Kissinger arguing that the South Vietnamese debacle was directly related to reduced aid, it was not surprising that Ford turned to Congress to demand additional infusions of U.S. military arms and equipment. On April 10, Ford asked "Congress and the nation" for $972 million in military and humanitarian aid for the Saigon government. To give South Vietnam a chance "to save itself," $722 million was requested for military aid; $250 million was requested for economic and humanitarian aid. Although Ford declared that Indochinese events had to be kept "in perspective," half of his speech was devoted to Indochina.[54]

Congressional reaction to Ford's request was negative. Senator Henry Jackson simply stated, "It's dead. I oppose it." John McClellan, chairman of the Senate Appropriations Committee, observed that the aid even if granted was "too late to do any good." Senator Mark Hatfield criticized Ford directly, saying he was "appalled that a man could continue in such a bankrupt policy."[55]

Such opposition to Ford's aid proposal was not surprising. During the preceding month, the House Democratic Caucus rejected 189-49 Ford's earlier request for supplemental aid for South Vietnam and Cambodia. The following day, March 13, the Senate Democrats went on record against supplementary aid to Cambodia by a 38-5 vote and to South Vietnam by a 35-6 vote.[56]

If there was little likelihood that Congress would accept his aid proposal, why then did Ford make the attempt? At least two answers are probable, and one extends beyond the immediate context of Vietnam. In the first place, the effort to secure aid may well have been intended to secure Thieu's cooperation in withdrawing American citizens remaining in South Vietnam. If no effort to obtain additional aid had been made, Thieu could have rendered such an evacuation nearly impossible. While the effort for more aid did not guarantee his acquiescence, it at least removed a potential rationale for his opposition to a withdrawal.

Second, and perhaps more importantly, Ford's aid request was made despite its certain rejection by Congress because Ford wished to maintain the appearance that the United States executive wanted to act but was being constrained solely by Congress. This was clearly intended for consumption in the capitals of American allies and enemies. In the week before the April 10 request, maintaining the credibility of America's other overseas commitments was often on Ford's mind. On April 3, the President declared,

> I specifically warn any adversary they should not, under any circumstances, feel that the tragedy of Vietnam is an indication that the American people have lost their will or desire to stand up for freedom any place in the world.[57]

Shortly thereafter, in a note sent to Hanoi in early April and released on April 11, Washington warned Hanoi that unless it "reversed its present military course, it should have no doubt that it [would] be held responsible for the consequences."[58] The note was clearly a piece of rhetoric, but by this time its purpose was less to intimidate Hanoi than to reassure American allies. Indeed, according to some State Department sources, Kissinger already considered a North Vietnamese military victory inevitable.[59] The Ford administration's primary concern, therefore, was to maintain the image of the United States as a good ally until the final collapse.

Why did the United States not support a political settlement to avert the final collapse? Again, two reasons are evident. On April 1 and again on April 2, the PRG had offered to negotiate on the basis of the Paris Agreement with any government that excluded Thieu and renounced an extreme anticommunist position.[60] The United States, however, refused to pressure Thieu into resigning.[61] Any effort to pressure Thieu had to be initiated by the Ford administration itself. If such an effort were made, then the on-going attempt to blame Congress for South Vietnam's predicament would have been thrown open to further question since it could then be argued that Ford and Kissinger themselves had abandoned Thieu. The effort to maintain the image of the United States as a reliable ally consequently precluded pressures to get Thieu to step down. Thieu's continued ascendancy, in turn, precluded a political settlement.

In the second place, there is considerable room for doubt over the sincerity of the PRG offer. While some sources argued that the PLAF scaled down its military activity after Thieu finally resigned on April 21, this in itself is no indication that the PRG would have accepted a political settlement if the resignation had come earlier. According to Radio Hanoi on March 31, events in South Vietnam had reached "a new turning point." On April 4, the PLAF ordered its units to prepare for a final assault on Saigon,[62] and the period between the PLAF order and Thieu's resignation was used to make the requisite preparations. With victory close at hand, there was no reason to assume that the PLAF would stop short of final success. When South Vietnam's final President Duong Van Minh offered to "hand over his administration" and surrender on April 29, he was told he could not "hand over what one does not control."[63] This was nearly as true in mid-April as in late April. From the perspective of the PRG there was no reason to seek a political settlement. The probability was, then, that the PRG offer of a political settlement was as much rhetoric as were Ford's veiled threats and promises of aid.

Nonetheless, in Washington, debate over the question of Ford's request for $972 million in aid continued. Sidestepping a final vote on the request, Congress instead contemplated a $200 million "contingency" fund and a $327 million evacuation and humanitarian relief bill. The White House itself opposed the contingency fund as inadequate, while on April 17 the House International Relations Committee accepted the relief bill provided the funds were channeled through international organizations and not Saigon. The Senate Armed Services Committee rejected a $215 million military aid bill for Saigon the same day.

Meanwhile, Ford and Kissinger still argued for supplemental aid. On April 16, the President addressed the American Society of Newspaper Editors and told them he was "convinced" that if the $722 million military aid package was approved, South Vietnam could stabilize the situation.[64] Two days later Kissinger appeared before the House Committee on International Relations and presented a less optimistic picture. According to the Secretary of State, the military situation was "very grim." Additional promise of military aid was simply "bargaining chips" in negotiations for a "humane transition of power" in Saigon, Kissinger informed his listeners. Even if the funds were voted, Kissinger could offer "no assurance" that the situation in South Vietnam could be saved.[65] Despite Ford's appeal, Kissinger's theorizing, and the worsening situation throughout Indochina (on April 16, the government of Cambodia surrendered to the Khmer Rouge forces), Congress refused to be swayed. On April 22, the House Armed Services Committee refused Ford's request for military aid to South Vietnam, 21-17.

The United States' involvement in the Vietnamese War was

finally, for all practical purposes, at an end. Ford realized this. Speaking at Tulane University the day after the Armed Services Committee's vote, the President urged Americans to "regain the sense of pride that existed before Vietnam." That pride could be regained, he emphasized, but not by "refighting a war that is finished — as far as America is concerned."[66] Later that night, at 2:40 a.m., April 24, the House accepted a bill authorizing $327 million for humanitarian aid and evacuation. For the United States, the war had truly ended.

Events in Vietnam proceeded rapidly. On April 21, Thieu finally resigned. His long time supporter, Tran Van Huong, succeeded to the Presidency. This, however, was insufficient for the PRG, which demanded that the United States abandon "the Thieu clique and not just the person of Nguyen Van Thieu."[67] On April 28, General Duong Van Minh replaced Tran Van Huong. The following day, he ordered South Vietnamese troops to end their resistance, and on April 30, the South Vietnamese government surrendered. Finally, for Vietnam, the decades of war had ended.

Repercussions of the collapse of South Vietnam continued well after the final fall. American foreign policy for some time after the surrender reflected the major consideration that had determined U.S. policy toward Vietnam during the last few months of Saigon's independence — the effort to maintain America's credibility as a reliable ally. Indeed, events surrounding the famed *Mayagüez* ship-seizure incident of May 12-15 suggests that the United States was more concerned with restoring its reputation than in obtaining release of the ship and its crew. This, however, was understandable. Throughout Southeast Asia, erstwhile American allies were reexamining their defense alliances with the United States in light of the fall of both South Vietnam and Cambodia. On May 17, the government of Thailand announced an immediate review of "all aspects of cooperation and commitments between the United States and Thailand," and set March 1976 as the deadline for the final withdrawal of the remaining 23,000 U.S. servicemen in Thailand.[68] Even more disturbing, from Washington's point of view, was the April 12 announcement from the Philippine government that it was "reassessing" its defense agreements with the United States in light of Washington's "apparent new perception" of its commitments. Four days later, President Ferdinand Marcos of the Philippines reiterated this position. According to Marcos, the "balance of quadrilateral power in Asia between the United States, China, the Soviet Union, and Japan has been disturbed" by events in Indochina.[69] The Philippine "reassessment" included both Clark Air Base and Subic Naval Base.

These and other similar occurrences served to validate Washington's belief that its credibility needed shoring. Without condoning the events surrounding the *Mayagüez* incident, it is easy to see why Ford felt he must act. Washington did not confine itself to military action or statements of continued support for alliances in its effort to shore up its image. It also resorted to questioning the veracity and conduct of both the Soviet Union and China.

On April 16, Ford argued that one reason North Vietnam and the Provisional Revolutionary Government were nearing victory was because the Soviet Union and China had "maintained their commitment," whereas the United States "had not."[70] The following day, Kissinger warned that the U.S. would "not forget who supplied the arms which North Vietnam used to make a mockery of its signature on the Paris accords."[71] Earlier, in mid-March, the Ford administration claimed that the Soviet Union and China had poured up to $1.7 billion of military aid into North Vietnam in 1974 alone.[72]

How true were these revelations? Assessments based on a number of sources throw doubt on the claims of massive quantities of new aid. Two independent sources claimed that there had been no substantial increase in Soviet or Chinese military aid in 1973 and 1974, and that the buildup of equipment in South Vietnam which preceded the final offensive was based on supplies that were in North Vietnam before the 1973 ceasefire went into effect.[73] During his trips to Moscow and Peking in 1972, Kissinger had received assurances in both capitals that aid shipments to the D.R.V. would be reduced following an agreement.[74] Ambassador Graham Martin and the Defense Intelligence Agency both confirmed that the communist countries had followed their promises during 1973 and were "not resupplying [the D.R.V.] with massive weapons of war."[75] The Defense Intelligence Agency dealt in dollar figures. In 1972, the Agency reported, the D.R.V. had received $600 million in arms aid from its allies. In 1973, the figure had plummeted to $290 million.[76] During 1974, according to an assessment of American and foreign estimates of Soviet and Chinese aid that the D.R.V. carried in *Far Eastern Economic Review*, Communist military aid to the D.R.V. had dropped still further to $200 million. Economic aid for 1974 had meanwhile reached only $1.2 billion, half the 1973 figure.[77] On the weight of available evidence, then, it is reasonable to argue that Washington's claims of stepped-up Soviet and Chinese aid were primarily intended to place the blame for Saigon's collapse on Soviet and Chinese shoulders rather than on American unreliability.

American unreliability, Ford well knew, was not the product of his own uncertainty or a change in policy. As previously seen, ever since becoming president, Ford had supported higher aid levels to Vietnam than Congress had been willing to approve. Congressional opposition, again as we have seen, was not a function of the Ford presidency alone, but stemmed directly from the Watergate affair itself. As Henry Kissinger candidly explained at his April 29 news conference when asked to discuss the cause of South Vietnam's demise, the reasons were several, but paramount was "the weakening of executive authority in the United States for reasons unconnected with foreign policy considerations."[78] Policy had not changed and neither had perceptions. Rather, ability to implement the same policy based on the constant perception had changed, and that, for Saigon, was fatal.

## The Kremlin's Double Vision

When the January 1973 peace agreement was finally signed, Washington's policy-makers were not the only national leaders who breathed a sigh of relief. Brezhnev and other members of the Soviet hierarchy had been faced with the difficult task of explaining why relations with the United States could be improved while at the same time the U.S. bombed a fraternal socialist nation. Even for a politician as skilled as Brezhnev, explaining the apparent contradiction was a formidable task, and there are indications that the Soviet leader and his supporters faced opposition within the Politburo itself on this issue. It may well be argued that the April 1973 Politburo reshuffling was precipitated by disagreement over policy toward the United States.[79]

To Brezhnev, then, the peace agreement was welcome. In the months following the signing, the Soviet media maintained both that the end of the war abetted détente, and that détente abetted the end of the war. Brezhnev himself wrote Nixon on February 21, informing the American President that the accord opened "new possibilities" for improved Soviet-American relations.[80] The authoritative *Kommunist* carried an Arbatov article which followed the General Secretary's line. According to Arbatov, the Vietnamese conflict had "prevented the normalization of the international situation," but since the war was now over, "improvements" in Soviet-American relations could take place.[81] Other Soviet spokesmen reiterated this point throughout 1973.[82]

On other occasions, however, Soviet officials argued that détente itself had led to the end of the war.[83] The most pronounced instance of this perspective appeared in Soviet Foreign Minister Gromyko's September 24, 1974 address to the United Nations. In his address, Gromyko told his listeners that peace had come to Vietnam because of détente.[84] Other sources attributed the peace to the "struggle for a better international climate"; in other words, détente.[85]

The different post-ceasefire Soviet perspectives on the relationship between détente and the peace agreement are of limited significance other than to underline the Kremlin's sizable interest in seeing the war ended. Indeed, Soviet coverage of Vietnamese events fell off sharply following the signing of the accord, particularly in the major Soviet journals. *Kommunist, Novaia Vremiia, Mezhdunarodnaia Zhizn',  Mirovaia Ekonomika i Mezhdunarodnaia Otnosheniia,* and other prominent periodicals all significantly reduced their commentary on Vietnam. In Arbatov's February *Kommunist* article discussing the 1972 world situation and the impact of détente, Vietnam was scarcely mentioned.[86] In his 1973 May Day address, Brezhnev himself completely ignored the Indochinese wars.[87] Even when the conflict was mentioned, it was more often than not relegated to the past tense.[88]

Soviet aid to North Vietnam, according to Western sources,[89] also dropped during 1973 and 1974, making it clear that the statements emanating from Moscow were more than mere rhetoric. It served the Kremlin's purposes to have the war over, and as far as was practicable, Moscow sought to propagate the fiction of a Vietnamese peace.

The Soviet leadership was well aware, however, that the Vietnamese peace was little more than a convenient cover for continued conflict. During his May 5-9, 1973, trip to Moscow, the U.S. Secretary of State Kissinger had "long discussions" with Brezhnev on reported violations of the Paris Accord. Meanwhile, throughout 1973 and 1974, the Soviet media and Kremlin leadership condemned South Vietnamese breaches of the terms of the accord, often going so far as to state that the United States supported South Vietnamese policy. Rarely, however, was the United States itself directly condemned. The August 11, 1973, issue of *Pravda* provided an excellent example of Soviet deference. *Pravda* noted that the United States had ceased its military operations and had withdrawn its troops in compliance with the accord, but observed that the U.S. had neither completed the minesweeping operations or begun providing development assistance to the D.R.V. as provided under the terms of the Paris Agreement. The Russian paper condemned the Thieu regime for on-going military operations, and then obtusely asked, "Are not such activities being supported and encouraged from outside by the most shameless international imperialist circles?" The reference, clearly, was to the United States. Just as clearly, on the other hand, Moscow was seeking to minimize the publicity it gave to Washington's support for continued ARVN activity.[90]

What accounted for the Soviet "cognitive dissonance?" In the first place, the Soviet leadership could not readily acknowledge that the ceasefire was a sham. If the Kremlin had made this acknowledgment, Brezhnev's policy of détente would have been once again subject to skeptical scrutiny. At the same time, however, Moscow was faced with the problem of extending support to the D.R.V. This presented a sticky

problem. Enough diplomatic and material support had to be extended so
that the North Vietnamese could not accuse the Soviet Union of abandoning a fraternal ally in the Kremlin's pursuit of détente, but at the
same time, too much diplomatic and material support may have endangered détente itself. To surmount these problems, the Kremlin tried
to find a middle ground: extend aid, but not too much; render criticism,
but keep it veiled.

In the second place, the Kremlin hierarchy undoubtedly
recognized that while improved relations with the United States presented great opportunities for change in international affairs, not all those
opportunities were favorable for the Soviet Union. Throughout 1973,
the Soviet media cautioned that though the United States had "failed to
attain any of its objectives" in Vietnam, the "end" of the Vietnamese war
and the "beginning" of improved Soviet-American relations did not
signify "the end of the world struggle against imperialism."[91] Soviet
allusions to continued U.S. involvement coupled with praises for peace
in Vietnam may thus have signified an effort to instill a degree of caution
into the more optimistic.

Finally, the apparent contradiction between public Soviet claims
that the war was over and Moscow's realization that it actually continued may have been attributable to the fact that the Soviet leadership was no longer sure what course American policy would take. Had
there been fundamental change in American foreign policy as seen from
the Kremlin? Evidence suggests that there was no consensus on the answer to that question in Moscow itself during 1973 and much of 1974.

Proponents of the view that American policy had not changed
pointed to the "dreams" of "monopolies and imperialists" of penetrating
Indochinese economies under the guise of "rehabilitation."[92] Other
authors pointed to continued U.S. support for Thieu in Vietnam and
Lon Nol in Cambodia as proof that Washington's policy was still
neocolonialistic. The Pentagon's early October 1973 announcement that
the withdrawal of American Air Force units from Thailand had been
suspended fit within this interpretation.[93] Even "triangular
diplomacy"—the Soviet terminology for American overtures to
Peking—was interpreted in light of the presupposition of unchanged
policy. American overtures to Peking stemmed from Washington's
reassessment of Mao's unwillingness to use military force to counter U.S.
initiatives in South and Southeast Asia, and on the American desire to
trade with the P.R.C., at least as far as one Soviet author was concerned.[94]

This traditional Soviet view of U.S. policy was challenged by a
much less doctrinaire supposition which recognized fundamental
changes in U.S. policy and at the same time cautioned against continued

imperialism. According to this school of thought, certain American leaders — and one would have to assume Nixon himself was included — had realized that many "far-reaching social-economic changes" were taking place in the world, and that the United States was both losing its preeminence in the capitalist world and its competition with the socialist world.[95] This on-going "change in the balance of power on the international scene in favor of socialism" had consequently prompted "U.S. ruling circles to take a fresh look at their foreign policy strategy."[96] Even more strikingly, according to one *International Affairs* article, "it may thus be concluded that the U.S. ruling circles are actively adapting their policy to the changing international situation."[97] American foreign policy was still "adventuresome," but it was changing. True, it was being forced to change, but at least as far as one school of Soviet thought was concerned, the change was real.

Not surprisingly, the pro-change proponents pointed to American domestic developments to support their arguments. Georgi Arbatov maintained that the "upsurge of mass democratic movements" in the United States during the late 1960s and early 1970s played a major role in ending the Vietnamese war and altering U.S. foreign policy as a whole.[98] Even more significance was attached to the wave of congressional activity during 1973 and 1974 limiting U.S. support for Thieu. By implication, *Pravda* practically admitted that congressional constraints on presidential action were fundamentally altering U.S. policy toward Vietnam even if Nixon himself preferred not to:

> The legislative actions of Congress and the public statements of Senators and Congressmen indicate that sentiments in favor of the U.S.A.'s noninvolvement in new military conflicts abroad, in favor of a cutback in American military commitments overseas and, on the contrary, the expansion of domestic social and economic programs are growing stronger in Congress and throughout the country. Congress has passed a law ending the financing of U.S. military operations in Indochina. A law has been passed that provides for restrictions on the President's power in the use of American armed forces abroad.[99]

The following August when Congress limited military appropriations to Saigon to $700 million the Kremlin appropriately observed that the President and the Pentagon no longer had license to determine policy by themselves.[100]

Nonetheless, the debate still raged in Soviet circles: had American policy toward Vietnam in fact changed, or had it once again adopted a more subtle stance? While there was no immediate answer to that question in the Kremlin, it was evident that Moscow itself was still seeking to maintain its appearance as a trusted ally of North Vietnam and the Provisional Revolutionary Government. Throughout 1973, on almost a monthly basis, D.R.V. and PRG dignitaries traveled to Moscow to negotiate aid agreements or discuss problems. In April, Pham Van Dong visited Moscow. Two months later, Le Duc Tho went to the Soviet capital. In July, a reconstruction agreement was initialed. Another D.R.V. delegation visited Moscow shortly thereafter. In August, Le Duan and Pham Van Dong met respectively with Brezhnev and Kosygin. In November, Pham Van Dong was again in Moscow. Finally, in December, both Le Duc Tho and NLFSV Chairman Nguyen Huu Tho visited the Kremlin. There could be no doubt that close relations were being maintained.

At the same time, however, the outcomes of the numerous visits appeared somewhat contradictory, not entirely unlike the previously examined Soviet attitude toward the "sham peace" and "real war." On the one hand, Brezhnev on at least two occasions supported the PRG and NLFSV as "the only genuine spokesmen for the aspirations of the South Vietnamese population."[101] The Russians may thus be seen as encouraging the PRG in the South. On the other hand, communiqués and agreements during the various visits often specifically referred to the need to develop socialism in the D.R.V.[102] The Russians may thus be seen as restricting their aid to the North.

What accounts for this seeming paradox? The most probable explanation was that the Russians once again found themselves caught in the midst of the détente dilemma. If no support was extended to the PRG, then Moscow would have been a "traitor" to the cause. Were too much unrestricted aid delivered to the North, then some undoubtedly would have been funneled South, thereby again jeopardizing détente. The solution? Extend a modicum of support to both sides of the demilitarized zone — limited and restricted material aid to the North, and limited diplomatic support to the PRG.

The D.R.V.'s leaders realized what Moscow's tactics were, and protested vehemently. Throughout 1973, as ARVN forces, in their "nibbling operations," attacked PRG-controlled areas in the South, the PLAF fought a defensive war. However, sometime during late 1973 and early 1974, the D.R.V.'s leaders confronted both the Soviets and the Chinese and told them that the PLAF would resume active and increased fighting unless they pressured the United States to stop interfering.[103] In the Soviet case, it is probable that Pham Van Dong and Le Duc Tho carried the unwelcome message to Moscow during their November and December, 1973 trips to the Soviet capital. It is similarly probable that Soviet (and Chinese) pressures on the United States were deemed either insufficient or nonexistent by the North Vietnamese. Within a month after the D.R.V.'s ultimatum to its allies became known in the West, Hanoi called on the PLAF to begin retaking the areas it had lost since the Paris agreement. The third and final stage of the ceasefire war had begun.

Throughout the remainder of 1974, the Soviet Union verbally supported the renewed PLAF activity. There were no public indications that Soviet support for the stepped-up activity included significant increases in Soviet material aid. On occasion, it was implied, however, that the Kremlin realized a turning point was approaching in Vietnamese affairs. For example, when Thieu reshuffled his government in October in order to quiet unrest in the areas under his government's control, *Pravda* commented on the reshuffling, the unrest, and the PLAF successes and declared that "the struggle of the population of the Saigon zone" for fulfillment of the accords was "passing through a qualitatively new period."[104] While the Soviet's "qualitatively new period" assessment may possibly be dismissed as rhetoric, it was impossible to dismiss the negotiations surrounding Soviet aid to the D.R.V. for 1975. In past years, annual Soviet aid agreements were concluded with the D.R.V. and PRG for fixed amounts during December. In early December 1974, both the D.R.V. and PRG again sent delegations to Moscow to negotiate agreements, respectively concluding them on December 8 and December 10.[105] In at least the D.R.V.'s case, however, the agreement remained open-ended, quite probably to await developments as the military situation evolved in the South.[106]

This is not to argue that the Soviet Union had suddenly come around to support increased PLAF activity in the South. Indeed not, for the same constraints operated on Soviet policy that had been extant since the signing of the Paris accord. Rather, the Soviet Union had concluded that the D.R.V.-PRG side would pressure Saigon regardless of Soviet policy, and was consequently moving once again to increase its options. The Kremlin realized the Thieu regime was in increasingly dire straits. The peace agreement was being "implemented" selectively, *International Affairs* announced. On the one hand, two of the most important provisions that had led to a "realization" of the peace were, "first and foremost," the cessation of U.S. "military operations against the D.R.V.," and secondly, the withdrawal of U.S. troops from South Vietnam. On the other hand, numerous other provisions were being ignored.[107] Other Soviet articles noted that unrest continued in South Vietnam, that the PLAF was steadily expanding the territory under its control, and that Thieu himself was doomed.[108] Shortly after the PLAF launched its highlands offensive, Moscow labeled the effort a "crucial turning point."[109]

For the most part Soviet coverage of the final offensive was straightforward and factual.[110] On occasion, however, the Kremlin sought to propagate the myth that the offensive stemmed from the South Vietnamese people themselves as they sought to "fight for their lives, their homes, their futures."[111] In almost every instance, the offensive was justified as a reaction to the "endless provocation by punitive expeditions from Saigon."[112] While the United States was from time to time castigated for "continued meddling," Soviet commentary on the United States involvement remained exceedingly low key.[113] In no small part, this was due to the American refusal to extend additional aid to Thieu. As far as the Kremlin was concerned, there was no reason to pique American sensibilities by hurling spurious claims.

During the last half of 1974, the school of Soviet thought arguing that genuine aspects of change had entered American foreign policy increasingly came to the fore. This was caused by the Kremlin's realization that congressional activism and the Watergate affair itself had practically immobilized the American executive branch.[114] Whereas in earlier eras Moscow had correctly observed that a U.S. president's request to Congress for additional aid to Indochinese clients as good as guaranteed the aid, this was no longer true by early 1975. A March *Pravda* article underlined just how far the Kremlin's thinking had evolved. While the Party paper cautioned that the Pentagon wanted to "land U.S. Marines in Cambodia," it stressed that if Congress did not approve Ford's $522 million aid request of January for Thieu and Lon Nol, then "these regimes will soon collapse." To *Pravda*, this was a distinct possibility since "many members of the U.S. Congress share the realistic appraisal" that both Thieu's and Lon Nol's defeats were "inevitable."[115] As the Saigon government's position deteriorated in March and April, this viewpoint solidified. "Rationally thinking Americans" wanted nothing more to do with Thieu since he had been "rejected by the people," one report noted,[116] while another "report from Washington" indicated that "the American public and the press [were] resolutely opposed to further military support for the Saigon regime."[117] *Pravda* sedately informed its readers that "broad segments of the American public, some representatives of the American press, and certain political circles" had a "realistic understanding of the situation" and wanted "total American noninvolvement."[118] The Kremlin clearly believed change had come to American foreign policy toward Vietnam, and even though that change was induced by factors beyond the control of the American chief executive, it was nonetheless real.

Soviet coverage of the collapse of South Vietnam was surprisingly restrained. In the days before Saigon's final surrender, the Soviet media factually reported Thieu's resignation, attributing it to "a widespread wave of indignation against the anti-popular policy of the regime he headed."[119] The Soviets waited until the PRG had rejected Thieu's successor Tran Van Huong as a legitimate spokesman for the government of South Vietnam before themselves denouncing the new government as "Thieu's administration without Thieu himself."[120] When Saigon finally surrendered, the Soviet Union simply launched the expected barrage of praise for the "heroic victory of the Vietnamese people."

Nonetheless, throughout the final stages of the offensive, the Soviet Union saw fit to minimize its own supportive role in the PLAF onslaught. *Pravda, Izvestiia,* and *Kasnaia Zvezda* rarely referred to Soviet aid to the D.R.V.-PRG side in their coverage of the fighting in the South, and much the same was true of the Soviet periodicals.[121] Even after the final surrender, Soviet leaders and media limited their comments on Soviet support. When Brezhnev, Kosygin, and Podgorny sent a congratulatory message of greeting to the NLFSV and PRG in early May, they merely observed that "the Soviet Union has invariably and firmly supported and will continue to support the patriots of South Vietnam and the Vietnamese peoples."[122]

The entire Soviet handling of the fall of Saigon was reminiscent of John Kennedy's instructions to his staff following Khrushchev's withdrawal from Cuba in 1962. In 1962, it was evident that the Soviet Premier had been embarrassed and even humiliated. Kennedy instructed his staff not to further Khrushchev's humiliation by proclaiming a major American success. In 1975, it was evident that the United States had been embarrassed and humiliated by South Vietnam's collapse. The Soviet Union evidently felt facts were clear enough, and attempted not to rub salt in the wound.

In the weeks immediately following Saigon's fall, the Russians maintained their posture. The Soviet government's May 1 message to the PRG did not refer to the United States, but remarked that "a most dangerous seat of international tensions and military conflict" had "been removed." Other Soviet publications noted that the final end to the Indochinese conflict meant that the world tension could now be reduced.[124] Even more strikingly, when Brezhnev delivered his May 8 speech marking the 30th anniversary of the end of World War II, he lauded détente and the end to the Indochinese wars, but directed absolutely no criticism at the United States itself. Instead, he reaffirmed that the wars' end would lead directly to improved Soviet-American relations.[124] The ongoing Soviet effort to save American face continued in the Soviet coverage of the *Mayagüez* incident in mid-May. For the most part, the Soviet media delivered factual accounts of the affair without overt condemnation, although foreign commentary was reported.[125]

While the Soviet Union clearly sought to downplay its own role in Saigon's collapse and to minimize American embarrassment, this should not be interpreted to imply that the Kremlin refrained from taking advantage of the crumbling American position in Indochina. In Cambodia, the Soviet Union had moved to improve its relations with Sihanouk as Lon Nol's regime lost territory. As the Khmer Rouge forces representing Sihanouk's National United Front of Cambodia encircled the Cambodian capital, the Kremlin increasingly condemned Lon Nol.[126] Finally, on March 28, the Soviets ordered Lon Nol's embassy in Moscow to close. Sihanouk's stayed open. Immediately after the Pnompenh government surrendered, the Russians expressed "solidarity" with the Cambodian patriots.[127]

Much the same scenario was followed in Laos. On August 28, 1975, the 185-man U.S. Agency for International Development team withdrew. A 1500 member Soviet aid and assistance delegation immediately replaced the Americans. According to the Laotian foreign minister, Laos preferred Soviet aid because it came "without any strings attached, unlike American aid."

In South Vietnam itself, Soviet ships began to call at South Vietnamese ports immediately after the final surrender. On May 4, the Soviet cargo vessel *Nina Sagaidak* and the tanker *Komsomolets Primorya* arrived at Danang, the first ships into Danang since the city was "liberated."[128] On May 21, three other Soviet ships arrived in Saigon's Nha Be port carrying fuel.[129]

Throughout Indochina, then, the collapse of the South Vietnamese state and the ensuing rollback of American influence was followed not only by increased North Vietnamese influence, but also by a corresponding Soviet effort to expand its influence into the void created by the American withdrawal. As far as the Soviet Union was concerned, the conclusion of the ceasefire war was a dream come true. The United States was retrenching, its credibility shaken; the Kremlin could move to take advantage of the American uncertainty. The D.R.V.-PRG side was victorious; Moscow could point to both a success for socialism and a reaffirmation of its own credibility as an ally. The war had ended, détente had survived, and Moscow's influence and prestige had expanded. Even the most optimistic Soviet leader could scarcely have hoped for more.

## China's View: Two Hostile Frontiers?

For China, the 1973 Paris Peace Agreement removed one of the major areas of contention preventing further improvement of Sino-American relations. To be sure, the question of Taiwan prevented normalizaton of relations, but at least one issue had been removed.

Chinese reaction to the Paris Agreement reflected Peking's relief that its diplomacy with the United States would no longer be endangered. *People's Daily* immediately declared that the agreement was in "everyone's" interest, including the United States, and urged all concerned parties to follow the terms of the agreement.[130] Peking's Foreign Languages Press quickly issued a propaganda booklet entitled *Welcome the Signing of the Paris Agreement on Vietnam!* Other reports emanating from Southeast Asia indicated that China was urging the D.R.V. and PRG to obey the agreement's provisions.[131] China's great interest in the success of the ceasefire was confirmed in February when Peking sent a high level delegation under Foreign Minister Chi Peng-fei to Paris for the International Conference on Vietnam. Of course, Mao had yet another reason to be pleased with the Paris agreement. His theory of protracted war had been "confirmed." Mao's message to the PRG after the agreement was signed illustrated this. The Chinese leader termed the peace agreement a "great victory won through self-reliance, arduous struggle, and perseverance in a protracted peoples' war."[132]

Throughout 1973, China continued to signal that it appreciated the legal end of American involvement in Vietnam. Kissinger visited Peking from February 15-19, 1973, and reached an agreement establishing liaison offices in both Peking and Washington.[133] Later in the year, in November, Kissinger met with Mao for almost three hours. According to the communiqué, the meeting was conducted "in a friendly manner." Kissinger also discussed Vietnam and "other issues" with Chou En-lai. The Secretary of State, probably because of the Watergate scandal then unfolding, assured Chou that "no matter what happens in the U.S. in the future, the friendship with the People's Republic of China is one of the constant factors of American foreign policy."[134] A more indirect reflection of improved Sino-American relations was trade between the two countries. In 1973, trade soared to $803.4 million, with estimates for 1974 ranging as high as $1.25 billion.

The Chinese desire to maintain good relations with the U.S. was similarly apparent in Peking's reaction to the ceasefire war in Vietnam itself. Throughout 1973 and 1974, the P.R.C. criticized South Vietnam for breaking the ceasefire, but more often than not simply offered that the United States "supported and instigated" the Thieu government.[135] The United States itself was verbally assaulted only on rare occasions. Indeed, as Congress moved to curtail U.S. involvement in Indochina, China realized that continued high levels of American support for Thieu were far from certain. The Chinese media gave factual accounts of the congressional vote both to end bombing in Cambodia and to ban the reintroduction of U.S. troops in Vietnam.[136] For its own part, the P.R.C. publicly played down the support it extended to the D.R.V. and PRG, but gave enough economic and military aid to keep its erstwhile allies basically satisfied. Generally speaking, then, Peking's overall reaction to the Paris agreement and the ceasefire war was not unlike the Soviet reaction — play up the peace and play down the fighting.

China, however, had additional considerations. While the Soviet Union (not to mention North Vietnam) hoped for an eventual full American withdrawal from Indochina, the P.R.C. did not favor a collapse of American positions throughout the area. To China, a united Vietnam acting on its own or, worse yet, under Soviet influence presented more of a threat to Chinese security than did a continued low-level American presence in Indochina. United States Ambassador William Sullivan, speaking in Paris on January 27, 1973, remarked that China preferred a "Balkanized Indochina."[137] Almost two years later, U.S. Senator Mike Mansfield returned from Peking convinced that the Chinese still felt the same way. According to Mansfield, the Chinese were "not terribly interested in Vietnam."[138]

What accounted for this Chinese attitude? At least two factors are apparent. In the first place, Sino-Vietnamese relations began to deteriorate shortly after the Peace Agreement was finalized. Secondly, Sino-Soviet relations remained strained, giving rise to the Chinese fear that American containment would be replaced by Soviet encirclement.

Problems began to crop up in Sino-Vietnamese relations at first over the issue of American support for Thieu's "nibbling operations" and how to react to it. China, as has already been seen, preferred to ignore the entire ceasefire war as much as it could. The D.R.V., on the other hand, still sought to reunify the two Vietnams, and could not. During early June, 1973, Le Duan and Pham Van Dong both journeyed to Peking, the first time the two North Vietnamese leaders had made the trip together. They successfully concluded an aid agreement with the Chinese, but in the final communiqué, it was apparent that some disagreement existed. While the communiqué stressed primarily the victory in the South as exemplified by the Paris agreement and economic reconstruction in the North, the North Vietnamese leaders strongly attacked South Vietnamese and American breaches of the Peace Agreement. China, on the other hand, carefully supported North Vietnam without directly criticizing the United States.[139]

The same pattern was followed in November when a Provisional Revolutionary Government delegation went to Peking. At a banquet given in the delegation's honor, Chou En-lai praised the PRG victory and condemned South Vietnamese violations of the Peace Agreement. He made no mention of American violations. Nguyen Hun Tho, speaking for the PRG delegation, criticized both South Vietnam and the United States.[140]

Sino-Vietnamese disagreements worsened during 1974. Two island groups off the Vietnamese coast, the Paracels and the Spratlys (to the Chinese, the Hsishas and the Nanshas, respectively) had long been claimed by both China and South Vietnam. In January 1974, 600 Chinese soldiers supported by 14 ships and several MIG aircraft stormed the Paracels groups and overwhelmed the 175-man South Vietnamese garrison.[141] Both sides claimed the other was responsible for the incident.[142] Nonetheless, the takeover had an impact in Hanoi as well. "Vietnamese" territory had been expropriated by China. Hanoi would remember the Chinese action.[143]

Other incidents reflected the deteriorating relations between the two Asian communist nations. In March, the D.R.V. suspended the activities of the Sino-Vietnamese Friendship Associaton, and the following month when Pham Van Dong went to Peking the Chinese pointedly failed to mention the necessity to unify Vietnam. In August, when Le Thanh Nghi, North Vietnam's leading expert on foreign economic assistance, went to Peking, he failed to conclude an agreement. Two months later he returned to the Chinese capital on a visit the Chinese termed "a continuation of his China visit last August." This visit was more successful. On October 26, four agreements on military and economic assistance for 1975 were finalized.[144]

Nonetheless, it was evident that China had no desire to exacerbate its relations with the United States over the Vietnam question or to see a powerful and united Vietnam, even if it was communist. North Vietnam's solidarity with the Soviet Union on any of a number of international questions led the Chinese to fear that Soviet influence in Vietnam could become so strong that China in effect would become encircled by the Soviets and their client states. North Vietnam sided with the Soviets on the question of the Portuguese communists, Allende in Chile, the Middle Eastern conflict, American forces in Europe and the Far East, and the Diego García naval base. Meanwhile, China implied that it favored the continuation of an American presence throughout these areas of conflict. On the Diego García question, for example, the Chinese argued that since the Soviet Union had put naval forces into the Indian Ocean, the United States was "bound to respond."[145] The Sino-Soviet rivalry thus continued to have definite ramifications for China's view of the ceasefire war. As long as Hanoi tilted toward the Soviets, the P.R.C. harbored misgivings about Hanoi.

Chinese distrust of the Soviet Union stemmed from, among other things, the continued Soviet buildup on China's northern frontier. In 1969, there were 30 Soviet divisions facing the Chinese. By 1973, that figure had grown by fourteen. Additionally, the Chinese accused the Soviets of numerous "provocations" including "61 air intrusions" between January 1973 and March 1974.[146] On occasion, fighting flared between the two communist giants along their common border.

Chou En-lai underlined Chinese antipathy for the Soviet Union in his political report to the Tenth National Congress of the Chinese Communist Party on August 24, 1973, and at the same time clearly delineated both the course of and motivation behind Chinese foreign policy.[147] Chou accused the Soviets of meddling in Chinese domestic affairs, striving for world hegemony, degenerating into a social-imperialist country, and having territorial ambitions directed against China. The United States did not escape criticism. It was castigated as seeking hegemony and striving to maintain its neocolonial empire. However, Chou emphasized, the United States itself had "openly admitted that it [was] increasingly on the decline; it could not but pull out of Vietnam." While Chou clearly feared that the two superpowers would patch up their differences so as to threaten China,[148] it was equally evident that he regarded the Soviet Union as China's primary enemy. Indeed, the Chinese Communist Party went so far as to add the Soviet Union to the Party Constitution as a "superpower to oppose."

In light of the expressed Chinese hostility to Soviet-American collusion, how then did Chou explain the P.R.C.'s own rapprochement with the United States? To Chou, the rationalization was simple: "necessary compromises between revolutionary countries and imperialist countries" had to be distinguished from "collusion and compromise between Soviet revisionism and U.S. imperialism." Chou then referred to a colorful story from Lenin's *Left-Wing Communism: An Infantile Disorder*, to further solidify his case:

> One must learn to distinguish between a man who gave the bandits money and firearms in order to lessen the damage they can do and facilitate their capture and execution, and a man who gives bandits money and firearms in order to share in the loot.

To Chou, China and the Soviet Union, respectively, were the two men, while the United States was the bandit. With this perspective on international affairs, it was apparent why the Chinese sought a continued U.S. presence in Southeast Asia. The United States was a declining power, and consequently presented a reduced threat to Chinese security. At the same time, however, a continued U.S. presence would act to balance Soviet influence in Vietnam, thereby reducing the threat of a Soviet encirclement of the Inner Kingdom. Chou and Mao were walking a delicate middle road, and fully realized it. Kissinger's November trip to Peking and his warm reception there were simply other manifestations of the Peking leadership's effort to bring off this difficult maneuver.

This does not imply, however, that the Chinese communist hierarchy was in total agreement. Shortly after the Tenth Congress, leftists within the party structure improved their position, and a major anti-Confucian and anti-American propaganda wave was launched. The leftist resurgence may be directly attributed to the fact that during late 1973, Chou En-lai was diagnosed as having cancer. The anti-Confucian, anti-American campaign may thus be viewed as the opening salvo in the struggle to replace Chou.[149] Nonetheless, it cannot be denied that this struggle had an impact on Sino-American relations. After Kissinger's November 1973 visit to Peking, an entire year elapsed before high level Sino-American discussions again took place. In his November 1974 trip, Kissinger was much less warmly received than the preceding year.[150] Aside from this cooling of rapprochement, the internal Chinese disagreements had little apparent impact on Chinese policy. The basic thrusts remained the same.

Meanwhile, in Vietnam itself, the PLAF had switched to the offensive. After some original hesitation, *People's Daily* came out in support of the offensive. A September 2 editorial urged the PLAF to "hit back with force at the [Thieu] clique's nibbling attacks."[151] Peking's short-lived hesitation to endorse the change in tactics stemmed from the P.R.C.'s hesitancy about the impact of the offensive on Sino-American relations. Peking's endorsement undoubtedly reflected a Chinese awareness that with the Watergate turmoil paralyzing Washington, the United States would attach little importance to Peking's verbal support for the offensive.[152]

The Chinese recognized that the South Vietnamese political and economic situation was deteriorating as rapidly as the military situation during the last half of 1974. To Peking, South Vietnam's problems were directly attributable to the "reactionary policies" of Thieu. Since Thieu had no intention of supporting or implementing the Paris agreement, in Peking's eyes, the fall disorders in the major South Vietnamese cities was further interpreted as demands for "the establishment of an administration in Saigon which has the sincerity to implement the Paris agreement."[153] Thieu's November government reorganization changed little. China simply denounced it as a sham.[154]

Throughout late 1974 and early 1975, the Chinese media gave factual accounts of PLAF successes. The lack of American response was seldom commented upon, but inside the Chinese hierarchy, it probably served to confirm the assessment of the United States as a declining power in Southeast Asia. In February 1975, the first Chinese military delegation to visit the D.R.V. since 1961 arrived in Hanoi. Little importance should be attached to this visit, however, at least in relation to the PLAF highlands offensive. The Chinese delegation was under Yang Uyng, commander of the Chinese People's Liberation Army in Sinkiang, and Tsao Li-hua, deputy commander of the nation's Air Force. Neither's expertise was particularly relevant to the new PLAF effort.

South Vietnam's rapid collapse surprised the Chinese as much as anyone. Though Peking had long predicted Thieu's demise, the disappearance of the South Vietnamese state presented China with an entirely new set of circumstances in Indochina. Immediately after Saigon surrendered, Mao and Chou had a congratulatory message delivered to the PRG embassy in Saigon. The following day, May 2, a mammoth rally was held in Peking commemorating the liberation of the former South Vietnamese capital. On the public level, at least, China was pleased.

In subsequent weeks, however, China's concern about the implications of the collapse of South Vietnam became apparent. Had the United States decided to retreat to a "fortress America" foreign policy? If it had, then Peking's intricate calculations of balancing the Soviet threat with an American rapprochement had failed. Deputy Premier Teng Hsiao-ping voiced this fear in early June, telling a group of American editors that the United States must continue to "attend its global responsibilities."[155] Other Chinese sources stressed the importance of a continued American presence in Europe.[156] Teng was even more explicit at a June 7 banquet in Peking honoring the visiting President Marcos of the Philippines. Teng praised the "great victory" in Indochina since it created "one family," but in an obvious and urgent allusion to the Soviet Union, cautioned that Asian nations must avoid "letting the tiger in through the back door while repelling the wolf through the front gate."[157]

Chinese uncertainty about the future course of U.S. policy was once again reflected by Peking's response to the *Mayagüez* incident. On May 16, the Chinese government released a brief statement accusing the U.S. of "piracy,"[158] and *People's Daily* made similar accusations. Despite Peking's comments, the P.R.C. made no threats, and did not even bring up the incident at the United Nations. The entire issue was dropped quickly, and had no lasting effect whatsoever on Sino-American relations. Chinese public statements were a function of China's close relations with the new Cambodian government,[159] and the quick disappearance of the statements reflected Peking's desire not to embarrass the United States further. In short, China did as little as it possibly could about the *Mayagüez*, and even that was to protect its close relationship with the revolutionary Cambodian government.

The United States, for its part, sought to quiet Chinese fears about the future of Sino-American relations. Even while the final offensive strangled Saigon, a congressional delegation under Speaker of the House Carl Albert and Republican Representative John Rhodes was in Peking, and in August, two more congressional delegations visited the P.R.C. More strikingly, Kissinger confirmed in June that President Ford's trip to Peking later in the year would go on as planned. This was in stark contrast to the cancellation of the scheduled Ford-Brezhnev summit. Peking (not to mention Moscow) could not miss the implications of the two different approaches Washington employed.

Nonetheless, for China, the end of the ceasefire war raised some fundamental questions. Could the United States be trusted to balance Soviet influence, even if only tacitly? Now that Vietnam was for all practical purposes united, would the D.R.V. itself present a challenge to China and Chinese policies in Southeast Asia? (Just before Saigon's surrender, the D.R.V. landed troops on the disputed Spratly Islands and took control of them, in a clear response to the P.R.C.'s seizure of the Paracels.) Even more ominously, would Hanoi "tilt" further toward Moscow, possibly even extending naval base rights to the Russian bear? Indochinese peace, as far as the Chinese were concerned, presented as many problems and uncertainties as had the ceasefire war.

The end of the conflict in Vietnam consequently represented different things to different governments. All realized that the status quo in Southeast Asia as a whole had been seriously upset, and in the months following the PLAF victory, the smaller Southeast Asian nations moved to accommodate themselves to their new facts of life. The Philippines, Malaysia, and Thailand, among others, all established diplomatic relations with the PRC before August. The D.R.V. was regarded with a new respect, even fear. Throughout the capitals of Southeast Asia, governments wondered if Hanoi would turn to internal development, or export revolution.

Meanwhile, in Washington, Moscow, and Peking, other questions were being asked. In Washington, national leaders sought to develop a new consensus on which to base American foreign policy, and at the same time wondered whether the executive-legislative stalemate made all efforts futile. While the final end of the war was welcomed, it also left the question, "What now? How can American credibility as an ally be restored, and how can face be saved?"

At the same time, in Moscow, Soviet leaders applauded the victory but wondered about its implications. Did the lack of American reaction to the fall of Saigon indicate a collapse of American will, or rather a momentary paralysis brought about by the Watergate affair? Did the new situation present opportunities for Soviet global initiatives, or would the American need to save face force U.S. policy makers to adopt a more forceful posture in response to Soviet initiatives?

Questions similar to these were also being asked in Peking. The P.R.C.'s primary concern, however, was whether the United States would continue to be a worthwhile counterweight to the Soviet Union. Despite American assurances, Peking remained unconvinced. Throughout the long war, the three capitals had had different views on U.S. policy toward Vietnam. Now, after the peace, they had different questions about where U.S. policy was headed. Each capital, for its own reasons, had a vital stake in the answers.

# VII
# The Lessons of Vietnam

The final collapse of the Republic of Vietnam, and the American inaction during that collapse, for the first time drove home to the international community that the post-World War II era "Pax Americana" had ended. Inevitably, the international community wondered what would replace it.

To a great extent, the answer to that question depended (and depends) on the lessons that national leaders learned from the American experience in Vietnam, and on how they adapt their on-going policies to accommodate those lessons. And, as might be expected, those lessons and the policy changes they induce are even more diverse than the perceptions of the conflict which preceded.

## The United States: Lessons of Losing

In the United States, the long years of war had destroyed the domestic consensus on which U.S. foreign policy had been based. Congress had lost its willingness to follow the presidential lead in foreign policy, and vast segments of the American public had lost their confidence in the government's ability to conduct a coherent foreign policy. With this disarray in the domestic body politic, it is not surprising that public perceptions of what lessons should be learned from Vietnam varied widely. Much of this debate has sought to establish criteria for conduct of American foreign policy in areas far removed from Vietnam in geographic, social, developmental, and historical terms.

Such debate overlooks a critical fact. The American experience in Vietnam was a unique series of events, determined by a unique set of factors not likely to be repeated. Any lessons to be learned must therefore be viewed in a highly selective context. It is only in such a context that Americans and American leaders may draw meaningful conclusions.

Perhaps the most striking lesson the United States government has learned is the degree of inter-relationship existing between military

204

force and social, economic, psychological, and other forces. Gerald Ford
made this point exceedingly clear upon his return from Peking and other
Asian capitals in December, 1975:

> The preservation of the sovereignty and independence of our Asian
> friends and allies remains a paramount objective of American policy.
> We recognize that force alone is insufficient to insure security. Popular
> legitimacy and social justice are vital prerequisites of resistance against
> subversion or aggression.[1]

This, of course, had been heard before, dating back to Johnson's
"two-front war" declaration of 1966 and even before. In previous instances, the will-o'-the-wisp of a military victory had always usurped
priority. Since 1975, however, facts had been different. There could be
no light at the end of the tunnel or victory just around the corner, for at
least as far as Vietnam was concerned, there was neither an American
tunnel nor corner. Past policy no longer acted as an albatross about the
necks of American policymakers, and opportunities for a genuinely
balanced policy toward Indochina and Asia were slowly opening. With
the 1976 election of Jimmy Carter, who in no way was connected with
either Vietnam or Watergate, the final links with past policy were
broken.[2]

Indeed, since Ford's 1975 statement, the United States has shown
a propensity to consider "popular legitimacy" and "social justice" in its
foreign policy. In most instances, this has led to American inaction in
crisis areas. In some cases, such an Angola, this inaction was the result of
a deadlock between Congress and the presidency. In other cases, such as
Ethiopia, Iran, and Nicaragua, this inaction was the apparent result of
the Executive's taking into account the limited indigenous support the
now overthrown regimes had. (This is *not* to argue that the new regimes
necessarily enjoyed "popular legitimacy" or guaranteed "social justice.")
Thus, a new balance has emerged in American foreign policy, the result
of an apparent willingness to recognize the inter-relationship of military
with social and other factors.

This, of course, places a premium on accurate and timely
analysis of those factors. John King Fairbanks has written that the root
cause of the American failure in Vietnam was "the profound American
cultural ignorance of Vietnamese history, values, problems, and
motives.... Now we are out, and still ignorant even of the depth of our
ignorance."[3] To a great extent, this is true. As we have seen in our
analyses of the perceptions of American policy-makers as they made
critical decisions about the U.S. involvement in Vietnam, a comprehen-
sive understanding of the Vietnamese situation was rarely sought.
Rather, emphasis was regularly placed on the military implications of
military actions.

Thus, the second lesson of Vietnam must be that the quality of

American understanding of other societies with which they have contact must be improved. This understanding must be developed devoid of ideological cant. While this is a recognizably difficult task, it is one that nevertheless must be undertaken, for it is only on the basis of perceptions developed through such understanding that cogent policies may be formed and implemented. To a degree, the United States government has learned this lesson. Gerald Ford and Jimmy Carter both sought to upgrade the quality of U.S. intelligence and analysis, but results have been mixed. The Iranian revolution illustrates this. The Central Intelligence Agency only belatedly recognized the tide of revolution that eventually ruined the Shah, and even after it reported the growth of anti-Shah sentiment, its reports were dismissed by senior policymakers. A lesson may be learned, but it may take time to understand how to use that lesson.

Successful policies also require an understanding of what national interests are. As we have seen, an understanding of what U.S. interests were in Vietnam did not always exist. Indeed, in his first State of the World message to Congress, Richard Nixon admitted this, declaring that "our interests must shape our commitments, rather than the other way around." Nixon, just like Johnson before him and Ford after him, was too caught up in the continuity of American perspectives of and policy in Vietnam to achieve this herculean objective. Even so, Nixon recognized the necessity of defining interests. These, then, are the final lessons of Vietnam: that American interests in the international arena must be defined, and that American policies to protect those interests must be altered as interests themselves alter.

If there are lessons to be learned from Vietnam, there are also lessons not to be learned. The failure of American military force to achieve its desired objective must not be interpreted to mean that conventional military forces have no utility in contemporary international affairs. The South Vietnamese collapse in no way implies that conventional military forces are irrelevant. Rather, it illustrates that an almost exclusive reliance on military forces is ineffective. Indeed, there are numerous instances since 1975 when conventional military forces have shown their utility — Vietnam (from the North's perspective), Angola, Ethiopia, and Nicaragua once again serve as excellent examples.

At the same time, the failure of American military force to achieve its desired objective must not be interpreted to mean that that objective could have been achieved by applying more military force while still ignoring social, economic, and psychological factors. The United States spent at least $160 billion on the war in Vietnam, dropped three times as many bombs on Indochina as all the Allies in World War II dropped on all their enemies, and lost over 50,000 American lives.[4]

These are not inconsequential figures. They argue that the war was fought on a large scale. Seeking to maintain an independent South Vietnam by fighting the war on an even larger scale could have yielded at best a Pyrrhic victory.

Yet another lesson which must be learned from the collapse of South Vietnam concerns the scope of U.S. overseas interests. It has rightfully been argued that South Vietnam's fall did not seriously damage U.S. overseas interests. This observation has on occasion been used to legitimize U.S. inaction in other overseas areas. A danger is that the inertia of continued inaction may evolve into a pattern of policy, just as the inertia of continued involvement of the Johnson and Nixon years evolved into a pattern of policy. During the Vietnam years, as we have seen, U.S. policymakers believed that the American pattern of involvement dictated continued involvement. Similarly, unless U.S. interests are clearly delineated and articulated, current and future U.S. policymakers may accept the argument that the current U.S. pattern of inaction dictates continued inaction. Such logic is dangerous at best, and disastrous at worst. Vietnam proves the point.

## The Soviet Union: Socialist Globalism

For the Soviet Union, the Vietnam War proved to be a godsend. Although during its early stages the conflict inhibited Soviet initiatives and concessions toward the West, by 1969 these inhibitions had disappeared. One benefit after another accrued to the Soviet account, all from Vietnam. Soviet prestige throughout the world soared as it extended aid to an increasingly successful national liberation movement. American prestige plummeted. The war cost the Soviet Union less than $1 billion per year. For the United States, some estimates place the cost as high as $30 billion per annum. America's problems in Vietnam combined with its difficulties as home served to promote the view of the Soviet Union as a "normal" state that threatened no one. Even strident Chinese warnings about "Soviet social imperialism," not to mention the Soviet invasion of Czechoslovakia, did little to undermine this image.

It should not be surprising, then, that the Soviet Union also learned some lessons from the American experience in Vietnam. At least three separate lessons are evident. The first is that the United States can be beaten militarily. To the Soviets, the United States is still strong militarily, economically, and politically, but it is in a noticeable decline. Much of this decline is directly attributable to the American experience in Vietnam. As one Soviet author noted as early as 1972, "it is unlikely that the United States will ever regain the international prestige lost over the dirty war in Asia."[5]

This of course, has been a long-standing argument in Soviet propaganda. It is impossible, however, to dismiss it as mere rhetoric. If anything, the Republic of Vietnam's downfall provided eloquent testimony for the Soviet line, at least as far as the Kremlin was concerned. Vietnam is regarded as "one of the series of staggering defeats of the imperialist system in the global confrontation between the two worlds ... one of a series of historically inevitable failures of neocolonial strategies directed against the national liberation movement."[6] The defeat in Vietnam did not signify that imperialism would terminate its neocolonial efforts, but rather that it would "only try to find new forms and methods of promoting its design."[7] To the Kremlin, then, the fall of Vietnam had global implications, particularly in application to the emerging areas. Thus, one of the lessons of Vietnam, at least in Soviet eyes, was that American military might could be defeated, and "that lesson has been grasped by people all over the world."[8]

The second lesson the Kremlin has apparently drawn from the American debacle in Vietnam is that the growth of Soviet military strength has contributed directly to American hesitancy to act in crisis areas. With the Soviet leaders seeing the United States implementing the "Johnson" and "Asian" doctrines under the protection of conventional and nuclear military superiority, they undoubtedly reasoned that the elimination of that superiority would lead to an American hesitancy to act in situations that could result in Soviet-American confrontation. During the period from 1966 to 1975, the Soviet armed forces, and especially strategic forces, enjoyed a startling growth that removed much of the U.S. military superiority. If military superiority was a prerequisite for the American "war on the national liberation movement," much of that superiority had been removed by 1975. And it is precisely during the period since 1975 that the United States has not acted in situations where it might previously have been expected to act. From Moscow's perspective, the growth of Soviet military might has in fact constrained the United States. Numerous Soviet discussions of the so-called "changing international correlation of forces" make this point exceedingly clear.[9]

Finally, the collapse of South Vietnam coupled with American inaction during the collapse implied to the Soviet leaders that a "new realism" had entered U.S. foreign policy. A leading indication of the "new realism" was the lack of American response to the Soviet-backed Cuban intervention in Angola, which Soviet officials attributed to "the lessons the United States learned in Vietnam."[10] It is in this light, then, that one can better understand Soviet activity in Ethiopia, Yemen, Afghanistan, and elsewhere, as well as, of course, Angola. What better place than underdeveloped nations in the throes of civil war to verify and take advantage of the Soviet image of a constrained United States? The parallels to Vietnam were many (though not strictly accurate), and the risks to the Soviet Union were small.

The lessons the Soviet Union learned from Vietnam were, and are, considerably different from those the United States learned. Nevertheless, it should be evident that the American experience in Vietnam has done much to alter the Soviet view of its own role—and of the American role—in the world.

## China: Encirclement and Abandonment?

One may well imagine the questions Mao and Chou were asking themselves as PLAF forces rolled toward Saigon: Why is the United States not responding? What effect will the defeat of South Vietnam have on Southeast Asia? Perhaps most importantly, of what value is our rapprochement with the United States in constraining the Soviet Union if the United States will not even come to the aid of its erstwhile ally?

The lessons that Mao and Chou originally drew from the collapse of South Vietnam and the accompanying American inaction were that the United States was indeed a "paper tiger," and that the U.S. had to be encouraged if it were to continue a global presence to balance the Soviets. Even though the Chinese had long argued that the American conduct of the Vietnamese War was proof positive that the United States was a declining power, the Chinese appeared shocked by America's lack of reaction to the PLAF offensive. Chinese encouragement of a U.S. presence in Asia, Africa, the Indian Ocean, and Europe in the days immediately after the end of the war made it clear that, from the Chinese perspective, the United States was developing a "fortress America" mentality. For Peking, the implications were dire, both in a regional and in a global sense.

In the words of one authority, the Chinese became "preoccupied with the fear that [Vietnam] would become a kind of Soviet satellite, a block in the wall of containment that Peking argues is Soviet strategy in Asia."[11] This preoccupation has in turn had two impacts, one on Chinese relations with the D.R.V. and the other on Chinese policy toward the rest of Southeast Asia. Sino-Vietnamese relations, already strained during 1973 to 1975, further deteriorated following the South Vietnamese collapse, finally culminating in open warfare in early 1979. The Chinese have regularly made known their fear of Soviet encirclement carried out through pro-Soviet surrogates,[12] and the steady growth of Soviet influence in Vietnam, combined with Vietnamese control of both Laos and Cambodia, has accentuated these Chinese fears. In the words of one China watcher, "The Chinese believe the Russian bear has had a cub."

To counter the threat of encirclement from the south, Peking sought to build its own anti-Vietnamese containment wall in Southeast Asia.[13] With some momentary lapses, Chinese relations with other states in Southeast Asia, with the exception of Laos and Indonesia, have improved. Until the Vietnamese invasion of Cambodia, Cambodia was for all practical purposes a Chinese client state. Indeed, when Teng Hsiao-ping toured the United States in early 1979, he made it clear on several occasions that the P.R.C. would welcome American support for ASEAN and a continued U.S. presence in Southeast Asia. Teng's tour of the United States, coupled with American recognition of the P.R.C., the summer 1979 announcement that American troop withdrawals from Korea would be ended, and the Carter administration's increase in defense expenditure have gone a long way to assuage Chinese fears that their American "ally" was abandoning them. Chinese fears of Soviet encirclement, however, remain strong.

An additional comment is pertinent here. It should not be assumed that all Chinese leaders necessarily supported Sino-American rapprochement. It may even be argued that the political positions of the "Gang of Four," all of whom apparently supported improved Chinese relations with the Soviet Union, were temporarily strengthened by the collapse of South Vietnam. Why, they may have reasoned, should we seek to rely on an unreliable "ally" as a counterweight to the Soviet Union? Should we not improve relations with the Soviets themselves?

The demise of the "Gang of Four" undoubtedly ended such reasoning, at least temporarily, among the Chinese leadership. Nevertheless, at least one of the four "modernizations" of the Hua-Teng government, modernization of the military, may in part be explained as indicative of both continued mistrust of American intentions to counterbalance Soviet influence, and continued fear of Soviet intentions.

For China, then, the end of the Vietnam conflict cast a shadow over one of the major tenets of its foreign policy, even though it at the same time appeared to confirm the long-standing Chinese ideological precept that "American imperialism" could be defeated. Mao and his successors, one might guess, viewed the North Vietnamese-PRG success with mixed emotions as the threat of the bear with its cub loomed larger.

## Vietnam in a Global Context

There can be little doubt that the American involvement in Vietnam was a seminal event, with repercussions that affected and continue to affect the farthest corners of the globe. In many respects, that involvement served to undermine the then-extant world order. We are now in a time of transition; what will replace the "Pax Americana" is as yet unclear.

One thing is clear, however: the new world order will be no more based on trust and consensus among nations than was the old, at least if the differing perceptions and differing lessons examined here are any indication. Indeed, with no single nation able to act as international arbiter, and with increased availability of arms, it may even be reasonable to assume that conflict among nations may grow increasingly frequent and increasingly violent.

If anything good may be said to have emerged from the United States involvement in Vietnam, perhaps it may be an increased awareness both by Americans and by others that different national policies are determined as much by differing perceptions as by universalist ideology, historical antipathy, or anything else. Perhaps this realization may in time lead the United States to more realistic interpretations of other nations' policies, objectives, and motives. In turn, it may be hoped, increased understanding of this diversity may lead to more realistic American policy responses than were evidenced in Vietnam.

# Chapter Notes

## NOTES TO CHAPTER I

1. See John F. Cady, *Southeast Asia: Its Historical Development* (New York: McGraw-Hill, 1964); Joseph Buttinger, *The Smaller Dragon* (New York: Praeger, 1958); and Philippe Devillers, *Histoire du Vietnam* (Paris: Éditions de Seuil, 1952).

2. Ellen J. Hammer, *The Struggle for Indochina 1940-1955* (Stanford: Stanford University Press, 1966), p. 11.

3. George McTurnan Kahin and John W. Lewis, *The United States in Vietnam* (New York: Delta, 1969), pp. 8-10.

4. For the North Vietnamese rendition of Ho Chi Minh's life, see *Our President Ho Chi Minh* (Hanoi: Foreign Language Publishing House, 1970). For an excellent brief Western biography, see Robert F. Turner, *Vietnamese Communsm: Its Origins and Development* (Stanford: Hoover Institution Press, 1975), pp. 1-75.

5. Turner, p. 6.

6. Melvin Gurtov, *The First Vietnam Crisis* (New York: Columbia University Press, 1967), p. 2.

7. J. J. Zasloff, *The Role of the Sanctuary in Insurgency: Communist China's Support to the Vietminh 1946-1954* (Santa Monica, Calif.: Rand Corporation, 1967), p. 5. (Hereafter cited as Zasloff, *The Role of the Sanctuary.*)

8. For several concise histories of the early years of the development of the Vietminh, see Hammer, pp. 94-105; Turner, pp. 75-167; and Jay Taylor, *China and Southeast Asia: Peking's Relations with Revolutionary Movements* (New York: Praeger, 1974), pp. 1-7. For an interesting Soviet assessment, see *Istoriia Vetnama v Noveishee Vremia 1917-1965* (Moscow: Izdatelstvo, 1970), pp. 78-159.

9. Kahin, p. 18.

10. *Ibid.*, pp. 18-19.

11. Ho Chi Minh, in Bernard B. Fall (ed.), *Ho Chi Minh on Revolution* (New York: Praeger, 1967), p. 143.

12. U.S. Department of Defense, *United States-Vietnam Relations 1945-1967*, Book 1, A (Washington: U.S. Government Printing Office, 1971), p. A15. (Hereafter cited as *United States-Vietnam Relations.*)

13. Kahin, pp. 23-26.

14. *United States-Vietnam Relations*, Book 1, I, A, p. A25.

15. Kahin, p. 27.

16. According to one writer, "Mao's strategic insights were influential to the point of being plagiarized." See Gurtov, p. 16.

17. Kahin, pp. 28-29.

18. *United States-Vietnam Relations*, Book 1, I, B, p. B1.

19. Kahin, pp. 29-31.

20. *Ibid.*, p. 32.

21. Gurtov, p. 35.

22. *United States-Vietnam Relations*, Book 1, I, A, p. A42.

23. *Ibid.*, p. A49.

24. *U.S. Department of State Bulletin*, Vol. 22, No. 554 (February 13, 1950), p. 244.

25. E. Zhukov, "Obostrenie Krizisa Kolonialnoi Sistemy," *Bolshevik*, No. 23 (December, 1947), p. 52.

26. *United States-Vietnam Relations*, Book 1, II, A, p. A45.

27. Zasloff, *The Role of the Sanctuary*, p. 9.

28. Dwight D. Eisenhower, *Mandate for Change, 1953-56: The White House Years* (Garden City, N.Y.: Doubleday, 1963), p. 167.

29. King C. Chen, *Vietnam and China, 1938-1954* (Princeton, N.J.: Princeton University Press, 1969), p. 276. *United States-Vietnam Relations* cites lower figures: 10 to 20 tons per month in 1951; 500 to 600 tons per month in 1953; and 4000 tons per month in 1954. Book 2, IV, A, 5, Tab 1, p. 20.

30. *United States-Vietnam Relations*, Book 1, II, A, p. A47.

31. *The New York Times*, March 6, 1953, and March 20, 1953.

32. *Ibid.*, April 17, 1953.

33. *Ibid.*, September 3, 1953.

34. *Pravda*, May 9, 1953.

35. Donald S. Zagoria, *Vietnam Triangle: Moscow, Peking, Hanoi* (New York: Pegasus, 1967), p. 40.

36. This is the argument adopted by Philippe Devillers and Jean Lacouture. See Devillers and Lacouture, *End of a War: Indochina 1954* (New York: Praeger, 1969), p. 104.

37. U.S. Congress, House, Committee on Foreign Affairs, *Report of the Special Study Mission to Pakistan, India, Thailand, Indochina Pursuant to House Resolution 113*, House Report No. 412, 83rd Cong., 1st sess. (Washington: U.S. Government Printing Office, 1953), p. 35.

38. *The New York Times*, January 28, 1953.

39. *Ibid.*, April 7, 1954.

40. Eisenhower, p. 339.

41. Matthew B. Ridgway, *Soldier: The Memoirs of Matthew B. Ridgway* (New York: Harper, 1956), p. 277.

42. *United States-Vietnam Relations*, Book 1, II, B, p. B10.

43. "Agreement on the Cessation of Hostilities in Vietnam," in Marvin E. Gettleman (ed.), *Vietnam: History, Documents, and Opinions* (New York: New American Library, 1960), p. 164, 169.

44. *Ibid.*, p. 175.

45. "Final Declaration of the Geneva Conference," in *Ibid.*, p. 181.

46. *United States-Vietnam Relations*, Book 1, III, D, "The Geneva Accords," p. D9.

47. *The New York Times*, July 25, 1954.

48. *U.S. Department of State Bulletin*, Vol. 31, No. 791 (August 23, 1954), p. 261.

49. *United States-Vietnam Relations*, Book 1, III, A, p. A11.

50. See Devillers and Lacouture, chapters 20 and 21, as well as D. Lancaster, *The Emancipation of French Indochina* (London: Oxford University Press, 1961), pp. 314-336.

51. The Soviet Union apparently did not comment on the regroupment of forces following the 1954 ceasefire. See Nadia Derkach, *The Soviet Union and the Early Phases of the Vietcong Armed Insurgency in South Vietnam (1958-1963)* (Santa Monica, Calif.: Rand Corporation, 1966), p. 9.

52. J. J. Zasloff, *Political Motivation of the Vietcong: The Vietminh Regroupees* (Santa Monica, Calif.: Rand Corporation, 1968), p. v. (Hereafter cited as Zasloff, *Political Motivation.*)

53. Kahin, pp. 71-75.

54. Jean Lacouture, *Vietnam: Between Two Truces* (New York: Random House, 1966), p. 105; and Bernard B. Fall, *The Two Vietnams* (New York: Praeger, 1964), p. 154.

55. Kahin, pp. 71-72.

56. George C. Reinhardt, *America's Crossroad — Vietnam* (Santa Monica, Calif.: Rand Corporation, 1967), p. 9.

57. Kahin, pp. 80-81.

58. *U.S. Department of State Bulletin*, Vol. 32, No. 837 (July 11, 1955), p. 50.

59. Kahin, p. 82.

60. *The New York Times*, January 13, 1955, March 13, 1955, June 2, 1955, and June 8, 1955. See also Turner, pp. 168-82.

61. J. J. Zasloff, *Origins of the Insurgency in South Vietnam 1954-1960: The Role of the Southern Vietminh Cadres* (Santa Monica, Calif.: Rand Corporation, 1968), pp. 5-6. (Hereafter cited as Zasloff, *Origins of the Insurgency.*)

62. *Ibid.*, pp. 15-18.

63. P. J. Honey, "The Problems of Democracy in Vietnam," *The World Today*, Vol. 16, No. 2 (February, 1960), p. 73. See also Philippe Devillers, "The Struggle for the Unification of Vietnam," *China Quarterly*, No. 9 (January-March, 1962), p. 12.

64. Zasloff, *Origins of the Insurgency*, p. 23.

65. Kahin, pp. 102-106.

66. William Henderson, "South Vietnam Finds Itself," *Foreign Affairs*, Vol. 35, No. 2 (January, 1957), p. 285.

67. Zasloff, *Origins of the Insurgency*, p. 23.

68. For differing interpretations of that relationship, see Turner, pp. 168-82; Zagoria, pp. 112-122; *United States-Vietnam Relations*, Book 2, IV, A, 5, pp. 1037; and Jeffrey Race, *War Comes to Long An* (Berkeley: University of California Press, 1972), among others.

69. Both charts are from *United States-Vietnam Relations*, Book 2, IV, A, 5, Tab 2, p. 58.

70. Kahin, p. 89; and Turner, pp. 109-146.

71. An account of Soviet and Chinese aid to North Vietnam is given in Charles McLane, "The Russians and Vietnam: Strategies of Indirection," *International Journal*, Vol. 24, No. 1 (Winter, 1968-1969), pp. 60-64.

72. Fall, *The Two Vietnams*, p. 177.

73. *United States-Vietnam Relations*, Book 2, IV, A, 5, p. 32.

74. For an examination of the debate in Hanoi over policy to the south, see Turner pp. 178-182; also Kahin, pp. 113-116.

75. *United States-Vietnam Relations*, Book 2, IV, A, 5, p. 24.

76. Kahin, pp. 110-111.

77. U.S. Congress, *Congressional Record*, Vol. 101 (Washington: U.S. Government Printing Office, May 2, 1955), p. 5290.

78. U.S. House of Representatives, *Supplemental Foreign Assistance Authorization Fiscal Year 1966*, 89th Congress, 2nd Session (Washington: U.S. Government Printing Office, 1966).

79. *The New York Times*, August 9, 1955.

80. N. Pastukhov, "Volia Narodov Azii i Afriki k Miru i Edinstvu," *Kommunist*, No. 5 (April, 1956), p. 89.

81. V. Semenov, "Raspad Kolonialnoi Sistemy Imperializma i Voprosy Mezhdunarodnykh Otnosheniia," *Kommunist*, No. 18 (December, 1956), p. 102.

82. R. Ulianovskii, "Ekonomicheskaia Nezavisimost-Blizhaishaia Zadacha Osvoboditelnogo Dvisheniia v Azii," *Kommunist*, No. 1 (Jan., 1962), pp. 96-107.

83. Adam Ulam, *Expansion and Coexistence: The History of Soviet Foreign Policy 1917-1967* (New York: Praeger, 1968), p. 699.

84. McLane, p. 50.

85. Paul M. Kattenburg, "Vietnam and U.S. Diplomacy," *Orbis*, Vol. 15 (Fall, 1971), p. 822.

86. See P. J. Honey, *Communism in North Vietnam* (Cambridge, Mass.: M.I.T. Press, 1963), p. 49.

87. McLane, p. 50.

88. Chou En-lai, *On Present International Situation, China's Foreign Policy, and the Liberation of Taiwan* (Peking: Foreign Languages Press, 1956), p. 11.

89. Turner, p. 293.

90. *United States-Vietnam Relations*, Book 2, A, 5, p. 36.

91. Zasloff, *Political Motivation*, pp. 82-119.

92. U.S. Department of State, *A Threat to the Peace: North Vietnam's Effort to Conquer South Vietnam*, Publication #7308 (Washington: U.S. Government Printing Office, 1961).

93. Arthur M. Schlesinger, *A Thousand Days: John F. Kennedy in the White House* (Boston: Houghton Mifflin, 1965), p. 547.

94. Roger Hilsman, *To Move a Nation* (New York: Doubleday, 1967), p. 413-421.

95. *U.S. Department of State Bulletin*, Vol. 46, No. 1175 (January 1, 1962), p. 13.

96. *The New York Times*, July 28, 1964.

97. For a detailed examination of the program, see *United States-Vietnam Relations*, Book 3, IV, B, 2, pp. 1-36.

98. For Khrushchev's entire statement, see N. S. Khrushchev, "For New Victories of the World Communist Movement," *World Marxist Review*, No. 1 (January, 1961), pp. 3-28. (Hereafter cited as Khrushchev, "For New Victories.")

99. P. J. Honey, *Communism in North Vietnam*, p. 197.

100. *Washington Post*, May 12, 1963.

101. Hilsman, p. 480. It was later revealed that those channels led through the head of the Polish delegation to the I.C.C. See *The New York Times*, January 27, 1975.

102. *United States-Vietnam Relations*, Book 3, IV, B, 3, p. 37.

103. For a study of the withdrawal program, see *Ibid.*, Book 3, IV, B, 4, pp. 1-40.

104. *Ibid.*, Book 4, IV, C, 9, p. 3. During 1961 and 62, Kennedy rejected a neutral solution for Vietnam because "the Communists had the upper hand and were the most forcible element in the South as well as in the North." See Theodore Sorenson, *Kennedy* (New York: Harper & Row, 1965), p. 64.

105. *The New York Times*, January 2, 1964.

106. *United States-Vietnam Relations*, Book 4, IV, C, 9, p. 7.

107. Ho Chi Minh, "Speech Opening the Third National Congress of the Vietnam Workers' Party, September 5, 1960" in Bernard B. Fall (ed.), *Ho Chi Minh on Revolution* (New York: Praeger, 1967), p. 317; and P. J. Honey, "North Vietnam's Party Congress," *China Quarterly*, No. 4 (October-December, 1960), p. 68.

108. John Donnel and Melvin Gurtov, *North Vietnam: Left of Moscow, Right of Peking* (Santa Monica, Calif.: Rand Corporation, 1968), p. 33.

109. Joachim Glaubitz, "Relations Between Communist China and North Vietnam," in Robert Repen (ed.), *Vietnam and the Sino-Soviet Dispute* (New York: Praeger, 1967), p. 63.

110. *Pravda*, July 27, 1964. This is not to say that the deterioration of Soviet-D.R.V. relations was the only reason for the Soviet threat. Rather, it is to imply that the Soviet leadership was sufficiently disenchanted with the entire Southeast Asian situation that it was willing to consider abandoning the limited influence in the area that it retained.

111. "Resolution of the Third National Congress of the Vietnam Workers' Party on the Tasks and Line of the Party in the New Stage," *Third National Congress of the Vietnam Workers' Party: Documents, Volume I* (Hanoi: Foreign Languages Publishing House, n.d.), pp. 225-226.

112. Kahin, p. 114. For a similar interpretation of North Vietnam's attitude toward the Southern insurgency, see Zagoria, pp. 104-106.

113. The U.S. Department of State "White Paper" of 1965 maintained that "the Liberation Front for South Vietnam ... was formed at Hanoi's order." U.S. Department of State, *Aggression from the North: The Record of North Vietnam's Campaign to Conquer South Vietnam*, Publication No. 7839 (Washington: U.S. Government Printing Office, 1965), p. 2.

114. Kahin, p. 119.

115. For a detailed account of the formation of the NLFSV, see Turner, pp. 224-247.

116. *Pravda*, January 31, 1961.

117. Khrushchev, "For New Victories," pp. 3-28.

118. For a deeper explanation of the Soviet ideological position, see Nadia Derkach, *The Soviet Union and the Early Phases of the Viet Cong Armed Insurgency in South Vietnam 1958-1963* (Santa Monica, Calif.: Rand Corporation, 1966), pp. 21-25.

119. *Pravda*, January 19, 1962.

120. Douglas Pike, *Viet Cong: The Organization and Techniques of the National Liberation Front* (Cambridge, Mass.: M.I.T. Press, 1966), p. 340.

121. The situation in Laos was, if anything, as complicated as the situation in Vietnam. On September 4, 1959, the Royal Laotian Government appealed to the United Nations for assistance, claiming that North Vietnamese military units had entered Laos and were aiding the Pathet Lao rebels. The United Nations appointed a committee to investigate the complaint. Although the committee found evidence that equipment, arms, ammunition, and political cadres had infiltrated Laos from North Vietnam, it could not ascertain whether regular troops had.

In December 1960, Souvanna Phouma, Laos' neutralist prime minister, was ousted and replaced by right-wing General Phoumi Nosavan. To regain his position, Souvanna Phouma accepted the support of the Pathet Lao, who were dominated by the Vietminh. In the last two weeks of December, Soviet aircraft flew 184 missions into Laos in support of the Pathet Lao (Zagoria, *Vietnam Triangle*, p. 42). With the Soviet Union supporting Souvanna Phouma and the

Pathet Lao and the United States supporting Phoumi Nosavan and the Royalists, a Soviet-American confrontation appeared imminent. To prevent the confrontation, negotiations were undertaken in May 1961 that eventually resulted in the July 1962 "Declaration on the Neutrality of Laos," signed in Geneva.

The role of the North Vietnamese and the Soviets in the Laotian war itself, however, needs to be further commented upon. Neutralist officers who had served in Hanoi and the Plain of Jars during 1960-61, later testified that Soviet supplies were first directed to the North Vietnamese in Laos, then the Pathet Lao, and finally the neutralists (P. F. Langer and J. J. Zasloff, *Revolution in Laos: The North Vietnamese and the Pathet Lao* (Santa Monica, Calif.: Rand Corporation, 1969), p. 97). In December 1964 Souvanna Phouma wrote, "... the principal actions in these combats [in Laos] have been led by the North Vietnamese troops, a fact which I have been able to verify myself.... That the Pathet Lao have not disappeared from the scene is due to the support of its ally of the North which has supported, armed, trained, and encadred its guerrilla activities" (Langer, p. 109n).

It appeared clear that the Soviet Union and North Vietnam were both extending support to the Pathet Lao. What, then, would account for the signing of the Geneva Agreement on Laos when the Pathet Lao-D.R.V. offensive was moving well?

Two explanations appear most likely. First, North Vietnam may have feared a massive American response to further pressure. Kennedy had sent 5,000 troops to northeast Thailand and appeared to be willing to send more. Second, the Soviet Union, having undoubtedly already decided on its Cuban missile gambit, may have desired to clear the scene of a bothersome peripheral issue, thereby permitting its own leaders to concentrate more fully on Cuba or lulling the United States into the false belief of imminent Soviet good will. On the U.S. side, Kennedy believed that by signing an agreement on Laos he could both avoid a confrontation with the Soviets and cool off the Vietnamese situation by closing the Laotian infiltration route to South Vietnam. See Sorenson, pp. 548-549.

122. For several references to the Soviet attitude toward negotiations, see Foy D. Kohler, *Understanding the Russians: A Citizen's Primer* (New York: Harper & Row, 1970), p. 386; *The New York Times*, July 27, 1964; and *Pravda*, July 20, 1964.

123. Interview with former U.S. Ambassador to the Soviet Union Foy D. Kohler, conducted by the author in Miami, Florida, March, 1973.

124. For example, see *Peking Review*, July 19, 1960, and April 28, 1961.

125. *Ibid.*, May 16, 1961.

126. *Ibid.*, July 27, 1962. Cambodia was also included in the so-called "neutral zone" along with Laos and Vietnam. See *Ibid.*, October 12, 1962.

127. Glaubitz, p. 63.

128. A captured North Vietnamese document later confirmed that 1964 and 1965 were to be the "years of decision" in South Vietnam. See the so-called CRIMP Document, captured by U.S. and South Vietnamese forces north of Saigon in early 1966.

## NOTES TO CHAPTER II

1. U.S. Department of Defense, *United States-Vietnam Relations 1945-1967* (Washington: U.S. Government Printing Office, 1971), Book 3, IV, B, 3, p. 43. (Hereafter cited as *United States Vietnam Relations*.)

2. *Pravda*, December 20, 1964; and *Istoriia Vetnama v Noveishee Vremia 1917-1965* (Moscow: Nauka, 1970), p. 375.

3. *United States-Vietnam Relations*, Book 3, IV, B, 3, p. 38.

4. *Ibid.*, pp. 39-40.

5. *The New York Times*, December 2, 1964.

6. *United States-Vietnam Relations*, Book 3, IV, C, 1, pp. a7-a9.

7. *The New York Times*, July 24, 1964.

8. *Ibid.*, July 26, 1964.

9. *Ibid.*, July 29, 1964.

10. *Ibid.*, July 1, 1964.

11. *United States-Vietnam Relations*, Book 3, IV, C, 1, pp. a4-a6.

12. *Ibid.*, Book 3, IV, C, 2, p. 2.

13. *Ibid.*, Book 4, IV, C, 9, p. 31.

14. *The New York Times*, July 27, 1964.

15. *Ibid.*, July 25, 1964.

16. *Ibid.*, June 29, 1964.

17. *Washington Post*, June 27, 1973.

18. U.S. Department of State Bulletin, Vol. 51, No. 1313 (August 24, 1964), p. 268. For different views on the Resolution, see Eugene G. Windchy, *Tonkin Gulf* (Garden City, N.Y.: Doubleday, 1970); and John Galloway, *The Gulf of Tonkin Resolution* (Teaneck, N.J.: Fairleigh Dickinson University Press, 1970). It is also interesting to note that some accounts declared that Johnson had the text of the resolution "in his pocket for days" before the incident.

19. *United States-Vietnam Relations*, Book 4, IV, C, 2, pp. 2-5.

20. *The New York Times*, November 27, 1964.

21. *Ibid.*, December 13, 1964. This debate was, in fact, occurring. See *United States-Vietnam Relations*, Book 4, IV, C, 2, pp. 1-42.

22. *United States-Vietnam Relations*, Book 4, IV, C, 2, p. 69.

23. *The New York Times*, December 16, 1964.

24. *United States-Vietnam Relations*, Book 2, IV, C, 1, p. 102.

25. *The New York Times*, September 26, 1964.

26. *Ibid.*, October 10, 1964.

27. *Ibid.*, November 24, 1964.

28. *Ibid.*, November 28, 1964.

29. *Ibid.*, October 2, 1964.

30. *United States-Vietnam Relations*, Book 3, IV, C, 1, p. a12.

31. *Ibid.*, p. a14.

32. *Ibid.*, Book 4, IV, C, 2, p. xv.

33. *Ibid.*, p. 74.

34. *Ibid.*, Book 7, IV, C, 9, pp. 33-34.

35. *The New York Times*, September 2, 1964.

36. *Ibid.*, September 13, 1964.

37. *United States-Vietnam Relations*, Book 4, IV, C, 2, p. viii.

38. *Ibid.*

39. *The New York Times*, December 11, 1964.

40. *Ibid.*, December 20, 1964.

41. *United States-Vietnam Relations*, Book 4, IV, C, 2, p. 69.

42. *Ibid.*, p. 70.

43. *Ibid.*

44. *The New York Times*, December 24, 1964.

45. *Ibid.*, December 26, 1964.

46. *Ibid.*, December 28, 1964. See also *United States-Vietnam Relations*, Book 4, IV, C, 2, p. 70.

47. *United States-Vietnam Relations*, Book 4, IV, C, 2, p. 71.

48. *Ibid.*

49. *Ibid.*, p. 72.

50. *The New York Times*, January 31, 1965.

51. *Ibid.*, February 5, 1965.

52. *Ibid.*, February 3, 1965.

53. *The Economist*, January 30, 1965.

54. *The New York Times*, January 31, 1965.

55. Douglas Pike, *Viet Cong: The Organization and Techniques of the National Liberation Front* (Cambridge, Mass.: M.I.T. Press, 1966), p. 341.

56. Item 302, translation of a letter dated March, 1966, presumably written by Le Duan, First Secretary of the Lao Dong Party Central Committee and member of the Hanoi Politburo, captured by units of the 173rd Airborne Brigade, January 21, 1967, during Operation Cedar Falls, released to the press by the U.S. Mission at Saigon on March 15, 1967.

57. *Pravda*, February 12, 1964; see also TASS press release, Feb. 25, 1964.

58. *Pravda*, February 15, 1964.

59. Joschim Glaubitz, "Relations between Communist China and Vietnam," in Robert A. Rupen and Robert Farrell, *Vietnam and the Sino-Soviet Dispute* (New York: Praeger, 1967), p. 63.

60. *China News Analysis*, No. 555.

61. *The New York Times*, March 27, 1964.

62. *Pravda*, July 5, 1964.

63. *Izvestiia*, June 25, 1964; V. Pechorkin, "Teoriia I Praktika Kontrpartizanskoi Voiny," *Mezhdunarodnaia Zhizn*, No. 10 (October, 1963), pp. 35-43; and *Pravda*, July 10, 1964.

64. Radio Moscow, June 24-26, 1964.

65. *Ibid.*, June 24, 1964.

66. Nadia Derkach, *The Soviet Union and the Early Phases of the Viet Cong Armed Insurgency in South Vietnam 1958-63* (Santa Monica, Calif.: Rand Corporation, 1966), p. 49.

67. *Pravda*, July 27, 1964.

68. *Izvestiia*, July 28, 1964.

69. *The New York Times*, July 29, 1964.

70. *Ibid.*, August 1, 1964. Former U.S. Ambassador to the Soviet Union Foy D. Kohler also believed the Soviet threat to be sincere. Interview with Foy D. Kohler conducted by the author in Miami, Florida, May 1, 1973.

71. Radio Tirana to Yugoslavia, 0530 GMT, August 18, 1964, *FBIS*, U.S.S.R. and East Europe, August 19, 1964, p. mml.

72. *The New York Times*, August 3, 1964. The Chinese note was made even more striking when *Pravda* revealed that the Soviet Union had called for a conference of world communist parties on July 30, three days before the Chinese note was sent. Since the conference was undoubtedly called for the express purpose of condemning the Chinese ideological line, the Chinese letter of appeal was rather out of place unless, for some reason, the Chinese genuinely feared a Soviet withdrawal from the cochairmanship. See *Pravda*, August 10, 1964.

Another indication that the Chinese believed the Soviet threat of withdrawal was real occurred over a year later. At that time, *Peking Review* declared that "when the struggle of the Vietnamese and the Laotian people grew acute, [the Soviet Union's] policy on the question of Indochina was one of disengagement." See *Peking Review*, November 12, 1965.

73. *Peking Review*, July 3, 1964.

74. *Ibid.*, July 10, 1964.

75. *The New York Times*, July 15, 1964.

76. *Peking Review*, July 24, 1964.

77. The Soviet Union called for this conference on July 30 — *Pravda*, August 10, 1964.

78. *Ibid.*, July 9, 1964.

79. *Izvestiia*, July 19, 1964.

80. *Pravda*, July 21, 1964.

81. One reflection of the limited Soviet aid to the NLFSV may be Soviet trade with the Democratic Republic of Vietnam. Between 1963 and 1964, Soviet exports to the D.R.V. declined from 51.0 million rubles to 42.5 million rubles. Soviet imports, meanwhile, declined from 31.8 million rubles to 31.3 million rubles. See *Vneshniaia Torgovlia SSSR za 1964* (Moscow: Vneshtorgizdat, 1965), p. 12.

82. Mao Tse-tung, in Edgar Snow, "Interview with Mao," *New Republic*, February 27, 1965, p. 22.

83. New China News Agency, July 19, 1964.

84. Allen Whiting, "How We Almost Went to War with China," *Look*, April 29, 1969.

85. *Pravda*, August 6, 1964.

86. *Ibid.*

87. *Izvestiia*, August 6, 1964.

88. *Pravda*, August 7, 1964, August 8, 1964, and August 9, 1964.

89. *The New York Times*, August 6, 1964.

90. For the text of the official Chinese statement, see *Ibid.*

91. *Pravda*, August 7, 1964. Other Chinese warnings included Chen Yi's August 5 statement that China "would intervene" if the war in Indochina were carried north (*The New York Times*, August 7, 1964) and Central Committee member Liao Cheng-chik's August 9 statement that China was "determined by practical deeds to volunteer aid" to the North Vietnamese if they were attacked again (*The New York Times*, August 10, 1964). These statements were apparently not carried by the Soviet media.

92. *Pravda*, August 7, 1964.

93. *Ibid.*, August 8, 1964.

94. *Ibid.*, August 9, 1964.

95. See *Peking Review*, August 14, 1964. Almost every article in the issue is concerned with Vietnam and the U.S. escalation.

96. New China News Agency, August 7, 1964.

97. *The New York Times*, August 12, 1964.

98. *Ibid.*, August 14, 1964.

99. *Ibid.*, August 11, 1964.

100. Iu. Igritskii, "Amerikanskie Ultra," *Mezhdunarodnaia Zhizn*, No. 6 (June, 1964), p. 76.

101. *Pravda*, July 20, 1964.

102. "Tekushchie Problemy Mirovoi Politiki," *Mirovaia Ekonomika i Mezhdunarodnye Otnosheniia*, No. 10 (October, 1964), p. 92.

103. *Sovetskaia Rossiia*, June 28, 1964.

104. *The New York Times*, August 6, 1964.

105. *Pravda*, August 7, 1964.

106. *The New York Times*, August 11, 1964.

107. *Ibid.*, October 2, 1964.

108. Iu. Shvedkov, "U Novogo Starta," *Mezhdunarodnaia Zhizn*, No. 1 (January, 1965), p. 39.

109. *Ibid.*, pp. 43-44.

110. "Memuary Eizenkhauera," *Mirovaia Ekonomika i Mezhdunarodnye Otnosheniia*, No. 10 (October, 1964), p. 126.

111. V. Shamberg, "Vybory v S.Sh.A.: Nekotorye Itogi," *Mirovaia Ekonomika i Mezhdunarodnye Otnosheniia*, No. 1 (January, 1965), p. 67.

112. *Pravda*, September 1, 1964.

113. *United States-Vietnam Relations*, Book 4, IV, C, 2, p. 3.

114. *Ibid.*, p. 4.

115. *The New York Times*, November 4, 1964.

116. *Pravda*, November 2, 1964, November 3, 1964, and November 4, 1964.

117. *Izvestiia*, November 29, 1964.

118. *Pravda*, December 20, 1964.

119. *Peking Review*, November 12, 1964.

120. Shvedkow, p. 46.

121. K. Bochkarev et al., *Programma KPSS — o Zashchite Sotsialicheskogo Otechestva* (Moscow: Voennoye Izdvo Minist. Oborony S.S.S.R., n.d.), p. 24.

122. *Izvestiia*, December 12, 1964.

123. *The New York Times*, November 8, 1964.

124. See, for example, *Izvestiia*, November 19, 1964, and TASS International Service, 1145 GMT, November 24, 1965, *FBIS*, U.S.S.R. and East Europe, November 25, 1964; p. BB5.

125. *Izvestiia*, November 19, 1964.

126. Moscow Domestic Service, n.d., *FBIS*, U.S.S.R. and East Europe, November 18, 1964, p. BB9.

127. *Izvestiia*, November 28, 1964.

128. *Izvestiia*, December 1, 1964.

129. *Ibid.*, December 4, 1964.

130. *Ibid.*, December 5, 1964.

131. *Ibid.*, December 9, 1964.

132. *Ibid.*, December 10, 1964.

133. *Pravda*, December 14, 1964, and December 21, 1964.

134. *Ibid.*, December 17, 1964; and *Izvestiia*, December 20, 1964.

135. *The New York Times*, December 28, 1964.

136. *Pravda*, January 5, 1964.

137. *Krasnaia Zvezda*, January 8, 1965.

138. *Pravda*, January 18, 1965.

139. *Ibid.*, January 23, 1965, and February 3, 1965.

140. For just a few of the many examples, see *Pravda*, December 22, 1964, December 25, 1964, December 26, 1964, January 3, 1965, January 8, 1965, January 22, 1965, and January 29, 1965; also *Izvestiia*, December 23, 1964, December 26, 1964, January 9, 1965, and January 29, 1965.

141. *Pravda*, February 1, 1965.

142. Shamberg, p. 69.

143. "Tekushchie Problemy Mirovoi Politiki," *Mirovaia Ekonomika i Mezhdunarodnye Otnosheniia*, No. 1 (January, 1965), p. 75.

144. See A. L. Hsieh, *Communist China's Military Policies and Nuclear Strategy* (Santa Monica, Calif.: Rand Corporation, 1965).

145. See any of a number of *Peking Review* articles throughout the fall of 1964.

146. *People's Daily,* quoted in *The New York Times,* October 23, 1964.
147. *The New York Times,* November 4, 1964.
148. *Peking Review,* December 4, 1964.
149. *Ibid.,* November 12, 1965.
150. Edgar Snow, "Interview with Mao," *New Republic,* February 27, 1965.
151. *Ibid.*

## NOTES TO CHAPTER III

1. *U.S. Department of State Bulletin,* Vol. 52, No. 1339 (February 22, 1965), p. 238.
2. U.S. Department of Defense, *United States-Vietnam Relations 1945-1967* (Washington: U.S. Government Printing Office, 1971), Book 4, IV, C, 3, p. 25. (Hereafter cited as *United States-Vietnam Relations.*)
3. *U.S. Department of State Bulletin,* Vol. 52, No. 1339 (February 22, 1965), p. 239.
4. *Ibid.*
5. *Ibid.,* Vol. 52, No. 1340 (March 1, 1965), pp. 290-91.
6. Some observers argued that North Vietnam fully expected American attacks on the North and even a possible invasion of the North. While the D.R.V.'s leaders were not blind to the possibility of such a turn of events, such an assessment requires acceptance that Hanoi was ready to see the results of its five-year-old industrial drive destroyed, as well as ignore all the signals the U.S. was sending that it would not intervene.
7. *United States-Vietnam Relations,* Book 4, IV, C, 3, p. 23.
8. *Ibid.,* p. 107.
9. *Ibid.,* pp. 31-34.
10. *Ibid.,* pp. 35-38.
11. *Ibid.,* pp. 40-42.
12. *Ibid.,* pp. 44-47.
13. *Ibid.,* p. 48.
14. On February 19, Colonel Pham Ngoc Thao attempted to oust General Khanh but failed. In light of the uncertain political situation in Saigon, Taylor recommended postponing ROLLING THUNDER I.
15. It does not appear as if the U.S. government seriously expected the conflict in Vietnam to be affected by the Soviet-British undertaking at Geneva. Rather, it appears as if the U.S. administration believed the Soviets could use their Geneva gambit as a way out of increasing their own commitment to Hanoi. See *United States-Vietnam Relations,* Book 4, IV, C, 3, pp. 55-57.
16. *U.S. Department of State Bulletin,* Vol. 52, No. 1343 (March 22, 1965), pp. 404-426. See also *U.S. Department of State Bulletin,* Vol 52, No. 1344 (March 29, 1965), pp. 442-448.
17. *United States-Vietnam Relations,* Book 4, IV, C, 3, p. 72.
18. *Ibid.,* pp. 85-89.
19. *Ibid.,* p. 85.
20. *Ibid.,* Book 4, IV, C, 4, pp. 19, 22.
21. *Ibid.,* Book 4, IV, C, 3, p. 97; pp. 113-124.
22. *U.S. Department of State Bulletin,* Vol. 52, No. 1349 (May 3, 1965), pp. 650-52.
23. *The New York Times,* February 26, 1965.

24. Philippe Devillers, "Preventing the Peace: Report from an Intermediary," *The Nation*, December 5, 1970.

25. *United States-Vietnam Relations*, Book 4, IV, C, 3, p. 100.

26. *The New York Times*, May 30, 1965.

27. *Ibid.*, June 4, 1965; and June 6, 1965.

28. *United States-Vietnam Relations*, Book 7, IV, C, 9, p. 3.

29. *The New York Times*, June 2, 1965.

30. Committee on Foreign Relations of the United States Senate, *Background Information Relating to Southeast Asia and Vietnam* (Washington: U.S. Government Printing Office, 1966), pp. 227-231.

31. *United States-Vietnam Relations*, Book IV, C, 4, pp. 113-123.

32. *Ibid.*, p. 120.

33. George McTurnan Kahin and John W. Lewis, *The United States in Vietnam* (New York: Delta, 1969), p. 243.

34. *U.S. Department of State Bulletin*, Vol. 54, No. 1392 (February 28, 1966), pp. 304-305.

35. See the February Bundy Memorandum, in *United States-Vietnam Relations*, Book 4, IV, C, 3, p. 32.

36. See, for example, *The New York Times*, September 1, 1965, and October 19, 1965.

37. *Ibid.*, August 21, 1966, and September 11, 1966.

38. *United States-Vietnam Relations*, Book 5, IV, C, 6, a, p. 82.

39. *The New York Times*, November 5, 1966. This was a restatement of the so-called "Manila Formula" of October.

40. *Pravda*, February 9, 1965, and February 10, 1965.

44. *United States-Vietnam Relations*, Book 4, IV, C, 3, p. 19.

45. *Ibid.*, p. 24.

46. *Pravda, February 1-7 inclusive, 1965*.

47. *Ibid.*, February 9, 1965.

48. *Ibid.*

49. *Krasnaia Zvezda*, February 10, 1965.

50. *Pravda*, February 10, 1965.

51. *Izvestiia*, February 11, 1965.

52. *The New York Times*, February 11, 1965, and February 12, 1965.

53. *Izvestiia*, February 12, 1965.

54. Some examples of this Soviet belief can be found in *Izvestiia*, February 17, 1965; *Pravda*, February 26, 1965; "Vneshniaia Politika i Sovremennyi Mir," *Kommunist*, No 3 (February, 1965); p. 10; and "Missii Mira i Druzhby," *Aziia i Afrika Segodnia*, No. 3 (March, 1965), p. 3.

55. *Pravda*, February 27, 1965.

56. *Izvestiia*, February 17, 1965.

57. "Vneshniaia Politika i Sovremennyi Mir," *Kommunist*, No 3 (February, 1965), p. 2.

58. *Ibid.*, p. 12.

59. *Pravda*, February 9, 1965, February 10, 1965, February 11, 1965, and February 27, 1965. See also *Izvestiia*, February 20, 1965.

60. *Krasnaia Zvezda*, February 26, 1965. It should also be noted that the Soviet Union made it clear that the threat of a large-scale war would not deter it from supporting various national liberation movements. See "Vneshniaia Politika i Sovremennyi Mir," *Kommunist*, No 3 (February, 1965), pp. 3, 9.

61. Radio Moscow to Yugoslavia, 1930 GMT, February 11, 1965, *FBIS*, U.S.S.R. and East Europe, February 12, 1965, p. bb14.

62. *Pravda*, February 14, 1965.
63. *Izvestiia*, February 16, 1965.
64. *Pravda*, February 17, 1965.
65. See O. Ivanov, "Dogovor Druzhby Sovetskogo i Kitaiskogo Narodov," *Kommunist*, No 3. (February, 1965), pp. 95-104; and "Missii Mira i Druzhby," *Aziia i Afrika Segodnia*, No. 3 (March, 1965), p. 3.
66. William Simons, *Coercion in Vietnam* (Santa Monica, Calif.: Rand Corporation, 1969), pp. 45-50.
67. See *Pravda*, March 3, 1965; *Izvestiia*, March 3, 1965; and *Krasnaia Zvezda*, March 3, 1965.
68. *Krasnaia Zvezda*, March 4, 1965.
69. *Izvestiia*, March 4, 1965.
70. *Pravda*, March 5, 1965.
71. *Ibid.*
72. *Ibid.*, March 10, 1965.
73. *Ibid.*, March 14, 1965.
74. *Krasnaia Zvezda*, March 21, 1965.
75. TASS International Service, 0725 GMT, March 18, 1965, *FBIS*, U.S.S.R. and East Europe, March 18, 1965, pp. BB1-2. It must have also been particularly foreboding to the Soviets that the Marines landed at Danang in northern South Vietnam. Soviet leaders possibly foresaw another "end run" amphibious assault such as the Inchon attack during the Korean War.
76. The only reference to "necessary assistance" from February 24 to March 2 was in Kosygin's television report on his Asian trip. On occasion, somewhat similar formulas were used. See *Pravda*, February 24-March 2, 1965, inclusive.
77. See *Ibid.*, March 3-10 inclusive, 1965.
78. This hesitancy to indicate strong support for North Vietnam in the event of resolute American action was not peculiar to the Soviet Union. For the Chinese position, see below.
79. For the full text of the NLFSV appeal, see *Pravda*, March 23, 1965.
80. *Ibid.*, March 24, 1965.
81. *The New York Times*, March 29, 1965.
82. See *Pravda*, March 24-April 1 inclusive, 1965.
83. *The New York Times*, April 11, 1965.
84. *Time*, April 1, 1966.
85. *Pravda*, April 18, 1965.
86. For a detailed discussion of this Soviet view, see Daniel S. Papp, "The Soviet Perception of American Goals in Vietnam: 1964-65," *Soviet Union*, Vol. 2, No. 2 (1975), pp. 147-151.
87. For the Soviet reaction to the Dominican intervention, see *Ibid.*, pp. 153-54.
88. "Sovetskaia Vneshniaia Politika i Obshchestvennyi Progress," *Kommunist*, No. 12 (August, 1965), p. 8.
89. *Pravda*, August 20, 1965.
90. V. Paramonov, "Profilpolitiki Dzhonsona," *Mezhdunavodnaia Zhizn*, No. 7 (July, 1965), p. 5.
91. *Izvestiia*, September 22, 1965.
92. E. Zhukov, "National Liberation Movements and Peaceful Coexistence," *Soviet Military Review*, No. 10 (October, 1965), pp. 7-9.
93. *Izvestiia*, September 22, 1965.
94. *Pravda*, June 30, 1965.
95. E. Konovalov, "Voenno-Kolonialnaia Strategiia Imperializma," *Mezh-*

*dunarodnaia Zhizn*, No. 12 (December, 1965), p. 43; and Matveev, p. 94.

96. "Dominican Republic: Latest U.S. Challenge to the Peoples," *World Marxist Review*, No. 6 (June, 1965), p. 5.

97. M. Stone, "U.S.A. Steps Up Aggression in Southeast Asia," *World Marxist Review*, No. 5 (May, 1965), p. 84.

98. V. Saprykov, "Vashington Maskiruet Svoin Agressiiu," *Aziia i Afrika Segodnia*, No. 10 (October, 1965), p. 7.

99. Norman Freed and Kjeld Oesterling, "Stop the Drift to World War," *World Marxist Review*, No. 7 (July, 1965), p. 6; Z. Mirskii, "Laboratoriia Voiny i Agressii," *Aziia i Afrika Segodnia*, No. 10 (October, 1965), pp. 11-13; and G. Gerasimov, "Kraka Ogranichennoi Voiny," *Ibid.*, No. 1 (October, 1965), p. 3.

100. Konovalov, p. 41.

101. Freed and Oesterling, p. 7.

102. V. Kudriavtsev, "Kollektivnyi Kolonializm, Individualnyi Grabezh," *Mezhdunarodnaia Zhizn*, No. 10 (October, 1965), pp. 9-18.

103. For additional discussion of the hypothetical Northeast Asian Treaty Organization, see De. Petrov, "Plany SShA i Politicheskii Klimat v Azii," *Ibid.*, No. 7 (July, 1965), p. 10; M. Markov, "Dalnevostochnye Kombinatsii Amerikanskikh Agressorov," *Ibid.*, No. 10 (October, 1965), p. 69; and Stone, p. 84.

104. *Pravda*, July 29, 1965; *Izvestiia*, July 29, 1965; and *Krasnaia Zvezda*, July 29, 1965.

105. *Pravda*, July 30, 1965.

106. *Ibid.*, August 4, 1965.

107. *Ibid.*, August 5, 1965.

108. *Ibid.*, August 7, 1965; and *Izvestiia*, August 7, 1965.

109. B. Teplinskii, "Obychnye Sily SShA vo Vetname," *Mezhdunarodnaia Zhizn*, No. 10 (October, 1965), p. 37.

110. *Pravda*, July 30, 1965.

111. *Izvestiia*, August 22, 1965.

112. Alekseev and Zhurkin, p. 83.

113. *The New York Times*, October 18, 1965.

114. *Ibid.*, November 9, 1965.

115. It was later confirmed that Soviet missile experts were, in fact, serving in Vietnam. See *Ibid.*, November 19, 1965.

116. *United States-Vietnam Relations*, Book 5, IV, C, 6, p. 24.

117. *The New York Times*, December 2, 1965.

118. *Ibid.*, December 21, 1965.

119. M. Stone, "U.S. Imperialists Bogged Down in the Dirty War," *World Marxist Review*, No. 9 (September, 1965), p. 88.

120. *Pravda*, December 2, 1965.

121. *Izvestiia*, December 22, 1965.

122. *Pravda*, December 10, 1965.

123. *Izvestiia*, December 18, 1965.

124. TASS International Service, 0637 GMT, December 17, 1965, *FBIS*, U.S.S.R. and East Europe, December 17, 1965, p. BB1.

125. *The New York Times*, November 2, 1965.

126. Radio Moscow, December 30, 1965.

127. *Pravda*, January 1, 1966.

128. *Izvestiia*, January 22, 1966.

129. *Ibid.*

130. *Pravda*, February 12, 1966.

131. Jan Prazsky, "Escalation of Miscalculation," *World Marxist Review*, No. 10 (October, 1966), pp. 71-72; also *Izvestiia*, May 23, 1967.

132. It was a considerable blow to Soviet prestige when North Vietnam refused to attend the Consultative Conference of Communist Parties in March 1965. The Soviet Union was probably determined not to suffer the same insult again. It must also be remembered that, in December, both the D.R.V. and the Soviet Union had considerably more to gain by professing unity than they had had in March. It was not too much of a surprise, then, when North Vietnam attended the Twenty-Third Congress of the CPSU.

133. For an assessment of the communiqué, see *The New York Times*, January 15, 1966.

134. For a more detailed analysis, see Charles B. McLane, "The Russians and Vietnam: Strategies of Indirection," *International Journal*, Vol. 24, No. 1 (Winter, 1968-69), pp. 47-64.

135. I. Miluson, "Imperialist Conceptions of Preventing Revolution," *International Affairs*, No. 2 (February, 1967), p. 84. See also *Pravda*, October 6, 1966.

136. D. Volsky, "U.S. Expansion and Peking Policy," *New Times*, No. 46-47 (November, 1967).

137. *Pravda*, October 21, 1966.

138. *Ibid.*, October 5, 1966.

139. I. Shatalov, "Southeast Asia in the Military-Strategic Plan of Imperialism," *International Affairs*, No. 4 (April, 1967), pp. 45-50.

140. Volsky, "U.S. Expansion and Peking Policy"; and Shatalov, p. 48.

141. *Literaturnaia Gazeta*, December 20, 1966.

142. *K Sobytiiam v Kitae* (Moscow: June, 1967), p. 62.

143. For a detailed discussion of American objectives in Vietnam under the "Asian Doctrine," see Daniel S. Papp, "The Soviet Perception of American Goals in Vietnam: 1966-70," *Soviet Union*, Vol. 4, No. 1 (1977), pp. 156-160.

144. L. I. Brezhnev, *Leninskim Kursom*, Volume 1 (Moscow: Izdatelstvo Politicheskoi Literatury, 1970), p. 228.

145. *The New York Times*, December 8, 1965.

146. *Ibid.*, August 8, 1965, August 29, 1965, and September 4, 1965.

147. "Ekho Vetnama v Zheneva," *Mezhdunarodnaia Zhizn*, No. 10 (October, 1965), p. 8.

148. *The New York Times*, December 5, 1965.

149. *Pravda*, March 30, 1966, and April 3, 1966. See especially the speeches by Brezhnev, Soviet Foreign Minister Gromyko, and Minister of Defense Malinovsky.

150. Franz Schurmann, *The Logic of World Power* (New York: Random House, 1974), p. 510.

151. *Jen-min Jih-pao*, in *The New York Times*, August 7, 1964; and August 10, 1964.

152. For the complete text of the Chinese government statement, see *Peking Review*, February 12, 1965.

153. William E. Griffith, *Sino-Soviet Relations 1964-65* (Cambridge, Mass.: M.I.T. Press, 1967), p. 75.

154. See any of a number of *Peking Review* articles throughout February and March.

155. New China News Agency, February 9, 1965.

156. *Peking Review*, November 12, 1965. See also *The New York Times*, February 26, 1965.

157. See for example New China News Agency, March 4, 1964.

158. *Peking Review*, March 12, 1965. The promises of volunteers appeared on March 28, April 11, May 10, May 29, June 2, June 18, and August 7. See Taylor, pp. 46-47.

159. For some fascinating accounts of these disagreements, see Donald S. Zagoria, *Vietnam Triangle: Moscow, Peking, Hanoi* (New York: Pegasus, 1967), pp. 67-98; and Jay Taylor, *China and Southeast Asia* (New York: Praeger, 1974), pp. 37-48.

160. For an expression of the views espoused by both factions, see *Peking Review*, May 14, 1965.

161. Edgar Snow, "Aftermath of the Cultural Revolution," *The New Republic*, April 3, 1971.

162. Edward Crankshaw in the *Observer* (London), November 14, 1965. See also *Peking Review*, November 12, 1965, in which China accused the Soviet Union of limiting its aid to North Vietnam so it could "keep the situation under [its control], to gain a say on the North Vietnamese question, and to strike a bargain with U.S. imperialism on it."

163. *Peking Review*, January 1, 1966, and July 15, 1966.

164. New China News Agency, June 1, 1965.

165. Peking Radio, March 13, 1965; and *People's Daily*, March 3, 1966, quoted in Kahin, p. 295.

166. New China News Agency, September 21, 1965.

167. *Peking Review*, May 13, 1966.

168. Le Duan, "We Will Certainly Win, the Enemy Will Certainly Be Defeated," quoted in Gareth Porter, *A Peace Denied* (Bloomington: Indiana University, 1975), p. 2.

169. *Peking Review*, August 6, 1965.

170. *Ibid.*, August 13, 1965. This was one of the last times the Chinese made this threat.

171. *Ibid.*, September 3, 1965.

172. David P. Mozingo and T. W. Robinson, *Lin Piao on People's War: China Takes a Second Look at Vietnam* (Santa Monica, Calif.: Rand Corporation, 1968).

173. For North Vietnam's hostile reaction to "Long Live the Victory of People's War," see Zagoria, pp. 83-86.

174. For a sampling of these statements, see *The New York Times*, February 20, 1966, July 12, 1966, and August 23, 1966. These statements were made by Hubert Humphrey, Lyndon Johnson, and William Fulbright, respectively.

175. *Peking Review*, No. 4 (January 21, 1966).

176. *The New York Times*, April 27, 1966. Reportedly, the President himself made this decision. See *China and U.S. Far East Policy, 1945-66* (Washington: Congressional Quarterly Service, 1967), pp. 185-86.

177. John Gittings, "A Diplomatic Thaw," *Far Eastern Economic Review*, December 19, 1968, pp. 663-65.

178. See *U.S. Policy with Respect to Mainland China: Hearings Before the Committee on Foreign Relations*, U.S. Senate, 89th Congress, 2nd Session (Washington: U.S. Government Printing Office, 1966).

179. *U.S. Department of State Bulletin*, Vol. 54, No. 1041 (May 2, 1966), pp. 693-95.

180. According to *Peking Review*, Chou's statement was made on April 10 in an interview with a Pakistani writer. However, in the full text of the interview printed in the Pakistani paper *Dawn*, the four points do not appear. Thus, it ap-

pears likely that *Peking Review* and Chou were in fact responding to Rusk. See Roderick MacFarquhar (ed.), *Sino-American Relations 1949-71* (New York: Praeger, 1972), p. 214n.

181. *Peking Review*, May 13, 1966.

182. *U.S. Department of State Bulletin*, Vol. 54, No. 1406 (June 6, 1966), pp. 880-881.

183. *Ibid.*, Vol. 55, No. 1418 (August 29, 1965), p. 303.

184. *The New York Times*, July 12, 1966.

185. Schurmann, p. 512.

186. *Peking Review*, May 6, 1966.

187. *Ibid.*, March 25, 1966.

188. *People's Daily*, April 30, 1967, quoted in Yin, p. 151. See also *Peking Re-View*, January 1, 1966.

189. *Peking Review*, August 12, 1966.

190. *Ibid.*, September 16, 1966.

191. For an interesting treatment of changing Chinese pledges of support to Vietnam, see John Gittings, "Will China Fight?" *Far Eastern Economic Review*, March 2, 1967, pp. 260-62.

192. Hugh Sidey, *A Very Personal Presidency* (New York: Atheneum, 1968), p. 238.

193. See Zagoria, pp. 63-98; and Taylor, pp. 36-43.

## NOTES TO CHAPTER IV

1. U.S. Department of Defense, *United States-Vietnam Relations 1945-1967* (Washington: U.S. Government Printing Office, 1971), Book 5, IV, C, 6, b, p. 1. (Hereafter cited as *United States-Vietnam Relations.*)

2. *Ibid.*, p. 2.

3. For a detailed discussion of this debate, see *Ibid.*, pp. 7-18.

4. Commander in Chief Pacific and Commander, U.S. Military Assistance Command, Vietnam, *Report on the War in Vietnam* (Washington: U.S. Government Printing Office, 1969), p. 31. (Hereafter cited as Cincpac.)

5. Lyndon Baines Johnson, *The Vantage Point: Perspectives of the Presidency 1963-1969* (New York: Popular Library, 1971), p. 367.

6. *United States-Vietnam Relations*, Book 5, IV, C, 6, b, p. 64.

7. *Ibid.*, p. 83.

8. Johnson, p. 262.

9. W. W. Rostow, *The Diffusion of Power* (New York: Macmillan, 1972), pp. 458-459.

10. Cincpac, p. 9.

11. *United States-Vietnam Relations*, Book 5, IV, C, 6, b, 146-150.

12. Johnson, p. 422.

13. George McTurnan Kahin and John W. Lewis, *The United States in Vietnam* (New York: Delta, 1969), p. 355.

14. For an overview of the maneuvering, see Kahin, pp. 347-354.

15. Johnson, p. 262.

16. For the statements of favorably-impressed observers, see *Ibid.*, pp. 264-265. For negative impressions, see Kahin, pp. 356, 408.

17. *U.S. Department of State Bulletin*, Vol. 57, No. 1475 (October 2, 1967), p. 421.

18. Walter Rostow views this somewhat differently, saying that it must be

viewed as the competition between two processes. One process, that of "nation-building," required time to be successful. These opposed processes were "the attrition of American will in the face of an indecisive protracted war and a gathering strength of South Vietnamese nationalism." See Rostow, *The Diffusion of Power* (New York: Macmillan, 1972), p. 437.

19. *The New York Times*, October 26, 1966.

20. For the text of Johnson's letter, see Johnson, pp. 592-595.

21. *Ibid.*, p. 250. For a detailed account of the failures of Marigold and the other peace efforts as well, see David Kraslow and Stuart H. Loory, *The Secret Search for Peace in Vietnam* (New York: Random House, 1968).

22. *The New York Times*, September 30, 1967.

23. Johnson, p. 262.

24. *Ibid.*, p. 372. For Johnson's own response to McNamara's proposals, see *Ibid.*, pp. 600-601.

25. *United States-Vietnam Relations*, Book 5, IV, C, 6, c, p. 1.

26. Rostow, p. 693.

27. Townshend Hoopes, *The Limits of Intervention* (New York: David McKay, 1969), p. 102.

28. Rostow, pp. 462-63.

29. Johnson, p. 279-380.

30. *United States-Vietnam Relations*, Book 5, IV, C, 6, c, p. 2. For a detailed account of the Tet offensive, see Don Oberdorfer, *Tet!* (New York: Arrow Books, 1972).

31. See, for example, Cincpac, p. 136.

32. Johnson, p. 383. There was an alternative theory, though not accepted by Johnson or his advisors, that the Tet offensive merely sought to force negotiations. See Gareth Porter, *A Peace Denied* (Bloomington: Indiana University Press, 1975), pp. 65-70.

33. See COSVN Resolution No. 6 in Cincpac, p. 168.

34. "Circular from COSVN Current Affairs Committee of the SVLAF Headquarters Concerning a Preliminary Assessment of the Situation," in Patrick McGarvey, *Visions of Victory: Selected Vietnamese Communist Military Writings 1964-68* (Stanford: Hoover Institute on War, Revolution, and Peace, 1969), p. 253.

35. Institute for Strategic Studies, *Strategic Survey 1968* (London: Institute for Strategic Studies, 1970), p. 644-45.

36. *Time*, February 9, 1968.

37. *United States-Vietnam Relations*, Book 5, IV, C, 6, c, pp. 12-15.

38. *Ibid.*

39. For a detailed examination of the reassessment process, see *Ibid.*, pp. 16-76.

40. Johnson, for example, later argued that one reason Westmoreland's requests were rejected was because future large-scale Vietcong attacks were deemed unlikely (Johnson, p. 415). *United States-Vietnam Relations* disputes this point. Similarly, Walter Rostow argued that the "slippage in pacification" was "limited and quite easily repaired" (Rostow, p. 468). *United States-Vietnam Relations* takes issue with this point as well.

41. Henry A. Kissinger, *American Foreign Policy* (New York: W. W. Norton, 1974), p. 106.

42. Johnson, p. 423. Soon after Johnson's resignation speech, Clark Clifford spoke of a "policy decision" that the "South Vietnamese will take over the war" (*Washington Post*, April 12, 1968).

43. *The New York Times*, April 3, 1968.

44. Cincpac, p. 167.

45. *Ibid.*, p. 166. See also Johnson, p. 508.

46. Johnson, p. 514.

47. During June and July, Hanoi did in fact curtail its military activity in the South, leading the head of the U.S. delegation in Paris, Averell Harriman, to suggest a total bombing halt to Johnson. Johnson, however, refused to view the curtailed activity as fulfilling demands for reciprocity, and the bombing continued.

48. Johnson, p. 509.

49. *The New York Times*, November 1, 1968.

50. The D.R.V.'s and Johnson's accounts of these preliminary steps are quite similar. For Johnson's version, see Johnson, pp. 516-517. For the D.R.V.'s, see *The New York Times*, April 21, 1972.

51. Johnson, p. 513.

52. Sudershan Chawla et al., *Southeast Asia under a New Balance of Power* (New York: Praeger, 1974), p. 17.

53. Richard Whelan, *Catch a Falling Flag: A Republican's Challenge to His Party* (Boston: Houghton Mifflin, 1972), p. 139.

54. Henry A. Kissinger, "The Vietnam Negotiations," *Foreign Affairs*, Vol. 47, No. 2 (January, 1969), p. 211-234.

55. Frank van der Linden, *Nixon's Quest for Peace* (New York: Robert B. Luce, 1972), p. 42.

56. *The New York Times*, January 28, 1969.

57. For details of "Operation Menu," see *Bombings in Cambodia*, Hearings before the Committee on Armed Services, U.S. Senate, 93rd Congress, 1st Session, 1973.

58. William P. Rogers, *United States Foreign Policy 1969-70: A Report of the Secretary of State* (Washington: U.S. Government Printing Office, 1971), p. 48.

59. *Ibid.*, p. 49.

60. Johnson, p. 524.

61. *Washington Post*, April 18, 1969.

62. Kissinger, *Foreign Affairs*, p. 234.

63. Marvin Kalb and Bernard Kalb, *Kissinger* (Boston: Little, Brown, 1974), pp. 105-135.

64. *Congressional Record* (May 11, 1972), p. E5025.

65. Averell Harriman, "Harriman Suggests a Way Out of Vietnam," *The New York Times Magazine*, August 24, 1969.

66. The most prominent alternative explanation was that Hanoi was husbanding its strength for a later offensive. See Porter, pp. 92-94.

67. *U.S. Department of State Bulletin*, Vol. 60, No. 1562 (June 2, 1969), pp. 457-461.

68. *Ibid.*

69. Rogers, p. 35.

70. *Ibid.*, pp. 36-37.

71. *Ibid.*, p. 36.

72. *The New York Times*, November 4, 1969.

73. Slobodenko, p. 4.

74. Y. Melnikov, "United States Foreign Policy — A Threat to Peace," *International Affairs* (Moscow), No. 8 (August, 1967), p. 67.

75. Johnson, pp. 256-57, 483-85.

76. *Pravda*, January 31, 1968.

77. *Ibid.*, February 8-28, 1968; and *Izvestiia*, February 8-28, 1968.

78. *Izvestiia*, January 31, 1968.

79. *Ibid.*, April 2, 1968.

80. *Pravda*, April 6, 1968.

81. *Izvestiia*, April 2, 1968.

82. *Pravda*, May 5, 1968. For a somewhat similar account, see "Washington Maneuvers at Paris Talks," *International Affairs*, No. 7 (July, 1968), pp. 52-54.

83. This hesitancy may have been connected to the fact that Lyndon Johnson had been the "peace candidate" in 1964.

84. V. Churanov, "Novoe Levoe Dvizhenie," *Mirovaia Ekonomika i Mezhdunarodnye Otnosheniia*, No. 1 (January, 1968), pp. 94-98.

85. "Tekushchie Problemy Mirovoi Politiki," in *Ibid.*, p. 67; V. Shamberg, "Predvybornaia Borba v SShA," in *Ibid.*, No. 9 (September, 1968); and *Pravda*, June 25, 1968.

86. *Izvestiia*, March 22, 1968.

87. *Za Rubezhom*, No. 6 (February, 1968).

88. "Tekushchie Problemy Mirovoi Politiki," *Mirovaia Ekonomika i Mezhdunarodnye Otnosheniia*, No. 7 (July, 1968), p. 84.

89. *Pravda*, November 3, 1968.

90. *Izvestiia*, November 16, 1968. See also "Tekuschie Problemy Mirovoi Politiki," *Mirovaia Ekonomika i Mezhdunarodnye Otnosheniia*, No. 1 (January, 1969), p. 83.

91. *Literaturnaia Gazeta*, December 18, 1968; *Izvestiia*, November 29, 1968; and Observer, "The 37th Presidency," *New Times*, No. 4 (January, 1969).

92. D. Volsky, "Americans and Vietnam," *World Marxist Review*, No. 48 (November, 1968), p. 20.

93. V. Dagmar, "The U.S. after the Presidential Elections," *World Marxist Review*, No. 1 (January, 1969), p. 12.

94. *Izvestiia*, November 29, 1968.

95. "Vo Poiskakh 'Novoi' Vneshnei Politiki," *Mirovaia Ekonomika i Mezhdunarodnye Otnosheniia*, No. 10 (October, 1968), pp. 98-102.

96. Radio Moscow, December 18, 1968.

97. *Izvestiia*, November 29, 1968.

98. D. Volskii, "Podvig Vetnama," *Kommunist*, No. 16 (November, 1968), p. 96.

99. Leontyev, p. 53; and *Krasnaia Zvezda*, March 2, 1966.

100. Slobodenko, p. 3.

101. Radio Moscow, January 19, 1969.

102. V. Shvedkov, "The Fruits of Global Policy," *International Affairs*, No. 8 (August, 1968), p. 26.

103. A. Sovetov, "The Present Stage in the Struggle between Socialism and Imperialism," *International Affairs*, No. 11 (November, 1968), p. 3.

104. *Izvestiia*, February 1, 1969.

105. Radio Moscow, January 22, 1969.

106. For additional examples of Soviet willingness to give Nixon time to formulate his Vietnam policy, see V. Dagmar, "The U.S. after the Presidential Election," *World Marxist Review*, No. 1 (January, 1969), pp. 15-17; Radio Moscow, February 27, 1969; L. Vidyasova, "The USSR and the Struggle against Aggression and War," *International Affairs*, No. 3 (March, 1969), pp. 65-70; and *Trud*, May 28, 1969.

107. J. Prazsky, "Vietnam: Harder Blows at the Aggression," *World Marxist*

*Review*, No. 10-11 (November, 1968), p. 29; I. Shchedorv, "Vietnam: The New Phase," *World Marxist Review*, No. 1 (January, 1969), pp. 10-14; Commentator, "When Will Realism Prevail?" *International Affairs*, No. 1 (January, 1969), pp. 62-63; I. Belyaev, "Washington's Asian Boomerang," No. 5 (May, 1969), p. 65; and "Tekushchie Problemy Mirovoi Politiki," *Mirovaia Ekonomika i Mezhdunarodnye Otnosheniia*, No. 4 (April, 1969), pp. 74-76.

108. *Izvestiia*, March 13, 1969.

109. *Ibid.*, April 26, 1969.

110. Radio Moscow, March 25, 1969.

111. *Pravda*, June 8, 1969.

112. *Ibid.*, July 11, 1969.

113. V. Shamberg, "Vnutripoliticheskie Dilemmy Pravitalstva Niksona," *Mirovaia Ekonomika i Mezhdunarodnye Otnosheniia*, No. 7 (July, 1969), p. 26; and "Tekushchie Problemy Mirovoi Politiki," *Mirovaia Ekonomika i Mezhdunarodnye Otnosheniia*, No. 7 (July, 1969), p. 80.

114. V. Kudryavtsev, "Two Spearheads of American Aggression," *International Affairs*, No. 5 (May, 1970), p. 76.

115. I. Antonov, "Washington's Asia Doctrine," *New Times*, No. 6 (February, 1970), pp. 10-11.

116. *Pravda*, January 24, 1970; I. Lebedev, "The New Political Geometry in the Pacific," *International Affairs*, No. 1 (January, 1970), p. 50; B. Teplinsky, "Some Aspects of U.S. Global Strategy," *International Affairs*, No. 5 (May, 1970), p. 70.

117. *Pravda*, August 12, 1969.

118. Y. Shtykanov, "The 'New' U.S. Policy in Asia," *International Affairs*, No. 10 (October, 1969), p. 69.

119. *Pravda*, February 1, 1970; *Izvestiia*, February 8, 1970; and L. Zavyalor, "Who Formulates Policy in America Today?" *International Affairs*, No. 5 (May, 1970), p. 53.

120. Shtykanov, p. 69.

121. J. Prazsky, "1969: A Political Survey," *World Marxist Review*, No. 1 (January, 1970); *Pravda*, November 6, 1969; December 25, 1969; and February 19, 1970; and *Izvestiia*, December 12, 1969; and January 8, 1970.

122. S. Verbitzkii, "Za Shirmoi 'Vetnamizatzii," *Mirovaia Ekonomika i Mezhdunarodnye Otnosheniia*, No. 5 (May, 1970), pp. 78-79.

123. *Izvestiia*, October 18, 1969; A. Ter-Grigoryan, "The Vietnamization Bluff," *New Times*, No. 1 (January, 1970), p. 23; Kidryavtsev, p. 76; and A. Varyshev, "New U.S. Doctrine, Same Old Aims," *International Affairs*, No. 12 (December, 1969), p. 14.

124. *Pravda*, April 15, 1970.

125. Shtykanov, p. 70; I. Shchedrov, "Indo-China: U.S. Aggression Continues," *New Times*, No. 8 (February, 1970), p. 9.

126. Radio Moscow, November 4, 1969.

127. *Izvestiia*, November 6, 1969.

128. *Pravda*, November 6, 1969.

129. *Ibid.*, November 7, 1969.

130. *Washington Post*, April 19, 1968.

131. New China Agency, April 5, 1967.

132. *U.S. Department of State Bulletin*, Vol. 56, No. 1440 (January 30, 1967), p. 162.

133. For different Western interpretations of the Chinese debate, see Franz Schurmann, "What Is Happening in China?" *New York Review of Books* (Oc-

tober 20, 1966), pp. 18-25; the articles by Donald Zagoria and Uri Raanan in Tang Tsou (ed.), *China in Crisis*, Vol. 2 (Chicago: University of Chicago Press, 1968); and John Gittings, "Will China Fight?" *Far Eastern Economic Review*, March 2, 1967, p. 360-362. For a fascinating account of the effect of the Cultural Revolution on the Chinese Ministry of Foreign Affairs, see Melvin Gurtov "The Foreign Ministry and Foreign Affairs during the Cultural Revolution," *China Quarterly*, No. 40 (October, 1969), pp. 65-102.

134. New China News Agency, May 22, 1967. See also *Peking Review*, February 24, 1967, April 28, 1967, and July 28, 1967.

135. Institute of Strategic Studies, *The Military Balance 1968-69* (London: Institute for Strategic Studies, 1969).

136. U.S. Department of State, *Background Notes: People's Republic of China* (Washington: U.S. Government Printing Office, 1971).

137. *The New York Times*, April 12, 1967.

138. *Ibid.*, July 7, 1968.

139. *Ibid.*, December 27, 1967; and *Christian Science Monitor*, November 18, 1967.

140. *Peking Review*, March 10, 1967.

141. *Izvestiia*, March 29, 1967. This charge was a repetition of earlier similar charges.

142. *Peking Review*, January 1, 1967, and February 10, 1967.

143. *Ibid.*, February 24, 1967, and June 30, 1967.

144. *Ibid.*, March 10, 1967, and April 28, 1967.

145. *Ibid.*, February 24, 1967.

146. See for example, *Ibid.*, April 21, 1967, April 28, 1967, and May 5, 1967.

147. *Ibid.*, April 28, 1967, and May 5, 1967.

148. New China News Agency, August 30, 1967.

149. *Ibid.*, December 19, 1967.

150. See David Schoenbrunn's introduction to Vo Nguyen Giap, *Big Victory, Great Task* (New York: Praeger, 1967), p. xiv.

151. *Peking Review*, July 28, 1967.

152. *Ibid.*, September 8, 1967, October 6, 1967, and October 13, 1967.

153. Significantly, when Mao, Lin Piao, and Chou En-lai congratulated Ho on Vietnamese National Day, there was no reference to China as a "reliable rear area." Two of the rare instances this formula was used during the second half of 1967 were in July and December. See *Ibid.*, July 28, 1967, and December 25, 1967.

154. *Ibid.*, December 25, 1967.

155. *Ibid.*, February 23, 1968.

156. New China News Agency, February 2, 1968. Other Chinese leaders and publications were equally laudstory. See *Peking Review*, February 9, 1967, February 16, 1968, and February 23, 1968.

157. *Peking Review*, October 27, 1967.

158. *Ibid.*, December 15, 1967.

159. *Ibid.*, July 28, 1967, and February 16, 1968.

160. New China News Agency, August 30, 1967. See also *Peking Review*, February 9, 1968.

161. "Far Eastern Round Up," *Far Eastern Economic Review*, May 2, 1968, p. 240. Moscow Radio reported that Chou told the D.R.V. delegation in Paris that, "In Mao's opinion, the talks are a mistake" — *China Quarterly*, No. 35 (July-September, 1968), p. 199.

162. *Peking Review*, April 12, 1968.

163. New China News Agency, October 19, 1968. See also *Peking Review*, October 25, 1968.

164. *Peking Review*, September 6, 1968.

165. *Ibid.*, October 25, 1968.

166. New China News Agency, October 1, 1968.

167. For some Western views of Peking's attitude, see *Washington Post*, November 4, 1968; and *The New York Times*, December 15, 1968.

168. *The New York Times*, June 28, 1968.

169. *Peking Review*, October 24, 1969. *Peking Review* even issued a special supplement on August 23, 1968, condemning the Soviet invasion.

170. *The New York Times*, November 27, 1968.

171. *Confession in an Impasse* (Peking: Foreign Language Press, 1969). Similarly, the January 23, 1969, issue of *People's Daily* described Nixon as "an agent of the American monopoly groups which have chosen him as their front man." See *China Quarterly*, No. 38 (April-June, 1969), p. 190.

172. *Peking Review*, April 28, 1969.

173. *The New York Times*, January 28, 1969.

174. See Clark Clifford, "A Vietnam Reappraisal," *Foreign Affairs*, Vol. 47, No. 4 (July, 1969), pp. 601-622.

175. New China News Agency, February 7, 1969.

176. For the official Chinese government statement on the border clash, see *Peking Review*, March 7, 1969.

177. See Robert Osgood et al., *Retreat from Empire?* (Baltimore: Johns Hopkins University Press, 1973), p. 11; Chawla, pp. 14-15; and A. Doak Barnett, "The Changing Strategic Balance in Asia," in Gene T. Hsiao (ed.), *Sino-American Detente and Its Policy Implications* (New York: Praeger, 1974), p. 24.

178. Rogers, p. 42.

179. *Ibid.*, p. 43.

180. *Ibid.*, p. 42.

181. New China News Agency, January 1, 1970.

182. *Washington Post*, September 10, 1969.

183. *The New York Times*, March 15, 1969, and May 8, 1969.

184. Taylor, p. 62.

185. New China News Agency, September 1, 1969.

186. *Ibid.*, September 4, 1969. See also *Peking Review*, September 12, 1969, pp. 3-4.

187. *Peking Review*, October 24, 1967, pp. 6-7, and October 31, 1969, pp. 6-7.

188. *Ibid.*, November 7, 1969, p. 27.

189. *Ibid.*, August 15, 1969, pp. 23-24.

190. Edgar Snow, "A Conversation with Mao Tse-tung," *Life*, April 30, 1971.

NOTES TO CHAPTER V

1. See Sudershan Chawla, "U.S. Strategy in Southeast Asia in the Post-Cease-Fire Period," in Chawla et al., *Southeast Asia under the New Balance of Power* (New York: Praeger, 1974), p. 28.

2. William P. Rogers, *United States Foreign Policy 1971: A Report of the Secretary of State* (Washington: U.S. Government Printing Office, 1972), p. 71.

3. *Ibid.*, 50-51; and p. 71; and William P. Rogers, *United States Foreign*

*Policy 1972: A Report of the Secretary of State* (Washington: U.S. Government Printng Office, 1973), p. 347.

4. Richard Nixon, *Public Papers of the President: Richard M. Nixon, 1970* (Washington: U.S. Government Printing Office, 1971), p. 37.

5. David Landau, *Kissinger: The Uses of Power* (Boston: Houghton Miffline, 1972), p. 106.

6. Edgar Snow, "A Conversation with Mao Tse-tung," *Life*, April 30, 1971.

7. Marvin Kalb and Bernard Kalb, *Kissinger* (Boston: Little, Brown, 1974), p. 151.

8. *The New York Times*, April 21, 1970.

9. For a more detailed account of this so-called "territorial accommodation," see Gareth Porter, *A Peace Denied* (Bloomington: Indiana University Press, 1975), pp. 89-90.

10. *Washington Post*, December 11, 1969.

11. *Ibid.*, May 6, 1970.

12. *The New York Times*, March 7, 1970.

13. *Ibid.*, May 1, 1970.

14. *Christian Science Monitor*, May 27, 1970.

15. *Washington Post*, May 11, 1970.

16. See *The New York Times*, February 24, 1973. Moorer stated that the Joint Chiefs of Staff felt that any escalation should be directed against the source of the problem, North Vietnam.

17. *Ibid.*, September 18, 1970.

18. Richard M. Nixon, *A New Peace Initiative for All Indochina* (Washington: U.S. Government Printing Office, 1970), DoS Publication 8555.

19. For a brief review of these secret negotiations and proposals, see Frank van der Linden, *Nixon's Quest for Peace* (Washington: Robert B. Luce, 1972), pp. 168-170.

20. *Washington Post*, January 26, 1972, and January 27, 1972.

21. *The New York Times*, February 1, 1972.

22. George Kahin, "Negotiations: The View from Hanoi," *New Republic* (November 6, 1971), pp. 13-16; and *The New York Times*, January 27, 1972.

23. Rogers, *United States Foreign Policy 1971*, p. 75.

24. *The New York Times*, February 1, 1972.

25. Rogers, *United States Foreign Policy 1971*, p. 81.

26. *Ibid.*, pp. 72-77.

27. Rogers, *United States Foreign Policy 1972*, p. 350.

28. Jean Lacouture, "Toward an End to the Indochina War?" *Pacific Community*, Vol. III, No. 2 (January, 1972), p. 330.

29. Michel Tatu, "Moscow, Peking, and the Conflict in Vietnam," in Anthony Lake (ed.), *The Vietnam Legacy* (New York: New York University Press, 1976), p. 31.

30. Linden, p. 170.

31. *Time*, April 17, 1972.

32. *The New York Times*, April 21, 1972, and April 22, 1972.

33. Linden, p. 179.

34. *The New York Times*, June 20, 1972.

35. Porter, p. 107-108.

36. This again was a political phrase employed by Secretary of State Rogers in his yearly foreign policy report. See Rogers, *United States Foreign Policy 1972*, p. 346.

37. Linden, pp. 170-171.
38. *The New York Times*, April 7, 1972.
39. *Ibid.*, May 9, 1972.
40. For the text of the Shanghai Communiqué, see *Peking Review*, March 3, 1972.
41. Rogers, *United States Foreign Policy 1972*, pp. 338-342.
42. Kalb and Kalb, pp. 293-94.
43. *The New York Times*, May 3, 1972. A total of 12 Soviet ships had been trapped in Haiphong Harbor.
44. Linden, p. 174. Other official commentary was equally blunt. Secretary of State Rogers told the May meeting of NATO ministers that the Soviet Union bore "a responsibility" for North Vietnam's invasion of the South (*The New York Times*, May 6, 1972). Shortly thereafter, Kissinger told a news conference that the Soviet Union was responsibile for "the evolution of the situation" in Vietnam since it had provided the D.R.V. with "offensive equipment." Continuing, Kissinger claimed he doubted whether Brezhnev intended to "inflict a humiliation" on the U.S., but rather the Soviet leader had not "considered the consequences" of "imposing a major setback" on the U.S. (*The New York Times*, May 10, 1972).
45. *Ibid.*, pp. 218-219.
46. Kalb and Kalb, p. 330.
47. *Washington Post*, November 12, 1972.
48. *The New York Times*, May 13, 1972, and October 26, 1972.
49. *Ibid.*, July 1, 1972.
50. *Ibid.*, July 6, 1972.
51. Porter, p. 120.
52. For further development of this theme, see Daniel Yankelovich, "Why Nixon Won," *New York Review of Books* (November 30, 1972), p. 7.
53. For North Vietnam's expectations of the future, see *Washington Post*, July 23, 1972.
54. This report emanated from Hoang Tung, a spokesman for the Central Committee of the Vietnamese Workers' Party. See Tom Hayden, "What Detente Means to the Vietnamese" (July, 1974), p. 3.
55. Porter, p. 121.
56. *The New York Times*, October 27, 1972.
57. For a more detailed analysis of these negotiations, see Porter, pp. 122-136.
58. *The New York Times*, October 27, 1972.
59. For a more detailed look at the behind the scenes maneuvering surrounding the October "agreement," see Tad Szulc, "Behind the Vietnam Cease Fire Agreement," *Foreign Policy*, No. 15 (Summer, 1974), pp. 54-55.
60. Kalb and Kalb, p. 357.
61. In the preliminary negotiations on the draft agreement, it had been decided that the agreement would be signed on October 31.
62. *The New York Times*, November 1, 1972.
63. For a fascinating look at Thieu and his point of view, see Oriana Fallaci, "An Interview with Thieu," *New Republic* (January 30, 1973), p. 17. See also *The New York Times*, November 1, 1972.
64. See *Washington Post*, November 9, 1972.
65. *The New York Times*, November 5, 1972.
66. Kalb and Kalb, pp. 377-378.

67. Kissinger maintained that the North Vietnamese "understood the need to reduce the number of their forces in the South."

68. For Kissinger's complete list, see Porter, pp. 145-48.

69. Rogers, *United States Foreign Policy 1972*, p. 347.

70. *Christian Science Monitor*, November 10, 1972; and *Wall Street Journal*, November 17, 1972.

71. See Kalb and Kalb, p. 400; and *The Guardian* (London), December 22, 1972.

72. Kalb and Kalb, p. 412; and *The Guardian* (London), December 22, 1972.

73. *Ibid.*

74. *Washington Post*, February 4, 1973. Pentagon officials according to *U.S. News and World Report*, January 8, 1973, privately conceded that the United States could not have continued the raids much longer because of the staggering losses.

75. *Washington Post*, December 30, 1972.

76. *The New York Times*, December 22, 1972.

77. *Ibid.*, February 4, 1973.

78. *Ibid.*, December 19, 1972.

79. *Ibid.*, December 23, 1972. Further insight to Nixon's thinking may be gained by his later statement that the bombings were designed to make the Russians and Chinese "think they were dealing with a madman and so had better force North Vietnam into a settlement before the world was consumed by a larger war." See Thomas L. Hughes, "Foreign Policy: Men or Measures?" *Atlantic* (October, 1974), p. 56.

80. *Washington Post*, February 4, 1973. See also T.J.S. George, "The Precinct of a Single Angry Man," *Far Eastern Economic Review* (January 8, 1973), p. 10.

81. For Le Duc Tho's statement, see *Baltimore Sun*, January 7, 1973. For Nixon's letter, see *The New York Times*, May 1, 1975.

82. It is true that North Vietnam totally abandoned its demand to change the period for release of political prisoners from 90 days to 60 days, but it must be remembered that this demand was not put forth until the January talks began. It must thus be construed as a bargaining tool rather than a legitimate demand.

83. See *Weekly Compilation of Presidential Documents*, January 29, 1973, pp. 45-64, for this agreement and adjoining protocols.

84. Philip Dion, "Fatal Ambivalence," *Far Eastern Economic Review*, March 20, 1971, pp. 24-26.

85. For just a few of the numerous Soviet statements on this, see M. Aleksandrov, "Guamskaia Doktrina: Illiuzii i Deistvitelnost," *Kommunist Vooruzhennykh Sil*, No. 22 (November, 1972), pp 80-84; G. Trofimenko, "Anti-Communism and Imperialism's Foreign Policy," *International Affairs*, No. 1 (January, 1971), p. 53; and V. Kuzmin, "The Guam Doctrine: Old Objective, New Technique," *International Affairs*, No. 12 (December, 1971), pp. 32-37.

86. L. Sasnovsky, "Strategy of U.S. Neocolonial Wars," *International Affairs*, No. 10 (October, 1971), p. 34. See also F. Billoux, "Peaceful Coexistence and Ideology," *World Marxist Review*, No. 1 (January, 1972), p. 52.

87. For in depth discussion of the "American global strategy," see O. Bykov, "O Nekotorykh Chertakh Vneshnepoliticheskoi Strategii SShA," *Mirovaia Ekonomika i Mezhdunarodnye Otnosheniia*, No. 4 (April, 1971), pp. 53-64; M. Milshtein, "Amerikanskie Voennye Doktriny: Preestvennost i Modifikatziia," *Ibid.*, No. 8 (August, 1971), pp. 30-41; Y Mikheyev, "The Peoples of Indochina in

the Struggle for Freedom and Independence," *International Affairs*, No. 8 (August, 1971), pp. 68-74; and B. Andre, Step toward 'Permanent War'?" *World Marxist Review*, No. 5 (May, 1971), pp. 145-148.

88. Kuzmin, p. 37.

89. For Soviet statements on Vietnamization, see V. Gantman, "Tekushchie Problemy Mirovoi Politiki," *Mirovaia Ekonomika i Mezhdunarodnye Otnosheniia*, No. 1 (January, 1972), pp. 85-87; V. Matveyev, "Washington's 'New' Doctrine," *International Affairs*, No. 4 (April, 1971), p. 29; A Poltorak, "Vietnamization: Aggression Continued and Expanded," *International Affairs*, No. 5 (May, 1971), pp. 38-43; V. Matveyev, "Vietnamization: A Dead End Policy," *New Times*, No. 11 (March, 1971), pp. 4-5; D. Volsky, "Washington's Indochina Impasse," *New Times*, No. 40 (October, 1971), pp. 10-12; and Nguyen Phu Soai, "Vietnamization: A Doomed Policy," *World Marxist Review*, No. 6 (June, 1972), pp. 122-126.

90. Poltorak, pp. 38-43.

91. *Pravda*, December 15, 1971; and Andre, p. 145.

92. *Pravda*, May 4, 1971.

93. G. Arbatov, "American Foreign Policy at the Threshold of the Seventies," *SShA*, No. 1 (January, 1970).

94. A. Zorin, *Kommunist*, No. 17 (November, 1970).

95. *Pravda*, April 5, 1970.

96. *Ibid.*, March 22, 1970. On May 10, Kosygin sent a telegram to Sihanouk confirming Soviet support for the exiled Prince, but diplomatically ignored the fact that the Kremlin still maintained full relations with Pnom Penh.

97. V. Kudryavtsav, "Escalation of Aggression," *New Times*, No. 18-19 (May, 1970), p. 23.

98. *Pravda*, May 5, 1970.

99. *The New York Times*, April 17, 1970.

100. See, for example, *Pravda*, April 27, 1970; June 17, 1970; and July 21, 1970.

101. *Ibid.*, June 13, 1970. Brezhnev's cautioning statement was further underlined by the fact that Hanoi and Moscow had concluded a military and economic aid agreement two days earlier.

102. *Pravda*, October 3, 1970; and *Izvestiia*, October 13, 1970.

103. *Pravda*, October 10, 1970; *Izvestiia*, October 13, 1970; and Wilfred Burchett, "The Nixon Plan and Indochina Realities," *International Affairs*, No. 1 (January, 1971), pp. 45-48.

104. *Pravda*, November 24, 1970; and November 26, 1970.

105. *Ibid.*, December 17, 1970.

106. M. Kapitsa, "American 'Diplomacy' and the War in Vietnam," *International Affairs*, No. 5 (May, 1971), p. 58; A.Vakhrameyev, "Stalemate for Washington's Aggressive Policy in Indochina," *International Affairs*, No. 3 (March, 1971), p. 67; and "Doctrine of Piracy," *New Times*, No. 5 (February, 1971), p. 1.

107. I. Shatalov, "The Aggressor's Defeat in Indochina and U.S. Moves," *International Affairs*, No. 6 (June, 1971), p. 78. See also *Izvestiia*, February 11, 1971, and I. Biryuzov, "Behind the Laos Invasion," *New Times*, No. 8 (February, 1971), pp. 8-9.

108. Andre, p. 148.

109. *Pravda*, February 26, 1971.

110. *Izvestiia*, February 26, 1971.

111. See *Twenty Fourth Congress of the Communist Party of the Soviet Union* (Moscow: Novosti, 1971).

112. *New Times*, March 31, 1971. p. 26.

113. G. Arbatov, "American Foreign Policy at the Threshold of the Seventies," *SShA*, No. 1 (January, 1970), p. 24.

114. *Pravda*, May 5, 1970.

115. *Ibid.*, April 5, 1970.

116. *Izvestiia*, August 5, 1971; *Pravda*, May 4, 1971; Shatalov, p. 78; V. Kozyakov, "From 'Hot Spring' to 'Hot Summer'," *International Affairs*, No. 8 (August, 1971), pp. 85-86; M. Kobrin, "Big Lie Nailed," *New Times*, No. 27 (July, 1971), pp. 8-9; and "Crisis Ridden," *New Times*, No. 29 (July, 1971), p. 1.

117. *Literaturnaia Gazeta*, April, 1970.

118. See *Pravda*, April 10-19 inclusive, 1971.

119. The Kremlin's last comment was a reference to Edgar Snow's interview with Mao, published in *Life*, April 30, 1971. For the Soviet commentary, see *Pravda*, July 9, 1971; and *Krasnaia Zvezda*, May 20, 1971. See also Iu. Iukhananov, "Voina vo Vetname i Evoliutziia Amerikano-Kitaiskikh Otnoshenii," *Mirovaia Ekonomika i Mezhdunarodnye Otnosheniia*, No. 1 (January, 1972), pp. 40-52.

120. A. Topornin, "Balance of Power Doctrine and Washington," *SShA*, No. 11 (November, 1970), pp. 8-20.

121. *Izvestiia*, July 16, 1971. For a Western assessment of this Soviet reaction, see Hsiao, p. 141.

122. *Pravda*, July 25, 1971; and *Izvestiia*, July 29, 1971.

123. *Pravda*, August 10, 1971.

124. *Facts on File 1971*, p. 847.

125. *Pravda*, October 5, 1971.

126. See Gene Gregory, "Moscow Awaits a Windfall," *Far Eastern Economic Review* (February 19, 1972), p. 16.

127. Nonetheless, Moscow was sufficiently aware of the potential criticism that could be levied against its own détente with the United States. Thus, immediately after it was announced that Nixon would visit the Soviet Union in 1972, *Pravda* reassured its allies in general and the D.R.V. in particular that "there can be no doubt" that "any [American] attempt to build political relations with the Soviet Union to the detriment of its fraternal ties with the D.R.V. and other socialist countries ... will be unsuccessful" (*Pravda*, October 15, 1971).

128. *Ibid.*, December 22, 1971, and December 28, 1971; and *Izvestiia*, December 31, 1971.

129. *Literaturnaia Gazeta*, February, 1972.

130. *Pravda*, December 31, 1971; and J. Prazsky, "Re China's 'Emergence' on the World Scene," *World Marxist Review*, No. 4 (April, 1972), pp. 131-32.

131. *Izvestiia*, February 19, 1972; *Pravda*, February 20, 1972; and *Literaturnaia Gazeta*, February, 1972.

132. *Pravda*, March 1-4, 1972, inclusive; and *Soviet News*, March 28, 1972. For Soviet reaction to the Shanghai Communiqué, see Hsiao, pp. 152-54.

133. Prazsky, p. 133; and Y. Nikolayev, "United States Foreign Policy: Real or Imaginary Changes?" *International Affairs*, No. 5 (May, 1972), pp. 63-66.

134. Porter, p. 104.

135. *Facts on File 1972*, p. 262.

136. Michel Tatu, "Moscow, Peking, and the Conflict in Vietnam," in Anthony Lake (ed.), *The Vietnam Legacy* (New York: New York University Press, 1976), pp. 31-32.

137. Kenneth P. Landon, "The Impact of the Sino-American Detente on the Indochina Conflict," in Hsiao, p. 210.

138. *Pravda*, March 28, 1972. Batitsky is currently commander of the Soviet Home Air Defense Forces.

139. *Ibid.*, December 31, 1971.

140. Quoted in *Facts on File 1972*, p. 401.

141. *Izvestiia*, May 7, 1972.

142. *Pravda*, April 5, 1972, and April 28, 1972.

143. For two of these infrequent references, see *Izvestiia*, April 29, 1972, and May 19, 1972.

144. *Ibid.*, April 9, 1972.

145. *Pravda*, April 13, 1972.

146. *Ibid.*, April 26, 1972.

147. Four Soviet vessels in Haiphong were damaged as well. The Kremlin did lodge an official protest about the damaged ships. See *Ibid.*, April 17, 1972.

148. *Izvestiia*, May 12, 1972.

149. A chart clearly illustrates the reaction of the Soviet press to both events in Vietnam and the Moscow summit. The numbers in columns 2 and 3 represent the number of words *Pravda* and *Izvestiia* respectively devoted to events in Vietnam during the listed week. Word totals were compiled from the relevant index of *Pravda* and *Izvestiia* published in *Current Digest of the Soviet Press*.

| *Week of* | *Pravda* | *Izvestiia* | *Major Events* |
|---|---|---|---|
| April 24-30 | 8450 words | 4500 words | '72 Offensive |
| May 1-7 | 9625 | 3925 | '72 Offensive |
| May 8-14 | 13975 | 7250 | U.S. mines Haiphong |
| May 15-21 | 3900 | 2250 | |
| May 22-28 | 1800 | 1700 | Nixon in Moscow |
| May 29-June 4 | 3875 | 1025 | |
| June 5-11 | 6450 | 1575 | |
| June 12-18 | 5400 | 4600 | |

Clearly, the Russian major press acted to "protect" the summit.

150. See *Pravda*, May 27-30, 1972, inclusive. For other Soviet commentary on the summit, see M. Kobrin, "Tekushchie Problemy Mirovoi Politiki," *Mirovaia Ekonomika i Mezhdunarodnye Otnosheniia*, No. 7 (July, 1972), pp. 69-77; J. Prazsky, "Significance of the Moscow Talks," *World Marxist Review*, No. 7 (July, 1972), pp. 135-139; and any of a number of articles in *International Affairs* and *SShA*.

151. *Izvestiia*, June 29, 1972.

152. An article in *International Affairs* later claimed that the United States promised to "enter into serious negotiations" with the North Vietnamese for a settlement "fair to all" and to "bring about the earliest end of the armed conflict in Indochina"—see Mikheyev, p. 74. Meanwhile, the United States later claimed that an "implied understanding" had been reached that the U.S. and Soviet Union together had to act to end the war. Since the Soviets continued to supply the D.R.V. and the United States did not alter its negotiating posture, the claims from both sides were either summit rhetoric, misunderstandings, or lies.

153. Podgorny's unusual interest in Vietnam affairs was easily explained. In October, 1971, Brezhnev told West German Chancellor Willy Brandt that Brezhnev's foreign affairs responsibility area was the United States and Western Europe; Kosygin's was the Third World, the Middle East, and trade; and

Podgorny's was "Vietnamese Affairs." See *The New York Times*, October 26, 1971.

Podgorny's trip to Hanoi coincided with a U.S. White House announcement that Secretary of State Kissinger would soon travel to Peking to conduct further negotiations. The Kremlin could not have missed the significance of the timing of the announcement or the destination of Kissinger's trip.

154. T.J.S. George, "Landslide Logic," *Far Eastern Economic Review*, (November 11, 1972), p. 12.

155. *Pravda*, June 20, 1972.

156. *Department of Defense Appropriations: Hearings before a Subcommittee of the Committee on Appropriations*, House of Representatives, 93rd Congress, 1st Session, 1973 (Washington: U.S. Government Printing Office, 1973), p. 5.

157. *Christian Science Monitor*, September 7, 1972. Estimated Soviet and Chinese aid (in U.S. dollars) to the D.R.V. during 1971 and 1972 is as follows (in millions). **Soviet:** *military* (1971) $100, (1972) $150; *non-military* (1971) $370, (1972) $350. **Chinese:** *military* (1971) $100, (1972) $110; *non-military* (1971) $110, (1972) $120. See Douglas Pike, "North Vietnam in the Year 1972," *Asian Survey*, Vol. XIII, No. 1 (January, 1973), p. 56.

158. *Izvestiia*, September 27, 1972.

159. *Pravda*, October 29, 1972.

160. For a few of the numerous Soviet commentaries on Thieu's "rebellion," see *Pravda*, October 31, 1972; *Izvestiia*, November 30, 1972; "The Peoples Demand Immediate Peace in Vietnam," *World Marxist Review*, No. 12 (December, 1972), pp. 55-56; S. Panov, "Tekushchie Problemy Mirovoi Politiki," *Mirovaia Ekonomika i Mezhdunarodnye Otnosheniia*, No. 1 (January, 1973), pp. 95-97; and I. Trofimova, "Vietnam: There Must Be No Delay," *New Times*, No. 46 (November, 1972), pp. 6-7.

161. *Pravda*, November 5, 1972; *Krasnaia Zvezda*, November 12, 1972; and "Good Will and Stalling Tactics," *New Times*, No. 48 (November, 1972), p. 16.

162. *Pravda*, October 28, 1972.

163. *Baltimore Sun*, November 7, 1972, and November 17, 1972

164. *Pravda*, December 20, 1972.

165. *The New York Times*, December 19, 1972.

166. *Pravda*, December 22, 1972.

167. *Ibid.*, January 23, 1973.

168. *Izvestiia*, December 10, 1972.

169. *Pravda*, January 2, 1973. See also O. Alexandrov, "The World Demands: Sign!" *New Times*, No. 2 (January, 1973), pp. 8-9.

170. *Sovetskaia Rossiia*, January 4, 1973.

171. *Izvestiia*, February 6, 1973.

172. *Ibid.*, January 25, 1973; S. Ivanshin and I. Osotiv, "Vetnam – Pobeda Istoricheskogo Znacheniia," *Kommunist*, No. 2 (January, 1973), pp. 15-23; and Iu. Iukhananov, "Pobeda Vetnama," *Mirovaia Ekonomika i Mezhdunarodnye Otnosheniia*, No. 5 (May, 1973), pp. 19-30.

173. "Victory for the Peoples, Defeat for Imperialism," *World Marxist Review*, No. 3 (March, 1973), p. 5; and G. Arbatov, "O Sovetsko-Amerikanskikh Otnosheniiakh," *Kommunist*, No. 3 (February, 1973), p. 104.

174. A Leontev, "Istoricheskaia Pobeda Vetnama," *Kommunist Vooruzhennykh Sil* No. 6 (March, 1973), pp. 87-88; M. Kobrin, "Tekushchie Problemy Mirovoi Politiki," *Mirovaia Ekonomika i Mezhdunarodnye Otnosheniia*, No. 4 (April, 1973), pp. 84-86; Y. Skvortsov, "The Victory of the Vietnamese People: A

Triumph of the Forces of Peace," *International Affairs*, No. 4 (April, 1973), pp. 63-65; D. Volsky, "Peace for Vietnam," *New Times*, No. 4 (January, 1973), pp. 6-7; and I. Ivkov, "Vietnam's Victory: Lessons and Prospects," *New Times*, No. 6 (February, 1973), pp. 4-6.

175. *Pravda*, January 31, 1973.

176. There are four major schools of thought regarding the change in Chinese foreign policy. First, the transformation was real and in response to changed policies on the part of others. Second, the change marked a fundamental switch in China's international strategy. Third, the so-called "revolution in foreign policy" was only a short-term swing, which would inevitably swing back. Finally, the change marked a return to a pre-Cultural Revolution trend of improved relations with the West. For a deeper discussion of these views, see Michael Oksenberg, "The Strategies of Peking," *Foreign Affairs*, Vol. 50, No. 1 (October, 1971), pp. 18-22.

177. See, for example, *Peking Review*, August 27, 1972.

178. Robert A. Scalapino, "China and the Balance of Power," *Foreign Affairs*, Vol. 52, No. 3 (April, 1972), p. 358.

179. *Facts on File 1970*, p. 569.

180. For just a few of the numerous Chinese condemnations of Vietnamization and the Nixon Doctrine, see *Peking Review*, May 8, 1970, July 3, 1970, and July 17, 1970.

181. *Ibid.*, January 2, 1970.

182. The best brief account of Cambodian-Chinese relations between 1967 1970 appears in Jay Taylor, *China and Southeast Asia* (New York: Praeger, 1976), pp. 145-151.

183. New China News Agency, March 19, 1970.

184. *Ibid.*, April 8, 1970.

185. *Peking Review*, April 3, 1970.

186. When Secretary of Defense Elliott Richardson was asked whether intelligence reports predicted possible Chinese intervention, he responded that such a possibility was "an acceptable risk." See *The New York Times*, May 11, 1970.

187. *Peking Review*, Special Issue, May 8, 1970.

188. *Ibid.*

189. *Ibid.*, May 29, 1970. See also L. F. Goodstadt, "China: Mister Moderation," *Far Eastern Economic Review*, May 28, 1970, p. 8.

190. For a few of China's "excellent situation" comments, see *Peking Review*, May 29, 1970, September 11, 1970, and November 13, 1970.

191. The two countries concluded aid agreements in June and in October.

192. *The New York Times*, August 3, 1971.

193. New China News Agency, February 7-11 inclusive, 1971; and *Peking Review*, February 12, 1971, and February 19, 1971.

194. New China News Agency, February 13, 1971.

195. *Peking Review*, February 12, 1971, and February 19, 1971.

196. *Ibid.*, February 26, 1971.

197. *Ibid.*, February 12, 1971.

198. *Facts on File 1971*, p. 71. See also *Peking Review*, March 12, 1971.

199. *Pravda*, April 1, 1971.

200. *Peking Review*, April 2, 1971.

201. New China News Agency, August 3, 1971.

202. *International Herald-Tribune*, July 29-30, 1972.

203. Edgar Snow, "A Conversation with Mao Tse-tung," *Life*, April 30, 1971.

204. Mao himself confirmed this account of Lin's death. See the *International-al Herald-Tribune*, July 29-30, 1972. The Russians indirectly supported the argument that Lin was leaning toward an accommodation with the Kremlin in a *Pravda* article on December 5, 1971. In the article, it was stated that the purge of Lin meant the ascendancy of "extreme anti-Soviet factions" in Peking. See also Wilfred Burchett, "Lin Piao's Plot — The Full Story," *Far Eastern Economic Review*, August 29, 1972, pp. 22-24.

One fascinating note on the evolution of Sino-American relations is that Lin lost favor because he rejected détente with the United States at least in part because he feared it would provoke the Soviet Union, whereas in 1966, Liu Shao-chi had been purged because he advocated improved relations with the Soviet Union since he feared an American attack on the P.R.C.

205. Rogers, *United States Foreign Policy 1971*, p. 62.

206. *Peking Review*, May 7, 1971.

207. Lawrence, p. 215. For another explanation of China's foreign policy revolution, see Jim Peck, "Why China Turned West," *Ramparts*, May, 1972, pp. 34-41.

208. Kalb and Kalb, p. 264; and *Facts on File 1971*, p. 544.

209. *Ibid.*, p. 563.

210. China News Analysis, December 7, 1971.

211. *Facts on File 1971*, p. 925.

212. *China Quarterly*, No. 49 (January-March, 1972), p. 205.

213. *Facts on File 1972*, p. 118.

214. *Peking Review*, December 31, 1971.

215. The text of the Shanghai Communiqué appears *Ibid.*, March 3, 1972.

216. *Facts on File 1972*, p. 158.

217. Nonetheless, Peking's statement on Vietnam in the Communiqué was viewed in Washington as "one of the most moderate statements Peking has made on this question." See the *Washington Post*, March 3, 1972.

218. *China Quarterly*, No. 50 (April-June, 1972), p. 390.

219. New China News Agency, March 10, 1972.

220. *China Quarterly*, No. 51 (July-September, 1972), p. 596.

221. On an NBC television program broadcast on April 19, Chou declared that if the bombing was not halted and the aggression ended, then "the free Indochinese people can only fight on to the end and the Chinese people will certainly support them to the end." Additionally, Chou called Vietnam "the most outstanding question" in Sino-American relations.

222. *Le Monde*, May 11, 1972.

223. *Peking Review*, May 19, 1972; and New China News Agency, May 12, 1972.

224. *The New York Times*, May 25, 1972.

225. *Ibid.*, June 27, 1972.

226. *Christian Science Monitor*, August 29, 1972.

227. New China News Agency, June 12, 1972.

228. *The New York Times*, June 25, 1972.

229. *Ibid.*, July 18, 1972.

230. New China News Agency, October 1, 1972; and *Peking Review*, August 27, 1972.

231. New China News Agency, September 2, 1972.

232. *Peking Review*, November 3, 1972.

233. *Ibid.*, December 8, 1972.

234. *Ibid.*, November 10, 1972.

235. *Ibid.*, December 30, 1972.
236. *Baltimore Sun*, December 30, 1972.
237. *U.S. News and World Report*, January 22, 1973, p. 8.
238. New China News Agency, December 20, 1972. For more on China's restrained reaction to the bombing, see Leo Goodstadt, "An Ulcer Between Lips and Teeth," *Far Eastern Economic Review* (January 8, 1973), p. 10.
239. *Peking Review*, February 2, 1973.
240. *Ibid.*

## NOTES TO CHAPTER VI

1. For two discussions of the "decent interval" theory, see *The New York Times*, March 11, 1973; and R.P.W. Norton, "Webbed Feet," *Far Eastern Economic Review*, April 23, 1973, p. 17.
2. *The New York Times*, January 29-31, 1973; *Washington Post*, January 29-31, 1973; "Back to Battle," *Far Eastern Economic Review*, February 26, 1973, p. 13; and "Shooting Holes in a Ceasefire," *Far Eastern Economic Review*, March 5, 1973, p. 13.
3. *Washington Post*, February 8, 1973; *The New York Times*, February 9, 1973; and *Christian Science Monitor*, March 20, 1973.
4. Maynard Parker, "Vietnam: The War That Won't End," *Foreign Affairs*, Vol. 53, No. 2 (January, 1975), pp. 365-67.
5. For an excellent account of Saigon's harassment of the Joint Military Commissions, see Gareth Porter, *A Peace Denied* (Bloomington: Indiana University Press, 1975), pp. 206-218.
6. *Christian Science Monitor*, March 16, 1973.
7. *Vietnam — A Changing Crucible: Report of a Study Mission to South Vietnam*, House Report 93-1196, 93rd Congress, 2nd Session, 1974, p. 4.
8. *The London Guardian*, February 23, 1973.
9. *Washington Post*, April 12, 1973.
10. Parker, p. 368; and *The New York Times*, December 6, 1973.
11. Hoang Nguyen, "The Paris Agreement on Vietnam: Glimpses of the Past and Future," *Vietnam Courier* (Hanoi), No. 16 (September, 1973), pp. 9-10.
12. *The New York Times*, January 24, 1973.
13. *Washington Post*, February 1, 1973.
14. Henry Kissinger on "Today" television program, transcript, February 25, 1973.
15. *Washington Post*, December 9, 1972, December 11, 1972, and March 20, 1973.
16. The assurances were in letters dated November 14, 1972, and January 5, 1973. Both were released to the public by South Vietnamese Minister of Planning Nguyen Tien Hung in April, 1975, during the collapse of the Thieu government. The Ford White House later confirmed the authenticity of the letters. See *The New York Times*, May 1, 1975.
17. *Washington Post*, February 2, 1973.
18. *The New York Times*, March 16, 1973.
19. *Ibid.*, April 12, 1973.
20. Hai Au, "A Disturbing Sign," *Far Eastern Economic Review*, October 8, 1973, p. 15; and Hai Au, "Vietnam: Here We Go Again," *Far Eastern Economic Review*, November 19, 1973, p. 12.
21. *Baltimore Sun*, December 21, 1973.

22. *Facts on File 1974*, p. 222. After the supplemental appropriation was defeated, the Pentagon "found an error" in its accounting for 1972 and 1973. According to the Pentagon, the United States had overcharged Saigon for military equipment during those years. This "discovery" permitted the U.S. to ship $266 million of additional military aid to South Vietnam despite the defeat of the supplemental appropriations. See *The New York Times*, April 16, 1974.

23. *Facts on File 1974*, p. 477.

24. *The New York Times*, June 12, 1974.

25. *Ibid.*, August 6, 1974.

26. *Ibid.*, September 24, 1974, and September 25, 1974.

27. For Asian commentary on the aid reduction, see James Laurie, "Reducing the Asian Commitment," *Far Eastern Economic Review*, January 3, 1975, pp. 30-31.

28. *The New York Times*, August 13, 1974.

29. Denzil Peiris, "Asia's New Godfather," *Far Eastern Economic Review*, August 23, 1974, p. 000.

30. *Facts on File 1974*, p. 633.

31. "Hanoi Resigned to War," *Far Eastern Economic Review* August 30, 1974, p. 20.

32. *Facts on File 1974*, p. 665.

33. Gareth Porter, "Report from Hanoi: Pressing Ford to Drop Thieu," *The New Republic*, February 8, 1975, pp. 19-21.

34. Parker, pp. 362-65.

35. See the *Washington Post* or *The New York Times* on almost a daily basis through September and October, 1974.

36. For detailed maps of who controlled which area in South Vietnam during the summer of 1974, see *Far Eastern Economic Review*, August 9, 1974, p. 19.

37. *The New York Times*, December 18-26, 1974.

38. For an outline of the note, see *Ibid.*, January 12, 1975.

39. *Washington Post*, January 15, 1975.

40. *Ibid.*, January 22, 1975.

41. *Facts on File 1975*, p. 41.

42. *Ibid.*, p. 68, 70.

43. *Washington Post*, March 3-4, 1975.

44. *The New York Times*, March 11, 1975.

45. *Time*, March 24, 1975. See also General Van Tien Dang's account of the offensive in *The New York Times*, April 25, 1976, as well as Laurence E. Grinter, "How They Lost: Doctrine, Strategies, and Outcomes of the Vietnam War," *Asian Survey*, Vol. 15, No. 12 (December, 1975), pp. 1114-1132.

46. *The New York Times*, April 24, 1975.

47. *Christian Science Monitor*, April 1, 1975.

48. *Washington Post*, April 7, 1975.

49. *Ibid.*, April 5, 1975.

50. *Ibid.*, March 21, 1975.

51. *The New York Times*, March 27, 1975.

52. *Ibid.*, April 4, 1975, and April 6, 1975.

53. *Ibid.*, April 16, 1975.

54. *Ibid.*, April 11, 1975. Ford also stressed that the United States would remain steadfast to its allies and would continue to pursue improved relations with the Russians and Chinese.

55. *Facts on File 1975*, p. 226.

56. *The New York Times*, March 13, 1975, and March 14, 1975.

57. *Ibid.*, April 4, 1975.

58. *Ibid.*, April 12, 1975.

59. Porter, p. 275. As one U.S. official in Cambodia earlier put it, "Sometimes you have to go through the motions. Sometimes the motions are more important than the substance." See *Newsweek*, March 24, 1975.

60. *The New York Times*, April 2, 1975, and April 3, 1975.

61. *Time* (April 21, 1975), p. 19.

62. *Washington Post*, April 20, 1975.

63. Interview with Hoang Tung by an American delegation in Hanoi, May 6, 1975, *Indochina Peace Campaign Newsletter*, May 18, 1975, quoted in Porter, p. 277.

64. *The New York Times*, April 17, 1975.

65. *Ibid.*, April 19, 1975.

66. *Ibid.*, April 24, 1975.

67. At a news conference on April 29, Kissinger pointed to the changed position of the PRG as proof that the PRG has "escalated [its] demands" as the military situation changed. To Kissinger, the PRG was looking for an unconditional surrender and a "substantial political takeover."

While Kissinger was undoubtedly correct in his assessment, the "escalated demands" of the PRG must be viewed in the proper context. Throughout the history of the Vietnam conflict, both sides had increased their political demands as their respective military situation improved. The "escalated demands" of the PRG were thus well within the dictates of past experience.

68. *The New York Times*, May 18, 1975.

69. *Facts on File 1975*, p. 273.

70. *The New York Times*, April 17, 1975.

71. *Washington Post*, April 18, 1975.

72. *The New York Times*, March 20, 1974.

73. *Ibid.*, March 28, 1975, and March 29, 1975; and Parker, p. 369.

74. *U.S. News and World Report*, April 23, 1973.

75. *Washington Post*, March 15, 1974. See also *Congressional Record*, April 4, 1974, p. 2022.

76. Letter from the Defense Intelligence Agency to Congressman Les Aspin, May 18, 1974, quoted in Porter, p. 188.

77. James Laurie, "Washington Still Calls the Tune," *Far Eastern Economic Review*, February 21, 1975, p. 25.

78. *The New York Times*, April 20, 1975. See also *The New York Times*, April 20, 1975. See also *The New York Times*, April 26, 1976, where victorious North Vietnamese General Dung closely tied South Vietnam's collapse to the Watergate affair.

79. In the April reshuffling, Pyotr Shelest, commonly viewed as a hardliner on Soviet-Western relations, was dropped from his Politburo position. This action culminated a year-long period of uncertainty for Shelest. In May 1972, he had been relieved of his duties as First Secretary of the Ukrainian Communist Party.

80. *Facts on File 1973*, p. 159.

81. G. Arbatov, "O Sovetsko-Amerikanskikh Otnosheniiakh," *Kommunist*, No. 3 (February, 1973), pp. 101-113.

82. *Izvestiia*, February 6, 1963; and A. Stepanov, "Soviet Foreign Policy and the Restructuring of International Relations," *International Affairs*, No. 1 (January, 1974), p. 5.

83. Soviet officials were not the only ones who took this point of view. On

March 15, 1974, President Nixon told a Chicago audience that the end of the Vietnamese War was a product of détente, and on September 19, 1974, Kissinger told the Senate Foreign Relations Committee that improved relations with the Kremlin had helped to "extricate" the United States from Vietnam.

84. *The New York Times*, September 25, 1974.

85. B. Ponomaryov, "The World Situation and the Revolutionary Process," *World Marxist Review*, No. 6 (June, 1974), p. 4.

86. Arbatov, pp. 101-113.

87. *Izvestiia*, May 1, 1973.

88. See, for example, *Pravda*, April 4, 1973; and July 22, 1973.

89. See above, notes 73 to 77 inclusive.

90. For other similar examples, see *Pravda*, March 1, 1973, June 6, 1973, December 25, 1973, and January 27, 1974; C. Ivanshin and I. Osotov, "Vetnam-Pobeda Istoricheskogo Znacheniia," *Kommunist* No. 2 (February, 1973), p. 15; E. Vasil'kov, "Iuzhnye Vetnam: Realnost i Perspektivy," *Kommunist*, No. 11 (August, 1973), pp. 98-108; Y. Skvortsov, "The Victory of the Vietnamese People: A Triumph of the Forces of Peace," *International Affairs*, No. 4 (April, 1973); pp. 63-65; and A. Sergeyev, "Along the Path to Genuine Peace in Indochina," *International Affairs*, No. 3 (March, 1973), pp. 18-25.

91. "Victory for the Peoples, Defeat for Imperialism," *World Marxist Review*, No. 3 (March, 1973), pp. 6-7.

92. *Izvestiia*, February 6, 1973.

93. *Pravda*, October 9, 1973.

94. V. P. Lukin, *SShA*, No. 2 (February, 1973), pp. 12-23.

95. Anat. Gromyko and A. Kokoshin, "U.S. Foreign Policy Strategy for the 1970's," *International Affairs*, No. 10 (October, 1973), p. 69.

96. V. Petrovsky, "Current U.S. Thinking on Foreign Policy," *International Affairs*, No. 11 (November, 1973), p. 74.

97. Gromyko and Kokoshin, p. 73.

98. *Pravda*, July 22, 1973.

99. *Ibid.*, November 15, 1973.

100. See, for example, *Ibid.*, August 15, 1974.

101. *Ibid.*, July 17, 1973, and December 21, 1973.

102. *Ibid.*, June 19, 1973, July 17, 1973, August 14, 1973, August 15, 1973, and November 4, 1973.

103. *China News Analysis*, No. 953 (March 15, 1974).

104. *Pravda*, October 28, 1974.

105. *Ibid.*, December 9, 1974, and December 11, 1974.

106. Nayan Chanda, "The Waiting Is Almost Over," *Far Eastern Economic Review*, June 13, 1975, p. 13-14.

107. Y. Yurtsev, "Indochina's Burning Issues," *International Affairs*, No. 2 (February, 1975), p. 53.

108. For example, see *Izvestiia*, January 14, 1975.

109. E. Vasilikov, "Crucial Turning Point," *New Times*, No. 15 (April, 1975), pp. 4-6.

110. See V. Trifonov, "South Vietnam: Spring of Liberation," *New Times*, No. 13 (March, 1975), p. 7; L. Vizen, "South Vietnam: Flames of Wrath," *New Times*, No. 17 (April, 1975), pp. 16-17; and *Pravda* and *Izvestiia* on almost a daily basis through March and April, 1975.

111. *Izvestiia*, April 2, 1975; and *Pravda*, April 5, 1975.

112. *Izvestiia*, April 2, 1975; *Pravda*, April 12, 1975; and D. Volsky, "Peace Comes to Indochina," *New Times*, No. 19 (May, 1975), pp. 16-18.

113. For example, see *Izvestiia*, March 29, 1975; and Vasilikov, pp. 4-6.

114. For further discussion of this Soviet view, see Daniel S. Papp, "Nixon, Brezhnev, Ford, and Watergate: International Implications of a Domestic Crisis," *Georgia Political Science Association Journal*, Vol. 4, No. 1 (Spring, 1976), p. 3-20.

115. *Pravda*, March 9, 1975.

116. *Ibid.*, April 5, 1975.

117. *Izvestiia*, April 23, 1975.

118. *Pravda*, April 30, 1975. See also I. Andronov, "The Lesson of Saigon," *New Times*, No. 19 (May, 1975), p. 19.

119. *Izvestiia*, April 23, 1975.

120. *Pravda*, April 30, 1975.

121. See, for example, V. Trifonov, "Patriotic Forces Sweep On," *New Times*, No. 14 (April, 1975), pp. 16-17.

122. *Pravda*, May 6, 1975.

123. Volsky, pp. 16-18.

124. *Izvestiia*, May 8, 1975.

125. See *Pravda*, May 15-20 inclusive, 1975.

126. *Ibid.*, February 7, 1975, and February 10, 1975.

127. *Izvestiia*, April 19, 1975; and *Pravda*, April 23, 1975.

128. *Pravda*, May 6, 1975.

129. *Facts on File 1975*, p. 351.

130. *Peking Review*, February 2, 1973.

131. Leo Goodstadt, "China's Advice Is to 'Play It Straight'," *Far Eastern Economic Review*, February 5, 1973, pp. 10-11.

132. *Peking Review*, February 2, 1973.

133. *Ibid.*, February 23, 1973.

134. *Facts on File 1973*, p. 940.

135. *Peking Review*, April 5, 1974, June 28, 1974, and October 25, 1974.

136. For example, see *Ibid.*, June 8, 1973.

137. Quoted in Gene T. Hsiao, *Sino-American Détente and Its Policy Implications* (Praeger: New York, 1974), p. 221.

138. James Laurie interview of Mike Mansfield, *Far Eastern Economic Review*, March 21, 1975, p. 12.

139. For the text of the joint communiqué, see *Peking Review*, June 15, 1973. See also Norman Peagam, "Loosened Lips?" *Far Eastern Economic Review*, July 2, 1973, pp. 14-15.

140. *Peking Review*, November 23, 1973; and November 30, 1973.

141. In addition to the South Vietnamese, one American advisor was taken prisoner. The Chinese desire to minimize the impact of the incident on Sino-American relations was so strong that the American prisoner was released two weeks after his capture without comment. A similar American desire was evident, if South Vietnamese sources are to be believed, since Saigon requested American support but was refused. Officially, the Department of Defense maintained that it was "unaware of the request."

142. For the Chinese account, see *Peking Review*, January 25, 1974.

143. In April 1975, just before the collapse of the Republic of Vietnam, Hanoi landed forces on the Spratlys and claimed the islands. The D.R.V. was obviously preempting China.

144. *Peking Review*, November 1, 1974. It should be pointed out that Sino-Vietnamese relations were not the only casualty of Peking's American connection. Deposed Cambodian leader Sihanouk damned China with faint praise in a

1973 speech in Algiers. According to the Prince, "China remains faithful to us, but China is playing the big power game with America now, and so cannot help as much as it would like." See T. D. Allman, "Sihanouk: Victim of Detente," *Far Eastern Economic Review*, October 1, 1973, pp. 13-14. See also *Le Monde*, October 26, 1973.

145. New China News Agency, March 23, 1974, and March 27, 1974.

146. *Ibid.*, March 23, 1974.

147. For the complete text of Chou's address, see *Peking Review*, September 7, 1973.

148. This was not a new Chinese position. China had accused "Soviet revisionism" and "American imperialism" of concocting "new dirty deals" directed at China and the rest of the world on numerous previous occasions. For one example, see *Ibid.*, May 4, 1973. See also *China News Analysis*, No. 938, 1973.

149. Chou's sickness may also explain Teng Hsiao-pings's rehabilitaton during 1973. Teng had been purged during the Cultural Revolution, but was brought back into favor as Chou's heir apparent.

150. For an account of Kissinger's 1974 trip to Peking, see *Peking Review*, November 29, 1974.

151. *Ibid.*, September 6, 1974.

152. The Chinese media gave a straightforward account of Nixon's resignation, but were clearly troubled by the change in administrations. Ford's statement that the U.S. foreign policy would not change was greeted with obvious relief in Peking. See New China News Agency, August 9, 1974, and August 14, 1974; as well as *Peking Review*, August 16, 1974.

153. *Peking Review*, November 1, 1974.

154. *Ibid.*, November 22, 1974.

155. *China Quarterly*, No. 63 (September, 1975), p. 609.

156. *Peking Review*, June 6, 1975.

157. *Facts on File 1975*, p. 422.

158. *Ibid.*, p. 332.

159. Despite Sihanouk's feeling that China could no longer extend as much aid to the Cambodians as it would like because of the "big power game" (see note 144 above), Chinese-Khmer relations remained close. China had supported Sihanouk ever since he was deposed, and perhaps more importantly neither the Chinese nor the Khmer's trusted North Vietnamese intentions. Thus, there was ample reason for close relations.

## NOTES TO CHAPTER VII

1. *The New York Times*, December 8, 1975.

2. For a discussion of Jimmy Carter's opportunities in Asia as they were perceived in 1976, see Ralph N. Clough, "East Asia and the Carter Administration," *Pacific Community*, Vol. 8, No. 2 (January, 1977), pp. 191-203.

3. John King Fairbanks, as quoted in Joseph Buttinger, *Vietnam: An Unforgetable Tragedy* (Horizon Press: New York, 1977), p. 175.

4. *Ibid.*, pp. 168-169.

5. V. Ardatovsky, "Imperialist Infamy in Indochina," *International Affairs*, No. 2 (February, 1971), pp. 69-70.

6. "The Victory in Vietnam and Its International Significance," *World Marxist Review*, No. 7 (July, 1975), p. 3.

7. J. Prazsky, "Realities of the Times and Imperialist Policy," *World Marxist Review*, No. 6 (June, 1975), pp. 131-133.

8. "The Victory in Vietnam and Its International Significance," p. 7. For a further discussion of this point, see Daniel S. Papp, "National Liberation During Detente: The Soviet Outlook," *International Journal*, Vol. 32. No. 1 (Winter, 1976-77), pp. 82-99.

9. For an excellent analysis of the Soviet view of the international correlation of forces, see Michael J. Deane, "The Soviet Assessment of the Correlation of World Forces: Implication for American Foreign Policy," *Orbis*, Vol. 20, No. 3 (Fall, 1976), pp. 625-636.

10. For just a few of these numerous examples, see *Izvestiia*, December 26, 1975, and January 10, 1976; and V. Pustov, "The Battle of Angola," *New Times*, No. 6 (February, 1977), p. 8.

11. Donald E. Weatherbee, *The USSR-DRV-PRC Triangle in Southeast Asia* (Carlisle Barrack, Pa.: Strategic Studies Institute, 1976), p. 11.

12. See, for example, Radio Peking, June 16, 1975, in *FBIS*, "Daily Report, People's Republic of China," June 19, 1975.

13. The dissolution of the Southeast Asian Treaty Organization in October 1975 provided an interesting study in contrasts. While both the Soviet Union and Vietnam loudly praised the end of SEATO, China said nothing.

# Index